Andro Linklater has been a writer for twenty years.

BY THE SAME AUTHOR

The Black Watch (with Eric Linklater)
Charlotte Despard: A Life
Compton Mackenzie: A Life
Wild People: Travels with Borneo's Head Hunters

The Code of Love
A True Story

ANDRO LINKLATER

PHŒNIX

A Phoenix paperback

First published in Great Britain in 2000
By Weidenfeld & Nicolson
This paperback edition published in 2001 by Phoenix,
an imprint of Orion Books Ltd,
Orion House, 5 Upper St Martin's Lane,
London WC2H 9EA

A CIP catalogue record for this book
is available from the British Library.

ISBN 0 75381 115 4

Printed and bound in Great Britain by
Clays Ltd, St Ives plc

CONTENTS

ILLUSTRATIONS

ACKNOWLEDGEMENTS

My debt to Pamela Hill, widow of Donald Hill, was so great that I often felt in writing this book that it almost amounted to a collaboration. I shall always be deeply grateful to her not only for her unstinted help but for her friendship, too. Her children, Joanna Wilkinson, Carolyn Morris and Christopher Hill have been equally generous with their time and memories, and I was also helped by a useful interview with Stuart Morris.

I am indebted to Brigit Ferguson and Sheila Froom, Pamela's sisters, who were informative, amusing and vastly patient in providing recollection and comment. I owe thanks also to Philip Aston, who decrypted the diary, for his guidance, and to his wife, Linda, for her help. I am grateful for Barbara Waterworth's information about Iraq in the 1950s.

My friend and neighbour Anne Sorby not only helped with reminiscence and books about Hong Kong but steered me towards crucial sources on the colony in wartime. Chief among them was Michael Wright who generously talked about his experiences as a prisoner. I also acknowledge with gratitude the help of Arthur Gomes MBE of the Hong Kong Prisoners' Association, Group Captain Bennet, John Harris, and Dr Peter Barham of the Wellcome Institute. To Dr Goorney, formerly of Ticehurst hospital, goes the credit and my appreciation for identifying the courageous Florrie.

The book is the brainchild of my editor at Weidenfeld & Nicolson Toby Mundy, who has overseen its genesis with a care and attention to detail for which I am continuingly grateful. I acknowledge the kindness of Russell Twisk, editor-in-chief of the *Reader's Digest* in the United Kingdom and of Susannah Hickling, senior editor, in giving permission to use material which first appeared in an article I wrote for the magazine. I am grateful to Emma Baxter of Weidenfeld & Nicolson for her extremely cogent comments on an early draft.

I acknowledge the advice and help provided by the staff of the Imperial War Museum, the Public Record Office, the British Library, the London Library and the Tunbridge Wells Public Library.

For permission to use quotations, I acknowledge:

W. H. Auden, 'September 1 1939': the permission of Faber & Faber.

Robert Graves, 'She Tells her Love while Half Asleep': the permission of A. P. Watt.

T. S. Eliot, 'Little Gidding': the permission of Faber & Faber.

W. H. Auden, 'Lay your Sleeping Head': the permission of Faber & Faber.

George Barker, 'Wild Dreams of Summer, What is your Grief?': the permission of Faber & Faber.

My final acknowledgement must go to the extraordinary, tortured character of Donald Hill. I hope that I have done him justice, for he had firm tastes in books. Among those that came under his critical eye in prison camp was a book called *Juan in America* by Eric Linklater. This was my father's first bestseller, and one of his finest novels. Donald awarded it just three stars meaning 'Fair'. I feel I have a lot to live up to.

INTRODUCTION

But this is now – you may depend upon it –
Stable, opaque, immortal – all by dint
Of the dear names that lie concealed within't

Edgar Allan Poe, 'An Enigma'

Pamela Hill died on 22 March 2000, sixty-one years almost to the day after she first fell in love. It had been a *coup de foudre*, a blinding revelation that came in the course of a dance, and from that moment she was never out of love. She experienced it in many different guises, as joy, agony, despair, renewal, but never did she find it to be sweet and sugary. There was only one person she loved, and constancy gave to that single attachment a quality which was epic in its depth and passion.

He was a young pilot in the Royal Air Force, who had just gained his wings. They met in March 1939. Thus the shadow of war hung over them from the start. There was nothing strange in that. It was the fate of an entire generation to live with the knowledge that the world was out of control. Like other lovers, they tried to ignore it, as though the high intensity of their feelings could keep the future at bay. What made them different was not something that could be recognized quickly, it was hardly apparent when war broke them apart, separating and scarring them, and it was only beginning to emerge when they found each other again after peace returned, in a way that later generations, searching for immediate fulfilment, would find increasingly hard to understand, it was a matter of keeping the faith whatever it cost . . .

★

In the evening of 7 December 1941 Flight Lieutenant Donald Hill began to keep a diary. He was stationed in Hong Kong, and his opening words explain clearly enough why he had chosen that moment to keep a record of events. 'Much talk about war with Japan,' he wrote, and then added guardedly, 'but no one seems to think anything will happen.'

The qualification was unwise. Far out in the north Pacific, Admiral Nagumo and a fleet of aircraft carriers were closing upon Hawaii. He had signalled to the aircrews waiting by their planes, 'The moment has arrived, the fate of the empire is at stake, let every man do his best,' and the message had been greeted by a storming cheer of 'Banzai! Banzai!' In something over seven hours, 140 Japanese bombers and 43 fighters would be launched into the dawn to attack the United States Pacific Fleet in Pearl Harbor. Within a week, every nation in the Far East would be at war.

If those first lines do not reveal foresight, at least the diarist could claim to share his ignorance with almost everyone else outside the Japanese High Command. Military experts in Washington and London, and from different perspectives in Berlin and Moscow, had studied Japanese intentions minutely, and come to the almost unanimous conclusion that, however bellicose she might appear, Japan would not go to war quite yet. Thus the quality that the diary's opening might have suggested to anyone who happened to read it was one of conventionality. It was an impression that would have suited Donald Hill.

His manner was quiet and reserved. For most of his life he had attempted to disguise himself, hiding feelings, concealing ambitions, narrowing the scope of desire to what was reasonable and attainable. After a childhood overshadowed by tragedy, and a deeply inhibited upbringing, he had dutifully begun his adult years by training to become an accountant. Nevertheless, if only for the intensity of the passion and physical sensuality he had begun to sense within him, he could not be called a conventional man.

Entirely by chance he had stumbled into joy. It came first

from flying, and nothing had prepared him for the sense of liberation he felt in the air. Yet it did not compare with the lightness of being that followed with the discovery that he was in love. From the cramped loneliness of what had come before, he was lifted to giddy heights, and the happiness he felt was to remain with him for the rest of his life. He could still fly every day, but being in love had become less easy. Barely three months after he first met Pamela he had been sent out to the Far East. They were engaged and would be married as soon as his tour of duty was over. So long as Japan did not go to war, he could expect to return home in the summer of 1942. Meanwhile the separation made him wretched, and he was not proud of his behaviour. The RAF had sent him first to Singapore, but there he had been involved in a notorious affair which had been brought to an end only by his transfer to Hong Kong. Until he and Pamela Kirrage were reunited, he would have preferred to be prone to less powerful emotions.

Thus the talk of war carried a double threat. At the least any serious conflict would delay his homecoming, but quite possibly it might cost him his life. At the age of twenty-eight he commanded a flight of five aircraft which represented the colony's only air defence. In battle, air superiority was a prerequisite for victory, and military logic meant that his aircraft would be among the first forces to be attacked. Death seems less daunting at his age than it does later; nevertheless its prospect concentrates the mind, even of a young man. He would not have been the first in those circumstances to want to leave a record of his life. If he did not survive the momentous days ahead, the diary would serve to tell the woman he loved what had happened to him.

On the morning of Saturday 6 December, he had joined a farewell party for his retiring commanding officer. The talk turned to the endlessly deferred possibility of a squadron of fighters being sent out to give protection to the airfield and their tiny force of two Walrus seaplanes and three Vildebeeste torpedo-bombers. Like so much of the British empire's defences, the chief function of these aircraft was display. For those who had never seen any other plane, a Walrus surging up from the sea between curtains of foam or the immense span of the Vildebeeste, almost 50 feet from wingtip to wingtip, roaring low over the rooftops, made an impressive spectacle. Put up against the latest generation of fighters which could fly at more than 300 m.p.h., they would be deathtraps. The Vildebeeste, which was a biplane with an open cockpit, had a top speed of 156 m.p.h., and the firing rings for the torpedoes it was designed to carry had been removed. Instead it was used mainly for reconnaissance, although it could carry two small 500-pound bombs. A year earlier, the Air Ministry had declared it obsolete, but its replacement had not yet arrived. There were rumours that some fighters would be sent to protect their antique bombers, and an Australian pilot called Frank Hennessy had arrived to set up a fighter operations room. No one quite believed reinforcements would arrive until the beginning of December when the Air Ministry in London authorized the construction of a new 500-yard runway. Work was due to begin on Monday 9 December.

That Saturday afternoon, Donald Hill and the new commanding officer, Wing Commander Sullivan, ran through the details of what needed to be done. Obstacles which had been placed on the existing runway to prevent it being used by enemy aircraft would have to be moved, and a detachment from the Hong Kong Defence Force Volunteers taking over guard duties had to be warned that there would be contractors on site.

Physically, the two officers made an incongruous pair as they surveyed the airfield – Sullivan, stocky, red-haired and inevitably nicknamed 'Ginger', and Hill towering over him, with dark hair and black, hawk's-wing eyebrows – but in character they were still more unlike. As his appearance and nickname indicated, Sullivan was energetic and quick-tempered, with an unquenchable desire to spur up people and ideas. Hill, known as 'Sammy', his second name, appeared to possess the solidity of a big man, slow to show his mood or even his thoughts. Yet he was a natural athlete, good at tennis and an instinctive, enthusiastic dancer, and women found him physically attractive. His fellow officers regarded him as 'a sound man', conscientious and careful, though a little remote. Despite these differences, he and Sullivan worked well together, and quickly cleared up the problems.

By mid-afternoon their work was finished, and the weekend began. Some of the small RAF detachment went racing at the Happy Valley racetrack, but for others there were rugger matches, football, swimming and sailing. All of these were mixed up with preparations for Christmas. Later, the atmosphere of shopping and partying struck many people as unduly frenetic – 'like Brussels before Waterloo' one participant later commented. At the colony's most luxurious hotel, the Hong Kong, the famous Gripps restaurant and ballroom was booked solid until Christmas for dances and parties. Those were the smartest events, but the colony's prosperity could be seen too in the fantastic entertainments put on at the Rose Room and Roof Garden at the Peninsula Hotel, and the dances organized at private homes.

'The evening ended at a typically bright young colonial party with discreet flirtations everywhere, sleek beautiful women and dashing young men in uniform,' wrote Emily Hahn, a sharp-eyed American-born resident, 'all being incredibly childish, so it seemed to me . . . we played our charades, we drank at the funny little bar, we giggled.'

In the red-light district of Wanchai, the bar-girls in their thigh-length *cheong-sams* offered more adult entertainment, and most of those among the 6,000-strong garrison who preferred alcohol to sex were crammed into the bars along Nathan Road.

Despite the general refusal to believe that the colony faced any real threat, Donald Hill took two measures which suggested that he viewed the situation more seriously. On Sunday morning, he climbed into one of the Vildebeestes, loaded it with two 500-pound bombs, and went out on a reconnaissance flight to see what targets the colony would present to an enemy pilot.

In the clear sunlit air, the scene looked too peaceful for it to be easily imagined as a battlefield. The streets were filled with traffic, ferries carved white wakes through the blue water, and a green and red tartan of intensively cultivated fields decorated the countryside. From 3,000 feet the three parts of Hong Kong were quite distinct. Disappearing into the haze of the Chinese mainland was the crumpled countryside of the New Territories. It was from here that any military force would attack. Below him the sprawl of Kowloon stretched inland from the long waterfront lined with tall brick-built stores and warehouses to a dense cluster of streets packed into a narrow coastal strip and eventually to straggling suburbs and steep hillsides dotted with the substantial red-tiled houses of the wealthy. A few hundred yards offshore lay Hong Kong island, consisting of little more than a crest of jagged hills with Victoria, the colony's capital, at its southern end.

In the previous month, he had taken up both the Governor, Sir Mark Young, and the General commanding the colony's forces, Major-General C. M. Maltby, to show them what they might have to defend. But this time he made himself view the scene as a Japanese pilot might, and, beside the short landing strip of the airfield, a target immediately presented itself. The two remaining Vildebeestes were lined up in the open side by side, and further out in the blue waters of Kowloon Bay the fat Walruses swung close together at their mooring buoys. When he landed, he ordered the old torpedo-bombers to be dispersed to opposite corners of the airfield, and he parked his own plane out of sight under the trees by the tennis court. There was nothing to be done about the seaplanes. Then he took another precaution.

The diary was his secret. During the First World War, soldiers on both sides had kept journals and when captured the intelligence services had found them invaluable sources of information. In consequence the Ministry of War in London had made it an offence for a serving soldier to keep any sort of daily record of his activities. The prohibition was not popular and thus was widely ignored. Officers far senior to a flight lieutenant kept personal diaries, and few even attempted to disguise their contents.

Donald Hill took a different approach. He would record what happened to him, but do so in such a way that no enemy would be able to read what he had written. Hiding his true feelings was second nature to him, and it was understandable that he should now have thought of using a code or cipher to conceal what he wrote. In the first instance, he wrote in a crude shorthand. But over the months ahead, as the danger of discovery grew, he responded by devising new layers of camouflage. One cipher overlay another, and eventually he tried to mask his secret so that it was impossible for anyone who had not been told even to recognize it as a diary, let alone be able to read it. So much of himself went into the disguise, it became an extension of his own enigmatic personality. In the end, it seems that he could only have wanted one other person in the whole world to be able to decipher the long columns of numerals into which it was transformed, because it was around her name that he devised his final cipher. If he wrote his diary for anyone other than himself, he wrote it for Pamela.

Long after the other officers went to bed, he remained awake writing in a stiff-backed notebook. By chance, 7 December was his night to act as duty officer, the one who would be woken if any urgent message had to be passed to the colony's air force. In his last entry of the day he questioned whether he would get any sleep at all.

In the event, it was shortly before dawn that an orderly shook him awake. The Colonial Secretary, Franklin Gimson, was on the telephone. Donald listened to the dry, tired tones, acknowledged the message, then put the phone down. In the early hours of 8 December, Tokyo Radio had interrupted its short-wave news broadcast to South-East Asia with a special announcement. It could hardly have sounded more innocuous:

'Allow me to make a weather forecast at this time: west wind clear.' But Donald was not the only one to disguise his secret in code. The attack on Pearl Harbor had begun, and now Tokyo was warning its embassies that it proposed to wage war against the enemy in the west, Britain.

Even after the other officers had been woken with the news, there was no urgency in their response. It was as though the jump in imagination they needed to make from the orderliness of a peacetime existence sheltered by the power of empire to the savagery of fighting for existence was too great for them even at that late hour. At 8.00 a.m. a few of the aircrew were strolling out to the airfield, but others were still eating breakfast when everyone heard an ominous roar to the north. Someone foolishly suggested it might be the long-awaited squadron of fighters arriving.

Donald began to run to where the Vildebeeste had been parked, but if there had ever been anything that could be done with such ancient aircraft, it was too late now. Nine bombers escorted by more than thirty Japanese Zero fighters came in at rooftop level. The bombers headed on for Kowloon, but the fighters swooped low along the length of the airstrip machine-gunning every target they could find.

The battle of Hong Kong had begun. It would not last long, but its resonance altered the rest of Donald's life. When he emerged from the maelstrom of battle and prison camp, the man he once was had been changed in almost every respect. There were, however, two crucial links between before and after – the diary and his love for Pamela. Each survived until his dying day, linked intimately for good and ill, but the secret that bound them together lasted longer still. It is the reason for this book.

CHAPTER I

ENIGMA

All longing converges on this mystery revelation, unraveling secret spaces, the suggestion that the world's valence lies just behind a scrambled facade, where only the limits of ingenuity stand between him and sunken gardens. Cryptography alone slips beneath the cheat of surfaces.

Richard Powers, *The Gold Bug Variations*

In his cramped office in the University of Surrey, Dr Philip Aston turned off his computer, and opened a large brown envelope that had arrived in the post for him that morning. Inside it he found about twenty photocopied pages. The first page had been taken from the cover of a notebook. The words, 'Russels Mathematical Tables', were written on it in block capitals. What caught his eye, however, were twelve pages filled with neat, closely written columns of numbers. They resembled old-fashioned logarithm tables, except that there did not appear to be any pattern to them. Another page contained elaborate, handwritten instructions showing how to use the numbers as a ready reckoner for multiplication. To multiply 83 by 26, for example, the reader was instructed to combine numbers from different columns in different ways 'so that the answer is found to be 2118'.

It did not look right, but, just to be sure, Philip Aston checked the calculation. One digit was wrong. It might have been a mistake, but a child equipped with no more than pencil and paper could work out that 83×26 came to 2158. As a senior lecturer in the Department of Mathematics and Computing Science, Dr Aston allowed himself to make the first, and in some ways most crucial, of what would be many deductions about the notebook. Whatever the numbers represented, they were not the mathematical tables they claimed to be.

It was only by chance that the package had been sent to him at all. A few days earlier, he had been copying some notes when the department's secretary looked up from her phone. 'There's someone on the line who wants to speak to a mathematician', she said. 'Will you deal with it?' There was no one else around, so he had taken the call.

The voice at the other end was clipped and military. The caller's name was Colonel Ian Quayle from the Soldiers', Sailors' and Airmen's Families Association (SSAFA). He had with him a notebook kept by a young RAF flight lieutenant, called Donald Hill, who had been captured by the Japanese after the fall of Hong Kong in 1941. It contained numbers arranged to look like a ready reckoner and conceivably, declared Colonel Quayle, that was what the notebook really was.

'That's why we want a mathematician to look at it,' he said briskly, seemingly unaware that getting a top-flight academic to check out what might be nothing more than multiplication tables was akin to asking a general to inspect a box of toy soldiers to ensure that they really were military figures. 'Would you be prepared to glance over it, and tell us what it is?'

Philip Aston had an international reputation for his research on such recondite branches of mathematics as bifurcation theory and chaos analysis. Someone of his academic standing might have felt slightly insulted, but instead he was intrigued, a response that marked him out from others who had heard about the tables. They had been sent to both the Imperial War Museum and the RAF Museum, and at neither place had anyone been tempted to give them more than a second glance before returning them. What interested Dr Aston was the story that Quayle had told.

There was a distinct possibility, the Colonel explained, that the notebook was in fact a diary. Donald Hill had died in 1985, but he had told his wife and children that the columns of numbers were a code, which concealed the record of his experiences in Hong Kong during the battle for the colony and later as a prisoner of war. What had happened to him then had remained a secret for half a century. Hill rarely referred to his wartime experiences, and understandably the family now wanted to discover what the notebook contained. Then Quayle added, 'And of course if it *is* a code, we wondered whether you would have a stab at decoding it?'

Philip Aston had enough to keep him busy. His heavy teaching workload ate into the time he needed for research and, like every academic, he knew that his reputation depended on having his research published. Yet his imagination was caught by the idea of finding out what had happened so long ago. Besides, he thought, if it does turn out to be a code devised by a prisoner of war with nothing more than pencil and paper, it should be easy enough to break. Aston had never really considered what life would have been like in a Japanese prison camp, but Hill had no computer, no calculator and, with all the pressures and privations he must have faced, he surely could not have had the time to work out anything too complex. It should not take long to crack it. Perhaps a weekend would be enough. He could spare a weekend. 'Send me a copy,' he said, 'and I'll see what I can do.'

Now he had the notebook in front of him. With it, Quayle had sent some details about Donald Hill. He had been in a prisoner-of-war camp in Hong Kong for three-and-a-half years. At the end of the war, he had been awarded the MBE, and had then left the RAF as a squadron-leader. Quayle did not say that Hill was 'a sound man', but it was there in those scraps. Studying the tables again, Philip Aston had a thought that was to return more clearly the longer he worked on them. The columns of tightly packed numbers made a direct connection with the man in the prisoner-of-war camp. What he sensed was that in their neatness and order, and their misleading instructions, and their seemingly impenetrable secrecy, they contained not just a record of events, but a flavour of Donald Hill himself.

Most people find numerals at least a little daunting, and so many, crammed on to the page with no clear purpose, might freeze the mind. For Philip Aston, however, they had an irresistible beauty. Even as a child, he had enjoyed the patterns that numbers make, and as he grew older the world that mathematics revealed often seemed more fascinating than the world revealed by sight and touch and smell.

The fascination lies in the way mathematics describes patterns to be found not only in abstract geometrical shapes like triangles and rectangles, but throughout nature, from the branched structure of a snowflake and the wave-like formation of dunes in the desert to the spiral of the Milky Way. Life itself, according to Ian Stewart, Professor of Mathematics at Warwick University, is built round the same kind of forms. 'There is mathematics in the molecular scaffolding of DNA,' he wrote in *Life's Other Secret*, 'and in the long-term evolutionary dynamics of the entire global ecosystem, in the glory of a peacock's tail, in the gaudy wings of butterflies and the markings on seashells, in the disposition of sunflower seeds, in the organization of ants' nests.' Even in the development of a human embryo, the multiplication of cells and the formation of organs and limbs exhibit mathematical regularities, and the branching of the circulatory system follows the same fractal model as the branching of a tree or a river.

As a child Philip Aston was brought up to believe in God according to the strict faith of the Plymouth Brethren. The Bible was interpreted literally, and their fundamentalist beliefs were diametrically opposed to the questioning, speculative outlook of a scientist. As he grew older, it was hardly surprising that he found himself having to reconcile the claims of religion and science, but everywhere in the natural world, as in mathematics, he discovered patterns of such intricacy and beauty that he could only believe that they were put in place by a creative God. 'I cannot believe that all this is the product of some meaningless process,' he declared. 'What mathematics reveals, at least it seems so to me, is evidence of a creator beyond the scope of human thought or imagination.' Today he spends his weekdays working on problems with daunting titles like Symmetry and Chaos in the complex Ginzburg–Landau equation, but on Sundays he plays the piano in Guildford Baptist church. From his point of view, each activity serves the same purpose.

Now with the numbers on the page before him, he instinctively began to search for patterns. Each page was filled with a tight latticework of boxes squeezed into twenty-three columns across and forty-seven rows down, and four tiny digits were crammed into each box. On the first two pages he saw that the numbers ranged from 1 to 26, with a dot placed either side of a single digit. On subsequent pages, a different set of numbers were used. These went from 10 to 35, and he suspected that this set had been adopted because double digits fitted more conveniently into the columns. What was significant was that Donald Hill had chosen to use no more than twenty-six different numbers. The first recognizable shape had emerged. If any meaning was to be extracted from the diary, at some point the numbers would have to be translated into words, and it was surely no coincidence that those words had to be made up from the twenty-six letters in the alphabet.

If there is one characteristic that mathematicians share, it is an enjoyment of meticulous work. One digit out of place, one equation misread, and the poison kills every subsequent calculation. The penalties are too great to risk anything less than perfect accuracy, and so the otherwise tedious business of achieving it becomes an ingrained and even pleasurable habit. The quickest way to transfer the numbers in the notebook to the computer would have been to put the sheets on a digital scanner which would have recorded them in a form the computer could read. But there was a danger that the scanner's Optical Recognition software might mistake a tiny 3 for a 5, or a 1 for a 7. In the end the human eye and intelligence were more reliable than a silicon chip, so he decided to type each number directly into the computer one by one. It was like a cabinet-maker putting a new edge on a chisel before beginning work. Getting the preliminaries right provided part of the satisfaction.

Tall and lean to the point of being cadaverous, Philip Aston possesses a sublime confidence in the power of numbers. He knew little about codes and ciphers except that there was a relationship between them and his field. It was enough to persuade him that he could master the discipline, and he looked forward to the intellectual challenge it would present. His guide was a book with the drab title of *Elementary Cryptanalysis: a mathematical approach* by Abraham Sinkov. One of the giants of modern cryptanalysis, Sinkov had in 1929 helped to set up the Pentagon's gigantic cryptographic section, now the National Security Agency and the largest ciphering and deciphering organization in the world. He had been recruited from New York University to this position at the heart of the United States military machine simply on the basis of his brilliance as a mathematician, and he never quite lost an academic's outlook. By a neat coincidence his most effective work was in cracking the codes of the Japanese air force which destroyed Donald Hill's planes. For this he was promoted to the rank of colonel and awarded the Legion of Merit, but even after four years of war his response to a crisp, military salute was a little wave of the hand and a cheerful 'Good morning'. For the next few weeks, his book led Philip Aston through the intricacies of his new subject.

Secrecy is the aim of all codes. The crucial word was 'crypt', whose Greek origin meant concealed or underground, hence the name for the little chapel hidden beneath the main body of a cathedral. The study of secret writing is 'cryptology'; creating codes, ciphers or any communication containing a hidden meaning is referred to as 'cryptography', and uncovering the secret messages is 'cryptanalysis'. From the start, mathematicians have been the supreme makers and detectors of this kind of secret communication – indeed the word 'cipher' itself once simply meant zero, the most basic of all mathematical terms.

There is a crucial difference between a code and a cipher. A code simply replaces a fragment of information, usually a word or sentence, with another symbol. Thus, to send a message from the front line, American troops in the First World War needed only to consult a codebook consisting of lists of letters referring to common situations, such as YB for 'Rifle ammunition needed', and AF for 'Enemy machine-gun fire serious'. The most widely used code in history, although many users have no idea they are employing it, is ASCII or American Standard Code for Information Interchange, which is part of the software of nearly all personal computers. Unusually for a code, individual characters are replaced in this case, so that each symbol on the keyboard has its counterpart in a string of seven '1's or '0's; thus the lower-case letter *a* becomes 1100001 and upper-case *A* becomes 1000001.

What makes a cipher different is that, when it changes the letters in the original message, it does so according to a rule which is defined by a secret key. The simplest example is the cipher devised by Julius Caesar and used by generations of schoolchildren since, in which *a* is encrypted as *d*, *b* as *e*, and so on. The key is that each letter is replaced by another three further on in the alphabet. The drawback, as generations of schoolchildren have also learned, is that this key is extremely easy to recognize.

'What you are looking for is a pattern; once you find that, you have the key,' Philip Aston explained. 'I think that's why so many mathematicians have taken an interest in cryptography. The two disciplines are quite compatible.'

A typical example of pattern recognition in a cipher, and the one that gives away the key to the Caesar cipher concerns the letter *e*, which occurs more frequently than any other letter in the English language. Thus, if an encrypted message contains more '*h*'s than any other letter, it is a good hypothesis that *h* stands for *e* in the original message, or plaintext as cryptanalysts prefer, and that quite probably the key is the one devised by Caesar. In fact the frequency with which different letters appear in English is astonishingly consistent. In any long text, the five letters used most often will almost invariably be *e*, *t*, *a*, *o*, *n*, in that order, and the frequency with which the remainder appear can be predicted with the same certainty.

Knowing this weakness, experienced cryptographers try to disguise the frequent appearance of *e* by throwing in complications. A second encryption might transform the first *h* in the Caesar cipher into *i*, the next into *j* and the third into *k*. They might also attempt to avoid using *e* in the original plaintext, following the example offered by Ernest Vincent Wright in his novel *Gadsby*. Summarizing its plot, he wrote, 'It is a story about a small town. It is not a gossipy yarn; nor is it a dry, monotonous account, full of such customary "fill-ins" as "romantic moonlight casting murky shadows down a long, winding country road". No. It is an account of up-and-doing activity; a vivid portrayal of Youth as it is today; and a practical discarding of that worn-out notion that "a child don't know anything".' Not a single 'he' or 'she' or 'the' or 'then' appears, and, to show it was possible, he went on to complete his 50,000-word story without using the letter *e* once.

In its final form, what confronts the cryptanalyst is designed to be as impenetrable as the shell on a tortoise. It is as though, out in the open, a secret needs protection as much as a soft-skinned animal, and codes have evolved as a defence against predators. However far-fetched it might seem, the analogy had a particular application to Donald Hill's code, for, had his diary been discovered, it could have put his very life at risk.

In *The Codebreakers*, his magisterial study of the craft, David Kahn commented, 'Cryptography is protection. It is to that extension of the modern man – communications – what the carapace is to the turtle, ink to the squid, camouflage to the chameleon . . . The objective is self-preservation. This is the first law of life, as imperative for a body politic as for an individual organism. And if biological evolution demonstrates anything, it is that intelligence best secures that goal. Knowledge is power.' Between the code-maker and the code-breaker, he argued, there existed a state of conflict as primal as the basic rivalry between prey and predator that drove evolution forward. 'Cryptography', he concluded 'seeks to conserve in exclusivity a [person's] store of knowledge, cryptanalysis to increase that store.'

The importance that Donald Hill attached to his secret could be measured by the effectiveness of the protection he created for it. At both the Imperial War Museum and the RAF Museum, the words 'Russels Mathematical Tables' had aroused enough doubts in the minds of whoever had examined the notebook to persuade them that it was not worth subjecting it to any further scrutiny. In the jargon of the code-breakers, this was a successful piece of steganography, concealing the very existence of the coded message. The fact that he had not only enciphered his diary, but set out to disguise the cipher as mathematical tables, indicated how essential to his life it was, and how greatly he feared the threat that would come from exposing its contents to outside view.

Philip Aston's initial difficulty lay in deciding where to start. In the end, he decided to find out whether Donald Hill had used a substitution cipher, replacing one letter with another or with a number, according to a secret formula. He chose to begin with the most basic of them all, beloved by generations of children needing to protect their secrets, which simply substitutes a number for a letter, so that $a = 1$, $b = 2$ and so on down to $z = 26$. It was simple to write a program for the computer to translate the numbers into letters, substituting a for 1, b for 2.

It was almost embarrassingly primitive, but the challenge had to begin somewhere. The computer on his desk could process ten million bits of information a second, sift the numbers for sequences, measure them for mathematical relationships, and compute every possible connection between them, all faster than he could read. Beyond that machine lay all the resources of a modern university's maths and computing department. It was a formidably powerful hammer to break open the little nut of Donald Hill's code. The date was 3 February 1996, and outside his window the short winter's day was turning to dusk. It was time to go to work.

The news that Colonel Quayle had discovered someone who was prepared to examine Donald Hill's notebook brought a curious kind of hope to Pamela Hill. Throughout the years of their marriage, she had known that the numbers were a code which contained his diary. Over ten years had passed since her husband's death, and the need to find out what it concealed nagged at her insistently. It was more than curiosity that drove her to search for someone to decode it. Her own past, almost all her adult life, had been intimately bound up with Donald Hill. From her early twenties when she first saw him, there had scarcely been a day when he had not occupied her thoughts and stirred her feelings. What he experienced during the period covered by the diary had profoundly affected their relationship, yet he had never been able to tell her what had happened to him.

At the same time, the sheer weight of expectation made her apprehensive. The contents of the diary were bound to affect her in ways she could scarcely imagine. Its secrets could explain the enigma of the man she had adored, but they might reveal some behaviour of his that she would find unforgivable. It was as though one crucial piece in the jigsaw of her own life remained face down, and the image it hid would change the picture she had of herself.

She was seventy-nine now, as fragile as porcelain but still, with enormous blue eyes beneath a wave of perfectly cut hair, recognizably the beauty she had been in her youth. Half a century had passed since she and Donald first fell in love. He had died in 1985, but still she thought about him every day, and on many nights saw him in her dreams. When she looked back on her own life, its shape was formed by that one relationship. It had not been entirely happy, but it had been all-encompassing, from its first beginning in spring to the final winter parting. They had loved and quarrelled, and said everything that could be said both in ecstasy and in anger. Each of them had regretted much, and loved more, and in the end forgiven everything. By the time death halted the dance, they had reached an understanding that united them in a way that went beyond the power of words to describe.

Yet at the heart of their relationship there remained this mystery of what had happened to Donald in Hong Kong. It was not just the experience of war, or even of a Japanese prison camp. There were histories and reminiscences which told of the general conditions the prisoners had endured. What mattered was the particular impact of those experiences on Donald's character. Any explanation he might have provided had been locked away so deeply that he had been unable to say it aloud. That was why she had to know what was in the diary, whatever its consequences. It was the last secret. Before his end, all others had been told and shared. Only this one had remained literally unspeakable. Behind the numbers were words that she should have heard while he was still alive. Until they had been spoken, the story was not complete.

In the years since his death, she had repeatedly tried to find someone who could decipher the diary. It had proved to be a frustrating search. Friends had been approached, acquaintances consulted, and the notebook had been sent to the sort of organizations that might be expected to crack codes. Some were simply daunted by the dense forest of numbers. Others wondered whether it was worth the trouble, or the risk of stirring up the past. And a few, without ever actually telling her she was being a fool, let it be known that perhaps the numbers actually amounted to nothing more than multiplication tables. None of them ever appreciated how compelling was her urge to know.

With the wilful confidence that a beautiful woman learns from her beauty and never forgets, she simply ignored a verdict that did not suit her. Regardless of what the experts might say, she remained certain that sooner or later someone would be found who could penetrate her husband's disguise. Her insistence had led her to SSAFFA, and eventually to the redoubtable Colonel Quayle. When he came up with Dr Aston, she was delighted that he had succeeded, but not entirely surprised. Men usually did what she asked of them.

'I wish I had that sublime confidence,' her eldest child Joanna once remarked. 'She will say outrageous things, without thinking about the impact they will have, and it doesn't matter. People enjoy her, and they don't seem to mind about the rest.'

While this book was being written, Pamela was taken into hospital to be treated for cancer. Convalescing in a ward where the inanities of daytime television blared out at an audience of weary patients, suffering from depression and other psychological wounds, she made it clear that whatever the outcome of her treatment, she was determined to face it in style. Day by day, she recycled the tiny wardrobe of clothes she had been able to pack into her suitcase, a silk scarf, a pretty blouse, a fire-engine red suit, a gold brooch, so that each morning she appeared beautifully dressed and made up.

'Of course most of them are loonies, mad as hatters', she exclaimed of her fellow-patients in a penetrating voice which was barely camouflaged by the raucous television. 'But who can blame them? Anyone would go mad in here.'

Her own protest against the system was an adamant refusal to eat any hospital food. The menu of muddy chunks of meat sited on banks of sludgy rice, alternating with sandwiches of grated orange cheese on stale bread, made it an understandable gesture although it did her health no good. To the despair of her family, she grew thinner and thinner, and her hunger strike brought her up against the formidable Sister Margarita who ran the hospital wing with fearsome authority. The untouched plates of stew were brought to the sister's attention, and Pamela was summoned to see her.

Large and domineering, Sister Margarita was too good a nurse to allow a patient to starve herself, and too imposing a character to tolerate any opposition to her rule. Evidently Pamela would have to put up with the food. What happened in the course of their confrontation remained private, but when they emerged into the corridor the outcome was there for everyone to see. The pair of them had their arms round each other, and while Sister Margarita beamed down at her impossible patient, Pamela sang in a wheezy soprano Georges Guétary's show-stopper from the 1947 musical *Bless the Bride*: 'La belle Marguerite, so beautiful to see. La belle Marguerite picking grapes with me.' A fortnight later, Pamela was sent home, officially cured, unofficially because keeping her there was more trouble than it was worth, but mostly as a reward for sheer *joie de vivre*.

In her flat, she kept the picture of Donald which a fellow prisoner had drawn shortly before he was released. In it he is still wearing his RAF cap, but he has grown a thick black beard and his face has a gaunt appearance. There are no other clues about what is happening to him. He is looking down as though to prevent the artist seeing into his eyes and revealing any more than that. It was one of the few items, other than the diary, that he brought back with him when he returned after the war, and it gave away no more secrets than the diary.

She did not have many other physical mementoes of him. Some had been destroyed in the turbulent years of their marriage, and more had disappeared in the decade since his death. What remained were the wedding photographs in their leather-covered frames standing on a cupboard by the wall, some letters kept carefully in a torn manila envelope, and a few pieces of furniture. Otherwise there were only her memories of him. Sometimes it seemed very little to show for the intensity of sharing a life for so long.

On the surface it had been a restricted existence. Unlike modern women who had careers and thought nothing of travelling around the world, Pamela had passed most of her life in the comfortable surroundings of Tunbridge Wells and, on the only occasion when she had spent any length of time abroad, had yearned to be back home. She had worked before her marriage, but afterwards her career was that of wife and mother.

Donald had kept her, and neither of them imagined there could be any other arrangement. From that perspective, it had been a model of post-war, middle-class English domestic life. Just occasionally, she wished it had actually been what it seemed.

There was no general formula for describing a life, she thought. The scope of it could be shown easily enough – went there, saw them, earned this, did that – but the intensity of living itself escaped. What remained of that intensity was the diary, and it came from the very heart of her invisible history.

Protected by the code, it had survived like a time capsule from a moment which was the turning-point in their lives. The suffering he had known then was to bleed into their love for years afterwards. Throughout their marriage that experience had been locked away. She could guess what pain it contained by the insistence with which he defended the secret. It was Bluebeard's room, the one part of his life that she was not allowed into.

Sitting in her comfortable armchair, she watched the light drain out of the February day, and wondered how long it would take Philip Aston to break Donald's code. She did not doubt that he would succeed in the end. Or, if not him, someone else. What sort of secret might emerge from his efforts? As she pondered the question, she realized the importance of what he was attempting to do. It was not just a matter of decoding a document. For Pamela Hill, it was a matter of decoding a man.

CHAPTER 2

FIRST LOVE

There is no such thing as the State
And no one exists alone;
Hunger allows no choice
To the citizen or the police;
We must love one another or die.

W. H. Auden, 'September 1 1939'

Pamela and Donald first met on the afternoon of Friday 31 March 1939. Since the course of her life was irrevocably marked by what happened that day, it was no surprise that in later years she remembered the date so well.

It was Derry McConnell who set it up. He was Irish in his birth and his charm, but pure pilot by temperament. Flying was what he lived for and, having trained at Cranwell, he was now a flying officer in the RAF. McConnell possessed the easy confidence of someone who had found his rightful place in the world. He might have been a fighter pilot, but instead was posted to Coastal Command at RAF Gosport, where they specialized in torpedo-bombing and anti-submarine warfare. His parents lived in Tunbrdge Wells in Kent, where he met Pamela Kirrage, as she then was, at a dance, and promptly enrolled as one of her impecunious admirers. These had the privilege of taking her to dances and to pubs, unlike the moneyed ones who took her to dances and the Savoy. Where she was taken was less important than being able to dance and have fun, and for both she liked to sense a certain confidence, an indefinable but instantly recognizable cocktail of zest and *savoir-faire*, in her boyfriends. And she could afford to be selective because membership of both groups was large.

She was just twenty-three. A photograph by the outstanding fashion photographer of the time, Angus McBean, shows her pale, serious face gazing out with enormous eyes from the moody black and white shadowed background that was his trademark. There is a vulnerable, almost waiflike look about her delicate features, emphasized by the thick, dark hair tumbling down to her bare shoulders. Not all of this was really her. In reality, the hair was chestnut-coloured, the eyes grey-blue, the character assertive and the look challenging, but the camera told no lies about her beauty.

When she was still seventeen and working as an au pair in France, she had been spotted in the street and offered a modelling contract. It was an occupation she had scarcely heard of, and which, until the 1920s, had hardly existed. Up to then, most new styles were still run up, as they had been for a century or more, by dressmakers and milliners following designs taken from fashion plates, mass-produced prints of the latest fashions. The change started when magazines like *Vogue* began using photographs rather than sketches to illustrate what Worth and Molyneux and the other Paris fashion houses were producing for the new season, and photographers like McBean and Edward Steichen looked for striking models to show the clothes off. Coincidentally, after the First World War a growing number of clothes shops, such as Simpsons and Selfridges, as well as textile companies produced their own particular look and hired mannequins to show it off for their favoured customers.

One of the very first models, Lucie Clayton, had just opened a school in London for those who wanted to learn the trade, and in 1936 after she returned to London Pamela took its six-month course. She was taught how to wear dresses and show them off, and given advice on how to put on make-up. They had foundation creams and rouge, but there was no eyeshadow, and for mascara the girls learned to dilute black paint with spit, applying the mixture with a large brush. Her first job on the catwalk was for the couturier Maggie Roulf, as desirable a label then as Nicole Farhi or Issey Miyaki is now.

In the respectable Tunbridge Wells of the 1930s, attitudes to modelling were as old-fashioned as the taste in clothes. According to the historian Richard Cobb, who grew up there during this period, fashion tended towards sensible tweed and Jaeger in winter, and vaguely Edwardian yellow tussore dresses with green parasols in summer. It was, he judged, 'a town built for leisure, for quiet and orderly enjoyment, for rather dowdy comfort and old-fashioned luxury'. On the whole models were regarded as not much worse than actresses and hardly better than chorus-girls. 'Racy' described their reputation, and raciness is not a quality that Tunbridge Wells has ever greatly cared for.

It was certainly not the career that might have been expected from a member of the Kirrage family. Pamela's father was general manager of the Scottish & Union National insurance company, and had sent his four children to the sort of schools which specified in the prospectus that they catered for the offspring of gentlemen. Their home was a substantial house near the top of the hill on Queen's Road where they were looked after by a parlourmaid, a housemaid called Sainter, a nanny called Quincy and a live-in cook called Edith. Faithful to the tenets of an unknown but unquestioned authority, the family ate a roast on Sundays, and ensured that the port circulated in a clockwise direction. But the picture of middle-class rectitude was not entirely unblemished.

'We were a respectable family but just slightly eccentric,' Pamela's younger sister Brigit remembers. 'My father, Henry, was a clever and determined man, who had gone to the same state school in Nottingham as D. H. Lawrence. He was popular with women and something of a flirt, but it was my mother, Marjorie, who ran things. She was round and fierce with a sharp tongue – I should describe her as an outspoken pudding.'

Recognizing that his daughters had inherited their mother's force of character, Henry Kirrage did not try to oppose their ambitions too strongly. When Pamela announced that she was going to be a model, he restricted himself to expressing his relief that she was not going to be an actress and paid her Lucie Clayton fees. And when Brigit declared that *she* was going to be an actress, he paid the fees for her training at the Old Vic without a murmur, no doubt silently relieved that she had not wanted to be a chorus-girl.

Perhaps this desire to show off was partly inherited, for very often Mr Kirrage would play the piano in the parlour, while Mrs Kirrage sang something from Gilbert and Sullivan. Frequently her selection included 'Three Little Girls from School Are We' with her daughters encouraged to join in, followed by 'Come into the Garden, Maud' from the Popular Home Songbook. Rather less often they organized musical evenings in a village hall where young men were expected to sing romantic or silly songs. In 1930 the local paper noted Miss Brigit Kirrage's performance as Mustard Seed in her school's 'admirable production' as *Midsummer Night's Dream*, and some time later commended Mrs Kirrage's 'remarkable concert' at St Barnabas Parish Hall where there had been humorous musical sketches, a Scotch dance, and Mr Elphick had contributed 'Old Barty' and 'The Skipper of the Mary Jane', which, the reviewer noted approvingly, were 'two very breezy songs'. Among their neighbours, the Kirrages were regarded as arty and rather odd.

Nevertheless, the family was entirely Tunbridge Wells in its solidity, and from that quality Pamela drew the memory of a completely contented childhood. She was the second of the four children, and the household in which she grew up was almost entirely female. Peter, the son and eldest by thirteen months, had gone to Cambridge and then Burma. Behind him he left three sisters, Pamela, Brigit, who was two years younger, and after a gap of seven years Sheila. Nanny Quincy and the beautiful Sainter, archly named 'The Fairest' by their father, acted as their proto-mothers, providing an affection that they missed from their real mother. As often happens, each of the daughters was deemed to have one quality only. Thus Pamela was the pretty one, Brigit the clever one and Sheila the sensible one, but regardless of character each in turn was sent to school at Hamilton House.

It was only five minutes down the road, but the two elder girls were taken as boarders because there was something ever so slightly common about being a day girl. The school was run by two lesbians, Miss Ferguson and Miss Body, known as Fugs and Bods, whose rigid sense of caste forced them to exclude any child with parents suspected of being engaged in trade, and at the same time prevented any but the most sordid minds imagining their sex lives. No one much cared if Miss Ferguson and Miss Body taught the girls little beyond some elementary Scripture, the offside rule in hockey and how to imitate the dashing Suzanne Lenglen's forehand drive on the tennis court. Sooner or later they would get married to a young man who would provide for them while they brought into the world another generation like themselves.

Buttressed by servants and convention, the pre-war family was a small society of its own, headed by the senior male and descending by gradations of age and sex and wealth to the youngest scullery maid. Consequently its values, particularly its respect for hierarchy, property and comfort, had an unmistakably municipal flavour. Tunbridge Wells liked to imagine itself reflecting those same values writ large. A handsome old town built on seven hills round a bowl in the Kent countryside, it had known a decent prosperity since the eighteenth century, when its water was found to contain chalybeate, or iron traces, which were thought to be health-giving. Transformed into a fashionable spa for London society, it never had to struggle very hard for its living. It avoided the raffishness of Brighton or Bath, missed out on the vulgarity of the Industrial Revolution, and was cushioned against the chanciness of farming life. Insulated from such life-giving turbulence, there was nothing to challenge its settled existence. Retired colonial officials, accustomed to the automatic deference of their inferiors, found Tunbridge Wells an attractive spot for their declining years. It was an hour from

London, but still in the country, and everyone knew their place. As an official guide in the 1920s put it, 'The town is never over-run with trippers, nor are its streets ever defiled by the vulgar or the inane. Its inhabitants are composed for the most part of well-to-do people who naturally create a social atmosphere tinged by culture and refinement.' To the outside world, it became synonymous with comfort, respectability and – although there may have been some envy in this – smugness.

The two elder Kirrage girls had a glamour that did not quite fit these surroundings. Richard Cobb, who for all his intellectual boldness was socially timid, remembered admiring them hope-lessly, but until the war broke out never plucked up enough courage to talk to either of them. First Pamela found her way on to the catwalk, then Brigit started to train as an actress, and, while she was still at the Old Vic, her elder sister was offered a lucrative contract by the British Cellanese Company. Men might not know what this bland name implied, but every woman could make the association, and it was certainly not one that any decent Tunbridge Wells family would choose for its daughter. Indeed it was the British Cellanese Company's products which provoked the original letter signed 'Disgusted of Tunbridge Wells'.

Although she worked regularly, Pamela was not ideal for the job. At five feet nine inches tall, she only just met the requirements for height, and her figure was slightly too full. Her official model sheet described her measurements as 35 inches at the bust, 25 at the waist and 37 at the hips. The boyish look of the 1920s had never quite gone away, and mannequins were required to be flat-chested or at least to bandage their breasts, with no hint of cleavage allowed. Such considerations did not apply to underwear, however, and underwear was what the British Cellanese Company manufactured. It was the drawing of a nubile young body in an advertisement for women's underwear in the *Courier*, which provoked one furious reader to tell the paper that in his opinion the floodgates to unbridled lust had wantonly been thrown open. In his outrage, he signed himself simply 'Disgusted of Tunbridge Wells'. The idea of a town so prim that its citizens might be overcome by the depravity of an advertisement for bras and knickers struck the outside world as too good a joke to be forgotten, and Tunbridge Wells has never been allowed to escape the connection. Mr Kirrage found it less funny.

'My father did not like the idea at all,' Pamela recalled, 'his daughter parading up and down in a skimpy bodice – how shocking. I think it must have been my mother who persuaded him that I wouldn't come to any harm because he did finally agree. And of course, as it turned out, it could not have been more respectable.'

What persuaded him was not just his wife's advocacy, but his daughter's enthusiasm. The nice conventional girl who was hopeless at schoolwork, and adored tennis and dancing, had developed a will of her own. It was a characteristic that remained apparent throughout her life. Convention depended on a young woman knowing her place and relying on her parents to support her until a husband arrived, but the attention that Pamela's looks attracted, and the income she earned, allowed her to insist on her own course. She travelled the country to model cellanese camisoles, knickers and bras to a select clientele in Selfridges in London, and in Jenners in Edinburgh, and Binns in Manchester. When Princess Marina became engaged to the Duke of Kent and went to Simpsons in Piccadilly to select her trousseau, Miss Kirrage was hurriedly summoned to model the underwear. Compared to other girls who became secretaries or schoolteachers, it was a glamorous career. She still lived at home, and still kept the same friends, but the narrow world was inexorably broadening.

There had always been a rivalry between the pretty sister and the clever one, made worse according to Brigit by their mother's clear preference for Pamela. It encouraged what her younger sister regarded as an already disagreeable expectation of getting her own way. Thus when they went to Stratford to see a production of *Richard III* and had to share a room, it seemed to

Brigit typical that Pamela should claim the best bed and strew her clothes all over the place. Her mood was not sweetened by the crowds of young men who used to cluster round her sister. They came in all kinds, from a handsome curate called Guinness to a smooth lounge lizard with greasy hair and a flashy style of dancing, from the charming, confident Derry McConnell to the bashful, brilliant Richard Cobb, whose hopeless adoration ultimately turned to a more realistic passion for Brigit. Meanwhile Pamela danced and flirted with them all, but emotionally remained utterly unmoved.

'She was like ice-cream,' Brigit exclaimed. 'It was extraordinary. She had innumerable young men queuing up to marry her, and on the outside she was sweet to them, yet quite cold on the inside.'

It was behaviour which Pamela herself found confusing. 'I loved dancing with them, but I never found any of them physically attractive,' she said. 'I think I must have been very shy deep down.'

She was, however, warmer than Brigit gave her credit for. It was after all the intensity of their feelings for each other that made their relationship so volatile. And Sheila, the youngest of the girls, remembered that it was Pamela rather than Brigit who helped her with all the problems of clothes and boys and growing up. In fact it was because she was a good sister that the meeting which was to change her life took place.

In 1938 Brigit suffered terrible injuries when a badly wired iron short-circuited, setting alight to her clothes. The right side of her body was so severely burned that for months her life was in danger. It was only the pioneering work of a plastic surgeon, Raynsford Mowlem, who took strips of skin from her thigh, and cultured them before applying them to the suppurating wounds that she survived at all. It put a halt to her theatrical ambitions, and her convalescence was slow. By the time she had recovered, a larger tragedy was beginning to loom.

Above the din of big bands blaring out 'The Black Bottom Stomp' and the chatter of gossip about Charlie Chaplin's new film, the drone of politics had become so insistent that no one could ignore it. Events in Europe were significant for some reason, and if the intricacies of treaties with France and guarantees to Czechoslovakia and Poland were too hard to understand, the threat of military aggression was something that young men instinctively responded to. Some volunteered for the Royal Navy, others enlisted in the army, and a minority put themselves forward for the Royal Air Force, the youngest service, and until then the least fashionable. But, for those who thought about it, warfare in the sky represented the last opportunity for single combat where one person pitted his fighting skill against another. And, compared to army discipline and naval anonymity, flying offered freedom and self-expression.

Long before war actually broke out, a new aristocracy had emerged among the young of Pamela's generation. They wore ashy-blue uniforms with white wings sewn above the heart to show that they were pilots. They had to be pilots. However much the experts tried to insist that the navigator or the station commander or even the artificer was equally important, civilians, especially female civilians, recognized only one hero in the line-up.

Derry McConnell had that mark on him, and he had too the cool RAF slang that diminished danger to a joke. When he 'pranged the kite', it meant a crash that could have killed him, 'daisy-picking' was coming in too low, and the day he 'bent the landing kit' referred to a slewed put-down with sparks cascading from a collapsed undercarriage. Nothing was that serious, not even death. And to ride the air at over a hundred miles an hour, to see the world as an eagle saw it looking down on the dusty lanes of Kent picked out from the green fields and ploughland by hawthorn hedges dusted in white blossom, to follow the silver snake of a railway line through the blackness of a night flight, to side-slip through the indigo canyons that twisted between mountainous bronze thunderclouds, that was – what

was the right word? – it was absolutely wizard. Small wonder
that pilots had sex appeal.

In the spring of 1939, the Gosport aerodrome decided to host
a dance to celebrate the twenty-first anniversary of the founding
of the Royal Air Force. It was to be a grand affair, and Derry
invited the most glamorous girl he knew. He would come and
pick her up on 31 March, then drive her down to Gosport. But
Brigit had returned home, and in the swirl of sibling rivalry and
affection Pamela was not going to let her be left out. Besides, it
was not absolutely certain that she would be allowed to spend a
night with a godlike pilot without a chaperone.

'All right,' said Derry, 'I'll get a date for Brigit as well.'

In the summer of 1937 the government had begun belatedly
to prepare for the worst. At that late stage, the priorities had
finally become clear, however impossible they were to achieve.
War would come in Europe. Defence had to begin at home,
and the first line would be in the air. It was not only girls in
their twenties who thought pilots were gods. In the huge
programme of rearmament which began that year, over 2,000
new aircraft were ordered for immediate construction, a string
of radar stations were to be built round the south and east coasts,
and an accelerated training schedule was set up for pilots. As an
added inducement, they were allowed to sign on for four years
instead of the normal twelve. By 1942, it was estimated,
Britain's air defences would be in good shape to deter German
aggression.

Even then, there would be gaps. As Alexander Cadogan, a
senior Foreign Office official, wrote in his diary in early 1937,
'We shall come to no good, and I don't see how we're to
defend our interests here, and in the Med or in the Far East.
Most depressing.' In other words, even in 1942 it might not be
possible to defend Hong Kong. A Japanese army had already
invaded Manchuria and northern China, and showed every
intention of moving south, but it appeared that the colony
would have no air defence for the foreseeable future.

Among the first of the 'short service' pilots was a tall, silent young man from the West Country who enlisted in 1937. He was sent to Perth on the edge of the Scottish Highlands where he was taught how to fly a Tiger Moth, and, having mastered the basics, moved on to a training squadron in Wiltshire to learn about more powerful military aircraft like Ansons and Harts, with their 1,000-horsepower Rolls-Royce engines. For day after day, he practised landings and approaches and side-slips and spins and aerobatics and night-flying, and on 11 September 1937 he was awarded his pilot's wings. For Donald Hill, that moment was the highest point so far of his young life.

'It was a terrific sensation, getting my wings,' he recalled in a tape recording made for his son many years later. 'I'll never forget it.'

What made it especially unforgettable was that it represented a double escape. When he first walked into the RAF recruiting office in London, he had been a trainee accountant living with his mother in a flat in Swiss Cottage. He had scraped through his preliminary and intermediate exams, but the thought of his finals depressed him almost as much as the prospect of a lifetime poring over account-books and preparing tax returns.

'I don't think I was born to be an accountant', he confessed. 'In fact, I don't think I should ever have been an accountant. Quite frankly, it was thrust upon me, and I wasn't very happy about it.'

The person who had thrust it upon him was his mother, and becoming a pilot meant release both from accountancy and from his mother's domination. What gradually dawned on him was something even more fundamental. In the air, he was in his element. In such a large man, and one so matter-of-fact, it was a surprising discovery. He did not have a pilot's flair like Derry McConnell – his instructors consistently marked him 'average', and when he came through his Tiger Moth training his report noted that he was 'quiet, hard-working, and very keen, with high average results, but needs more spirit in his flying'. Nevertheless, he had the balance and speed of a good athlete, and more importantly the desire to roam the vastness of the sky.

In the brief happiness that was about to enfold him, one crucial ingredient was the pleasure he took in that newfound freedom.

In January 1938, after six months with a training squadron in Wiltshire, he was posted to the drably named Coast Artillery Co-operation Unit at Gosport. It was part of Coastal Command, and provided airborne spotters for land-bound gunners aiming at targets in the Channel. The task demanded exact calculation and suited his temperament. On his first flight at the base, he met Derry McConnell and their friendship was as immediate as it was unexpected. Donald was a mere pilot officer, the lowest form of flying life, and on a short-service commission, while Derry was a regular, one rank higher, and had an extravert dash which was the opposite of Donald's reserve. Nevertheless, they immediately became the closest companions, and in March 1939 when Derry needed someone to take Brigit Kirrage to the RAF's twenty-first-anniversary dance, he turned automatically to Donald. Rather to his surprise, his friend's response was not enthusiastic.

'I was not very keen on girls in those days,' Donald later explained awkwardly. In fact, given his mother's inhibiting presence there had hardly been any opportunity to become keen on them. Emotionally he was hardly more experienced than he had been as a trainee accountant.

'You can't come to the party without a girl,' Derry pointed out forcefully, 'so you've got to get a girl, and here is one.'

It was irrefutable logic, and gilding the lily he added that she was bound to be good-looking because her sister was utterly ravishing. In fact, as he made plain, the situation left a real friend with no choice. Derry's only transport was a sporty two-seater, but Pamela would come only if Brigit was invited, and, with two girls to transport, a larger car was needed. And his quiet friend had just lashed out £13 on a piece of kit that any pair of girls would be proud to be seen in.

On the afternoon of 31 March, a massive car the size of a Bentley drew up in front of 2 Queen's Road in Tunbridge Wells. Even without the croaky, bullfrog rortling from its big three-litre engine, it would have been hard to miss. It had an immodestly large chrome radiator grille, swollen silver head-lights and running-boards wide enough to hold a sheep, and it weighed rather more than two tons. A company called Whitlock had built it, but the expense left them with no profit and they had gone bankrupt, survived by only a few hundred of their giant cars. Gleaming and engorged, this example dwarfed the thin Austin and Morris saloons in the street. Unfortunately its owner did not yet have a driving licence, and so Derry had driven it for all but the last hundred yards.

Watching from the window, Pamela saw Derry get out from the passenger's seat, followed by the driver, a tall, dark-haired young man wearing the blue uniform of the RAF. He was standing beside Derry when Pamela opened the front door.

'This is Donald,' said Derry. 'Donald Hill.'

She remembered later how white the pilot's wings had appeared against his uniform.

They were invited in so that her mother could inspect the young men who were to look after her daughters. It gave Pamela the opportunity to satisfy her own curiosity. She liked Derry, but there was nothing new to learn about him. His friend offered more scope for imagination. The wild car, the romantic wings, the big shoulders, those were enough to catch her attention. She liked his quiet self-possession, and even her mother was reassured when he told her how careful he was about driving. He had a faint Devon accent which sounded rural and trustworthy.

They quickly found out that the stuff about his driving was nonsense. Donald drove slowly to the end of the street, and there they switched over so that he was in the back with Brigit, his date for the dance. 'He's barely been driving more than ten minutes,' Derry said as he took the wheel.

Pamela saw him smile, a sudden boy's grin as though he had got away with something. The road to Gosport curled over the chalky back of the South Downs, and offered them a sight of the English Channel merging into the grey winter sky beyond before they plunged down to the coast. They talked of friends and flying and films. The Gosport aerodrome specialized in gunnery and torpedo-bombing, where the pilots had to approach low over the water to launch their weapons. It was possible to tell from the jokes about being overtaken by slow-moving seagulls that they had to sacrifice speed for precision, but there was nothing to suggest that what they did was particularly dangerous. Or perhaps events had now put all their lives in danger.

A fortnight earlier Hitler had annexed another of those middle-European nations, and every newspaper in the land had printed the long list of his broken promises – in 1936 Saarland had been all the Germans wanted, in March 1938 they had taken Austria, and assured everyone that this satisfied their final requirement, then it was the Sudetenland in September 1938. For a week, they had all been digging trenches and trying on gasmaks, certain that the bombing would start at once. The Prime Minister had gone to Munich, and Mr Hitler had given a solemn promise that 'This is the last territorial claim I have to make in Europe.' They could all remember the relief when Neville Chamberlain had flown back waving the agreement and saying it was 'Peace in our time'. Now Hitler's forces had taken over another gallant little nation, and each one of them was living in a split world, with the present going on as peacefully before and the future unwatchably violent. War was going to happen, and nothing could be done about it.

At the top of the Downs, Donald told Derry to stop, and announced that he would drive the rest of the way. Brigit remembered how wobbly the Whitlock's steering was, but Pamela enjoyed watching him drive. The car was too big for the narrow strip of tarmac, but any cars they met hugged the verge at the sight of their bulging bonnet, and he hardly slowed as they passed. His confidence was catching. Long before they arrived at Gosport, Pamela began to wish that she, rather than her sister, was to be Donald's partner.

The girls were dropped at a hotel near the base so that they could change. Pamela had a strapless dress, silk taffeta in midnight blue, cut low in the back, boned to the waist, with a full ruched skirt. It was a dress that bred confidence, that any girl would look good in, and Pamela knew she looked terrific. The question was, would he think the same?

Presumably Derry was with him when Donald picked the girls up from the hotel, but only the most important details of that night were to survive through all the trials of a long life. Donald was in full evening dress, black tie, airforce-blue mess jacket with gold-braided epaulettes and black satin lapels, and evening trousers. As was proper, they danced the first dance with their partners, and then changed over.

'Do you like dancing?' Donald asked Pamela.

'I love it,' she said eagerly.

He smiled back at her. 'So do I.'

Standing six feet two inches tall, he towered over her, but it did not matter. He danced beautifully, and she felt herself floating in his arms. Telling the story, she laughed at herself for using such a tired phrase, but insisted that it was exactly how she had felt – dancing with him she had floated. They danced a foxtrot, then a waltz, then a Charleston, and, as one dance followed another, each of them found that it was only the other who would do as a partner.

'It was like a dream,' she said. 'I kept telling myself that it didn't happen like this in real life.'

There was no point in pretending to keep up the formalities. What was happening was so electric that even those on the sidelines felt its intensity. 'It's something that remains absolutely vivid in my memory,' Brigit said sixty years later. 'I can see Pamela in her evening dress, it was dark-blue taffeta, I can see the two of them walking very close together, Donald and her. It's something I've never forgotten. And then they disappeared.'

The foxtrots became more frenetic, the waltzes a little closer, but in public that was as far as one went. What hands spoke and eyes read had to be understood without other signals. If they could dance for long enough, they might never have to explain anything. Then there was a break for a buffet supper, and voices were needed again. Pamela found herself laughing too loudly and trying to balance a tongue salad on her lap and at the same time say something eloquent enough to tell him how happy she felt. But afterwards the band played more loudly, and they turned and whirled in each other's arms until every secret had been exchanged and he led her out into the privacy of the night and kissed her, sealing up the inadequate words in her mouth.

The national anthem had been played, the last dancers were leaving, and Brigit and Derry were sitting in the front of the vast Whitlock when Donald and Pamela emerged from the darkness and climbed into the back seat.

The next day was 1 April. When the two young airmen came to the hotel to pick up the sisters they had so carefully left there in the early hours of the morning, the porter informed them with suitable gravity that the Miss Kirrages had already left. Leaning over the banisters, the girls could hear their confused voices – was he sure? they were supposed to meet, had they left a message? – but, as they ran down the stairs shouting 'April Fool!', Pamela saw the look on Donald's face, and never forgot it. It was an expression of pure relief. Oh, she thought, sharing the emotion precisely, he *does* care.

Tunbridge Wells exacted its dues. Having returned the two girls to the safety of 2 Queen's Road, Donald was taken through the ritual of the middle classes at dinner, the need to address Mr Kirrage as 'Sir', to pick out the correct fork, to reassure Mrs Kirrage about the RAF's efficiency, to pass the port from right to left, while every atom of his being was concentrated on the hot hand clutching his beneath the tablecloth. It was a qualifying ritual. There would have been nothing dramatic had he failed, just a corrosive perception that he was not quite what he seemed to be.

Anxiously Pamela noted the obstacles, and admiringly saw him take each in his stride until at last the decanter of port came round. It would have been easy to push it over to her on his right, and if he had a social chasm would have opened up between the two men she loved most deeply. Everything that was really important to that generation was contained in silence.

'It seems utterly absurd now, incomprehensible,' she exclaimed, 'but in those days it felt so important. If he had passed the decanter the wrong way, it would have been a terrible thing, as though he did not belong there.'

He pushed the port to his left. It seemed as though there was nothing he could not do utterly perfectly.

When she saw him to the door, he said quietly, 'Can I ring you?'

'Yes,' she whispered, 'please ring.' And she gave him what she hoped was an adoring smile.

He kissed her. There were maids and parents and sisters about and the kiss was quick and polite. She watched him walk down the path, then ran upstairs to her bedroom and hurled herself on her bed and burst into tears. It was the smile that was wrong. Gawping at him like a lovesick schoolgirl. And the hand-holding under the table, that had been completely wrong. How he must despise her for being so forward. She had shown no poise, no dignity, no self-restraint. Nothing she had done was worthy of him.

All through the next day, the black Bakelite telephone, Tunbridge Wells 744, stood squat and silent on the hall table. But that was a Sunday, and perhaps the RAF did not permit frivolous calls on a Sunday. There had to be a different reason why he did not ring on Monday. Or on Tuesday. Or on any other day of the week. It was not his fault. In all that he did, he had shown himself to be honourable and well behaved. It was she who had behaved so badly. Now he would find someone else. It would not be difficult. There would be no shortage of girls to snap up a man like Donald.

A week passed. In memory the party grew even more vivid, as though it were a perfect work of art, from the opening discovery that the blue of her dress went so well with the colour of his mess jacket through the excitement of the dance to the sunlit world laid open by his kiss, and the knowledge when she ran down the stairs to him in the hotel that he shared her feelings. For a few hours it had created a happiness higher and wider than any she had experienced. Now it was over. And she was to blame for ending it. Every day that the telephone did not ring made its ending more final. And it was her stupidity that kept it from ringing. Another week passed, and the distance between the happiness she had known and the misery she lived grew greater. And it was all her fault.

In the middle of April, the black phone rang.

The voice at the other end was tentative. 'Is Miss Pamela Kirrage there?'

She was, but hardly able to breathe. Like a fisherman who had thought the catch of a lifetime was gone but now felt the faintest tug on the end of the line, her one thought was not to frighten him off. 'Oh it's you,' she said as though the memory had almost lost itself among a multitude of distractions. 'I did enjoy the dance, such fun.' Her voice was light, bright, false.

His remained unsure. He had thought that perhaps she was only being polite when she had said he could ring her. 'I didn't know whether you really wanted me to,' he said. Then a hell of a flap had broken out, he explained, and life had suddenly become hectic. She jumped at the excuse. Of course that was the reason, she should have guessed. Apparently the international situation was getting worse. In the race to prepare its pilots for war, the RAF had extended training to fill every available hour of flying time. But she could not care less about the international situation. All she knew was that his not calling her had not been her fault.

'I thought you might have found someone else,' she burst out.

'I'm not like that,' he answered, and the reply was something else she never forgot. She believed it, partly because she wanted to, but partly because she sensed that it was true.

Yet on his side it had been a little more complicated than he suggested. For a fortnight he had in fact had no flying duties at all. There had been nothing to stop him getting in touch with her, except his own hidden doubts. He had been touched as deeply as her by the magic of the evening, and it had come as no less of a surprise. Telling his grown son about it more than forty years later, he remembered how badly it had started when he found himself lumbered with Brigit, who was bossy and sharp-tongued.

'Then before I knew what had happened I was dancing with Pamela,' he went on. 'Well, when I saw her, I suddenly realized she was the most beautiful girl I had seen in my life.' On the tape recording, a note of wonder enters his Devon voice. 'I don't think I had ever seen a more beautiful girl. She had the most glorious eyes, and I completely fell for her.' Then he laughs. 'Old Derry was a good sport about it and he realized the situation.' There is another pause as though the memory demands one more taste. 'We spent the whole time dancing together. She was a beautiful dancer, and we danced ourselves off all night. That was the beginning of it.'

What he admitted to neither Pamela nor his son was that a fortnight after the party he had a crucial exam in order to be promoted to flying officer. He must have realized that, once he saw Pamela again, he would have no more time for study. If so it was his last act of caution.

He told her that he had some leave due to him that weekend, and arranged to pick her up. They would drive somewhere. It did not matter where.

He arrived with an orchid in his hand, a piece of extravagance that she learned to appreciate over the weeks ahead. A pilot officer's pay on the brink of war was £17 a month, and, once the petrol and the car's fiendishly expensive repair bills had been paid, there was little left for lavish gestures.

The details of where they went that day have merged into the glow of the golden summer. Hardly a weekend passed when they were not together. Crowding close to one another on the Whitlock's bench-like seat, they drove off into the country, to the seaside, to the cool shade of Epping Forest, and the long sunlit rides of the New Forest. In 1939, the south-east of

England enjoyed its finest summer in years, with day after day of sunshine. The May blossom came early in the hedgerows and the apple and cherry blossom in the orchards. Then the white flowers gave way to green leaves, and in the summer heat the hop bines climbed their poles with tropical speed until the gardens looked like jungles.

They drove down narrow lanes where the dust rose in a cloud behind them, and stopped at tea-shops with painted signs advertising cream teas at 1/6d. Occasionally, when only the best would match their mood, they took the Whitlock to the Criterion restaurant in Piccadilly Circus and invested a week's pay in the best American highballs. Eating there was out of the question, but just down the street there was the Lyons Corner House in the Strand where they could have a three-course meal served by a smart, white-aproned nippy for the price of a Criterion highball.

They held hands and kissed, and began to find out who they were and what attracted each to the other. His quietness seemed endlessly appealing. At twenty-six he was older than most of the RAF's young guns, but his reserve made their puppyish enthusiasm seem adolescent. He had come late to flying, but there was another reason for his more adult manner.

His family came from south Devon near Sidmouth, where they had farmed for generations. Samuel Hill, his father, had bought Leighs Farm, a large dairy farm, overlooking Lyme Bay and become one of the most successful milk producers in the area. Donald was the second of three children, with an elder sister nicknamed Billie, and a younger brother called Ralph. Numbers had always come easily to him, and at the local school in Branscombe he was recognized as something of a maths prodigy, taking every available prize. To Maud, his mother, this was evidence that he was a genius, too good for a life on the land. Perhaps for that reason, or perhaps because she was desperate to escape herself, she insisted that the farm be sold so that he could receive the best education that money could buy. In 1924 Samuel Hill reluctantly sold his beloved farm and the family moved to a large house in Honiton while eleven-year-old Donald was sent to Mount Radford, a prep school in Exeter with a reputation for high academic standards. Barely a year later, his father went out rabbit shooting, and did not return alive.

'The story was he was trying to get over a hedge, and he slipped and the gun went off,' Donald later told his son. 'Well, I just don't know. I've always had a feeling at the back of my mind it wasn't an accident – that possibly he shot himself. He was only forty-seven and a crack shot, not the sort of person to have an accident like that. It's possible that there might have been trouble between my father and my mother, but I just don't know.'

Donald's doubts were well justified for, although the coroner ruled that his father's death was 'accidental', the verdict hardly tallied with the evidence. Samuel had been found on hands and knees in a stream with his shotgun underneath his body. A shot had been fired against his right temple from a range close enough to singe his hair and it had blown away the top of his skull. The court's sympathies were accorded to the victim's family, and a huge crowd filled St Michael's church in Honiton for the funeral, but once the facts emerged local opinion arrived at a different verdict. Samuel Hill, it was generally agreed, had put the barrel of his gun to his head and killed himself out of despair at losing the farm he had adored.

Not surprisingly the boy's educational career failed to flourish. At sixteen he was brought back to Honiton to go to the local public school, All Hallows, but when he was eighteen Maud decided on a new ambition for him. Samuel had left a substantial sum of money in trust for the education of his children, and there was enough too for his widow to buy her own home. In 1932 she boarded Billie out with relatives, sent Ralph to a public school in Sussex, and took Donald to live with her in London. It was not a move he wanted to make. His memories of his Devon childhood were of freedom, of stealing apples from a nearby orchard, of being endlessly indulged by a father whom he loved. 'My father wasn't a stern disciplinarian,' he recalled, 'he never beat me, which he probably should have. He was a very gentle man.' His mother, he admitted, was 'something different'. No one in the family, least of all his father, was able to resist her forceful character. Like the others, Donald passively accepted the plans she made for him.

'I imagine my father wanted me to become a farmer,' he told Pamela, 'but my mother's very ambitious, and she had other ideas.'

Determined to make the best use of his gift for numbers, she had him articled to a firm of accountants, Clemons Midgely, and there he might have remained had it not been for the country's sudden need for pilots. His father's death had required him to take on the role of senior male in the family. To cope with his mother's domineering nature, he had learned to suppress his own wants and inclinations. The ugly rumours about his father's death had taught him not to dwell on the emotions it aroused in him. Flying revealed a romantic streak he had never suspected in himself, and now a beautiful woman who loved him as he loved her was uncovering depths of feeling of which he had known virtually nothing until then.

In the next few weeks, they realized how improbable it was that they should have fallen in love. They were like mirror images of one another: Pamela had come from an extraordinarily secure background and grown up volatile and passionate, while Donald had developed solidity and maturity against a background of anxiety and rootlessness. In the course of a single summer, each appeared to borrow something from the other, she growing more adult, he more adolescent.

One Saturday, they found themselves driving through Epping Forest. Impulsively he swung off the road down a forestry track, which bounced through the green-dappled shade. Showing off with one hand on the steering-wheel and the other round her waist, he failed utterly to see a tree-stump which tore away the Whitlock's running-board with a hideous clatter of exploding rivets. A younger Donald would have been made distraught by his carelessness, but this one laughed. The big car began to look its age. A few days later, while reversing into a parking space, he happened to catch Pamela's eye as he turned to look over his shoulder. One passing glance was not enough. He could not tear his gaze away, and with his eyes locked on hers ran gently into the car behind. A bumper absorbed most of the impact, and it did not matter that the chrome was starred or the metal buckled. So long as they were together, nothing mattered.

Through the heat of summer, the inexorable descent into war accelerated and every moment together became more precious. They had disagreements. Accustomed to having her own way, Pamela resented furiously the time that the RAF demanded of its pilots, and for all Donald's protestations refused to believe that it could not find other officers to undertake the mundane chores of inspecting stores or filing reports.

His frustrations were no less powerful and irrational. The thought of Pamela modelling lingerie, parading half naked up and down beneath the eyes of strangers, provoked his jealousy, and more than that – a feeling that his girl should not have to display her body to earn her living. For the first time in her adult life, Pamela acknowledged a will stronger than her own. She tore up her modelling contract, and with the impetuosity of a romantic heroine took up the most self-denying work she could find, cooking in a youth hostel in Bermondsey.

'How I must have loved him,' she sighed looking back. 'I adored modelling and the freedom it gave me – nobody else could have made me give it up.'

With the cool appraisal of hindsight, she could see that their opposites fitted. Emotionally, she was the more extravagant, he the more stable, but while she drew confidence from his calmness, it was apparent that with her he expanded and let himself give expression to feelings which might otherwise have remained buried. It was as though in her he had found an element which welcomed him as completely and unexpectedly as the air. He was learning to let go, to fly emotionally.

Years later, when he wrote to her recalling their summer

together, each tiny incident had become charged with the romance of that golden season: 'The evening you drank too many highballs and developed girlish giggles – early morning cups of coffee in some snack bar – I lost my hat in a tea house – nearly got chewed up by a pack of hounds. Our last few days in London. I remember everything as if it were yesterday.'

Others were struck by the quality of the man who had fallen in love with Pamela. Although the youngest of the sisters, Sheila had an intuitive good sense that carried weight in the Kirrage family, and Pamela waited anxiously for her opinion. Her reaction was favourable, and even today she can remember the impression he created.

'He was tall and good-looking, which helped of course,' she says, 'but what struck me was how quick his mind was. It was easy to miss because he was quite reserved, but Donald was a very clever man.'

Once she had given her approval, he was adopted as part of the family. He would stay with them for the weekend, playing tennis on the court in their garden, and on Saturday night take Pamela to a dance. The next day, flying out of Gosport, he would detour over Tunbridge Wells, and swoop low over the rooftops until one of the girls ran out into the garden to wave at him.

He might almost have been regarded as an extra brother, except that an unbrotherly problem grew inexorably from their pleasure. Until they met, neither of them had found a partner who excited them physically. Now their kisses grew longer and more passionate. In the heat of one of the hottest Julys on record, fingers grew heavy and would not lift unaided from a breast or a thigh. In the dark, limbs stretched involuntarily, and by day desire weighed on the brain like a thunderstorm.

One evening they went to a dance in Windsor, and when it ended they could neither leave one another nor satisfy what they wanted. They kissed until their lips were sore, and drove slowly through the sallow dawn clutching hands as though something might turn up which would relieve the terrible longing. For an hour they escaped it in the unromantic surroundings of a transport café, where they drank mugs of tea and stifled desire in a vast plate of bacon and eggs. The ordinariness of it brought them back to reality and they smiled at each other as though they had come through an ordeal. But, when they went outside again, the sun had risen above the horizon, and they could feel its rays relight the warmth of their dangerously combustible bodies.

It seemed hardly possible that they would not soon fall into bed or simply lie down where they were and make love. But it was 1939 and most brides were virgin when they married. Nowhere was that more true than in Tunbridge Wells, where it was unthinkable that a well-brought-up girl should have sex before marriage.

'I was terrified of becoming pregnant,' Pamela recalled. 'At that period, nothing could have been more dreadful for me and for my family and for Donald. It would have been an utter disaster.'

Although the consequences were less drastic, men were expected to observe the same canons of behaviour. An officer who made an unmarried woman pregnant would have to resign his commission. A gentleman would lose his reputation and be branded a rotter. Sexuality itself, so openly discussed today, was scarcely talked about except in medical terms or as a music-hall joke. Smart young people could earn a reputation for raciness by referring to Krafft-Ebing or Freud.

'I can remember the embarrassment when an older woman told me that Miss Ferguson and Miss Body were lesbians,' Pamela exclaimed. 'I didn't even know what "lesbian" meant until she explained. I was so innocent.'

By itself the sexual restraint might seem inexplicable, but it was part of a much wider pattern of self-restraint. Rules which had been shaken by the slaughter of the First World War, and by the consequent imbalance of the sexes during the 1920s, were re-establishing their power. Throughout the western world, the jazz age was in retreat before the forces of conformity, a retreat epitomized by the censorship imposed on Hollywood by the Hays Office, which prohibited any displays of nudity, or even the portrayal of a woman in a bedroom unless she had at least one foot on the ground. In the newly fascist and communist countries, even more than in the old kingdoms and republics, there was pressure to regulate individual behaviour in the wider interests of society.

The films they watched carried the same message. In *The Drum*, Roger Livesey, as a beleaguered British colonial officer, leaves the safety of the fort knowing that he will be killed by the wicked khan, but prepared to make the sacrifice because his death will inspire others and thus save the empire. In the United States, Jimmy Cagney played a condemned killer in *Public Enemy* who agrees to fake cowardice as he is taken to the gas chamber so that his contemptible example will dissuade impressionable kids from following his criminal career.

Fashion mirrored the restoration of the old rules. Women's clothes had almost abandoned the hard tubular shape of the 1920s. The fabrics were soft and clinging, crêpe, sharkskin and silk, dresses were calf-length, cut on the bias to show off the curve of the body, and nipped in at the waist with a sash or belt. The last remnants of the masculine look was a jaunty line in fedora-like hats with tilted brims. Meanwhile men's clothes had drifted towards an almost defiantly uncivilized male look. Their suits were made of tweed, preferably hairy and Harris, beneath it they wore Fair Isle sweaters and loosely knotted ties, and on their feet solid brown brogues. The sexes knew their places once more.

It was this unspoken pressure towards conformity which constrained Donald and Pamela. Later generations sometimes look back on the 1930s with a nostalgic envy for its innocence and honesty, but it was all of a piece. The sexuality and the clothes, the attitudes of Hollywood and Tunbridge Wells, the same moral values ruled them all.

Nevertheless, before the summer was over, it had become evident that either a wedding must take place or convention would be blasted apart. One Sunday, as he was having breakfast in Queen's Road, Pamela's mother asked him bluntly what his intentions were. Between themselves, he and Pamela had talked vaguely about marriage, but now a definite answer was required. He remembered how nervous he felt, and how he had stuttered over the crucial phrase, 'We want to get married.' She had countered with the traditional question, 'What are your prospects?', and he began to feel that it was all slipping away. On £17 a month he could hardly support the Whitlock and his mess bill, let alone a wife as well. But he need not have worried. For the first time in her life, Mrs Kirrage's eldest daughter was in love. It would take a lot to persuade her of his unsuitability. Not even when he careered off the tennis court and destroyed a bed of fragile peonies did her mother complain.

On a walk over the South Downs, he asked her to marry him. It came as no surprise, but she cried all the same before she could say yes. The next weekend, he drove Pamela with more than usual speed up to London, and stopped outside Gieves, tailor and jeweller to the armed forces. He left her outside while he went in himself, and emerged a few minutes later with a small box. At a quiet table in the Criterion he produced the ring, a gold hoop with a single diamond surrounded by diamond half-circles. It was far too expensive for a newly promoted flying officer to pay for outright, but Gieves knew that an officer would not welsh on a debt, and it was put on his account. In the event, the bill was not paid until after the war.

For one blissful week, Pamela and Donald tasted the delight of being an engaged couple. Her family and his mother were told, and gave their blessing. Congratulations frothed up from friends and relations, and plans were made for a wedding in the autumn. To cement the bond, she bought him a gold ring and slipped it on his little finger. Then unexpectedly he was given a fortnight's leave.

It should have been good news, but she knew by his expression that it was bad. It was pre-embarkation leave, because in July he was being posted to Singapore. Nothing could have prepared her for the total extinction of all her happiness. In desperation, she clung to him tightly as though that might prevent him going.

'We'll be married whatever happens,' he promised. 'Next year you will come out to Singapore, and we'll have the wedding there.'

It was all that she had for comfort. They spent the last days of his leave together in London. To keep herself from bursting into tears, she joined in his elaborate plans for what they would do after they got married. They would have a vast wedding and a sumptuous honeymoon, but most important of all they would spend their wedding night in the Savoy Hotel. It was a dream to which she would cling for many years.

On 12 July he drove for the last time to the Bermondsey youth club where she worked. The only place they could find to be alone was a room at the top of the building. All the kisses and unvoiced desires had to be compressed into one final embrace, then he pulled himself away and walked downstairs. Outside the front door, he looked up and through a blur of tears saw her on a small balcony waving to him. He waved back and went down to the street. A policeman was examining the Whitlock's out-of-date licence, and jotting down details in his notebook.

'I'm sorry,' Donald said. 'I've been ordered abroad, and I had to come and say goodbye to my fiancée before I left.'

The policeman looked at him and the sight of a young pilot with tear-reddened eyes must have touched him. He put away his notebook. 'I don't know if you'll get away with it,' he said, 'but the best of luck.'

From the balcony, Pamela watched the man she loved get into his big black car. It began to move. A hand waved from the window. Then the car rounded a corner and he was gone.

CHAPTER 3

THE BATTLE
FOR HONG KONG

She tells her love while half asleep,
In the dark hours,
With half-words whispered low:
As Earth stirs in her winter sleep
And puts out grass and flowers
Despite the snow,
Despite the falling snow.

Robert Graves, 'She Tells her Love While Half Asleep'

The opening sentence of Parker Hitt's *Manual for the Solution of Military Cyphers* lists the four ingredients needed to break a code. In order of importance, these are 'perseverance, careful methods of analysis, intuition, luck'. As events were to show, Philip Aston had an abundance of the first three qualities. It was the last that he lacked.

The weakest point of a code is the key. Since this must be known to the person who is to read the message, the lucky code-breaker may find help at two points – the encoding stage and the deciphering stage. Even in the most famous, sustained and demanding exercise of cryptanalysis – the reading of the Enigma codes used by the German navy during the Second World War – the code-breakers at Bletchley Park outside Cambridge relied on this sort of luck. They had versions of the Enigma encrypting machines, and thus knew the technology used to create the constantly changing codes, but at crucial periods they acquired code-books retrieved from damaged U-boats. It was Philip Aston's bad luck that the encoder and intended reader of Russels Mathematical Tables had been the same man, and he had died taking the key with him. If he was to find a way into Donald Hill's mind, he would have to rely on perseverance, analysis and intuition alone.

Philip understood numbers almost aesthetically, and derived a deep satisfaction from their undeviating logic. Almost the only decoration in his drab office with its grey linoleum floor and cream walls were the photographs of his wife and two children on his desk and the rows of books with titles like *Chaos and Fractals* and *Complex Analysis and Applications* arranged on shelves above his computer. At thirty-six, with chronic lung problems, and a young family to bring up on an academic's salary, he might have been forgiven for worrying about health or money. Instead, mathematics seemed to give him the serenity of a priest secure in his faith.

His first attempt on Donald Hill's code was aimed at discovering whether he had merely substituted numbers for letters. Knowing the *e*, *t*, *a*, *o*, *n* frequency of letters in English makes it simple to test for a substitution cipher. He wrote a quick computer program to list the frequency with which different numerals appeared on the first page. The top five were 5, 20, 1, 14, 15. It seemed almost disappointingly simple: *e* was the fifth letter in the alphabet, *t* the twentieth, *a* the first. Could Donald Hill simply have used the basic schoolchild's substitution, 1 = *a*, 2 = *b*? Using that key, he programmed the computer to substitute letters for the numbers on the first page of the diary.

It took seconds for the numerals on his screen to be replaced by letters. Sure enough, the order was *e*, *t*, *a*, *o*, *n* and so on, following the characteristic order almost exactly. With his first effort, he had blown away part of Donald Hill's code. He was almost embarrassed.

Then he tried to make sense of the letters which now filled the mesh of tiny boxes on his screen. With luck they should have made up words. Unlike numbers, which may contain many different patterns, letters resolve themselves into just one sort that make sense, words. And if words did not appear in the usual fashion read from left to right, then a reader had to find them reversed, or running vertically or diagonally. It was like a puzzle. Somewhere in the chaos, the letters would become orderly and could be read, and a meaning could be understood. But it was not to be found in their present arrangement. However much Philip Aston studied the screen, and later the print-out of the diary's opening page, no words appeared. When he switched off the computer on that first evening, it was with a sense of something like satisfaction. This might turn out to be a task worthy of a mathematician.

The basic substitution cipher was only the outer covering. Inside it, Donald Hill had evidently constructed another. The problem was to identify what it was. The computer's grey screen offered no clues, and Philip decided to go back to the diary itself. Its neatness was remarkable. Row after meticulous row of numerals running across the full width of the page, split up by columns exactly half an inch apart to make a grid of 1,081 tiny boxes. And each box held four minute numerals.

Examining the first page, his attention was caught by some faint pencil marks. Some numbers had been marked out with a little square pencilled round them. He counted along the rows. The thirty-fourth number had a square round it. With mounting anticipation, he discovered that so did the 68th, the 102nd, the 136th and so on. Each square enclosed a multiple of 34. Then in the margin he found an almost obliterated arrow pointing to the right with the number '340' written beside it.

Philip drew breath and considered the possibilities. The '340' might refer to something else, but the coincidence of that 34 was too great to be overlooked. Cautiously, he let himself hope that Donald had simply added a zero as another part of his camouflage. In which case, he thought, trying to contain his excitement, the arrow must indicate that the numerals are to be read from left to right, with some sort of limit being reached at the thirty-fourth. What then? For want of anything better, he decided that then a new row would begin below the first. He went back to the original page of numerals on his computer screen, and tentatively rearranged the dense forest into this new, neater shape with each row restricted to thirty-four numerals. As the pattern imposed itself, he almost gave a whoop of triumph. Another part of the jigsaw had fallen into place.

At the end of the thirty-third row, there was a box with four zeroes, as though it marked the end of a section. He made another block with thirty-four numerals in each row, and sure enough the thirty-third row ended 0000. He was certain now that this was the way the diary should be arranged. As though he needed the confirmation, he found on the margin of the first page a second faint arrow, this time pointing down with the figure '330' beside it.

Now the pattern he had was a block – thirty-four numbers in a row, thirty-three rows in a block. If he could believe the evidence, he had cracked Donald Hill's code. It was time to run again the program to translate numbers to letters. Once more the magical transformation took place on the screen, and again Philip scanned the arrangement of letters, hoping to find that they had made themselves into words. As he studied the screen, his excitement faded. The diary kept its secret. The pattern had changed, but the letters still made no sense. This would be more than a weekend's work.

There was at least a third step built into the code. Of that Philip was sure. The text was somewhere among the scattered letters on the screen. His task was to find out the key formula Hill had used to mix them up, and use it to rearrange them into their original sentences.

Now began long hours of painstaking work. Since single letters offered no clue, he began to search for pairs of letters, known as digraphs. Centuries of research had shown that in normal English, the letter *h* was to be found paired with two other letters, *t* and *e*, more often than in any other combination. From the ubiquitous 'the' through pronouns like 'she' or 'that' and prepositions like 'though' and 'here', the digraphs *th* and *he* appeared again and again. Philip tried to pair off the letters in different ways, reading them forwards, backwards and up and down. When this produced nothing, he searched for less obvious links. He counted the letters between each *t* in a block of letters and each *h*, hoping for a regular number of intervals which would indicate another pattern. When this failed, he tried to relate the position of each *t* in one block to every *h* in the next. Through the last weeks of February and the first weeks of March, he wrote program after program, sweeping electronic nets through the clutter in an attempt to catch its invisible patterns. Time after time it came in empty, and on each occasion he tried to imagine another way in which the natural pairing could have been concealed.

Without his realizing it, the diary was gradually working its way into his mind until he could not shake it free. He tried not to bring his work home, but it was during that spring of 1996 that Linda, his wife, guessed from his increasingly abstracted silences that his mind kept returning to the problem of the cipher.

'At first it was nothing more than a diversion', she observed. 'I remember him telling me about it, this interesting little challenge he had set himself. It was not anything important. But the longer he worked on it, the more obsessed he became.'

In fact, any code sets a special trap for its would-be breaker. Making sense of a perplexing world is what the mind has evolved to do. When it is confronted with something strange and incomprehensible, it strives to perceive a pattern in these random stimuli. In psychological terms, the moment at which it recognizes a pattern is called a Gestalt perception (literally 'a shape perception'). The urge to make that mental construct is so deeply rooted that neuropsychologists today believe it to be innate. Thus someone who sets out to decipher a code is engaging in a highly specialized version of what people do constantly in everyday life, but in this case failure carries a particular danger. To be perpetually frustrated in the search for a pattern is to feel that the brain is failing or that the world is mad. A cryptanalyst who knows that apparently meaningless letters must contain a meaning is especially vulnerable. William Friedmann, head of the American Signals Intelligence Service which eventually broke the Japanese variation of the Enigma, the 'Purple' machine, suffered a complete nervous breakdown in December 1940, and spent almost four months in hospital, but was never able to work at the same intensity again. At Bletchley Park, code-breakers were closely monitored, yet frequently worked themselves to the point of mental collapse before they could be taken off the job. Even after being relieved, they found it hard to stop their minds churning away at the problem.

As his frustrations increased, Philip Aston began to think more about the man who had unknowingly set him this task. The care he had taken to conceal his message went much further than the straightforward disguise that he had expected of someone in a prison camp. This, the most frustrating step he had encountered, was the third that Donald Hill had built into his code. It was the work not of an amateur but of a person who enjoyed the intellectual challenge of concealment for its own sake.

Nobody knows how he or she will react to a violent attack until it happens. It calls up responses buried too deep for normal use. Even in war, where violence is the norm and participants are specifically prepared for it, the first attack reveals depths of character which no other situation evokes. For Donald Hill, as for every other person in Hong Kong, the Japanese onslaught that took place in December 1941 was to reveal aspects of their inner selves in a manner which could not be camouflaged.

When he said goodbye to Pamela, the pain of leaving her had plunged him into savage despair. An unsuspecting young airman with whom he shared a cabin on the troopship to Singapore made the mistake of trying to tease him out of his gloomy mood. Suddenly Donald leaped across the cabin and, as he later confessed, 'hammered the hell out of him'. The days at Gosport, and especially the few months with Pamela, had been like no other. Even golden childhood could not compare. To the end of his time, he would always say quite simply, 'Those were the happiest days of my life.'

Before leaving he had traded in the Whitlock to pay for its last lot of repairs. All that he had to remind him of his happiness were Pamela's photograph, the ring she had given him on their engagement, and her cigarette case. As the troopship plunged through the Bay of Biscay, sweated into the Red Sea and rolled across the Indian Ocean, he went morosely about his duties, sea-sick and depressed.

It was in Singapore that he discovered how much he had been changed. He who had 'never been very keen on girls' before he met Pamela suddenly found them irresistible, and the attraction was mutual. Physically he was tall and good-looking with an inexhaustible appetite for dancing, and, as married women seemed to sense more hungrily than others, there was a banked-up reserve of sensuality in him waiting to be released. His most frequent partner beneath slowly turning fans in the ballroom of the Raffles Hotel was the thirty-five-year-old wife of a naval officer who had the misfortune to be away at sea on night patrols.

He was not proud of himself. 'I don't have good memories of Singapore,' he remarked years later when he told his son of the episode. He could not shake off the misery of parting from Pamela, and in her absence grasped at the opportunity of a purely physical affair. 'I loved dancing, and this woman she loved dancing too – her husband was always on duty at night,' he said by way of excuse. On the tape recording, there is a short, uncomfortable silence, then 'I'm afraid I was a rather naughty young man.'

Their relationship could not be kept secret in Singapore's expatriate community. Gossip there was such a finely developed art that, when Somerset Maugham came to stay in the 1930s, he was able to lift chunks of it almost verbatim to serve as the basis of some of his best short stories. As the talk about Donald's affair spread, word reached his superiors. Frequently he was sent up-country to the airfields being opened up in Malaya to deter the Japanese, but whenever he returned the relationship blazed up again. In less dangerous times, the scandal might have ruined his career, but he was recognized not only as a pilot whose skill was now rated 'above average', but as a first-class officer. Promoted to flight lieutenant, he was transferred in June 1941 to Hong Kong.

To his embarrassment the naval officer's wife followed him there, swearing that she would never leave him. Firmly he pointed out to her the central reality of all his thoughts, that he intended to spend the rest of his life with Pamela Kirrage. 'There were a lot of tears,' he remembered, 'but I was engaged and I was going to stick to that.'

It did not prevent him having an affair with another married woman, the Chinese wife of a Hong Kong police officer. Her name was Foo Ling, which was shortened to Florrie. Born into a westernized family, she too was in her mid-thirties, and loved dancing. This was a deeper relationship about which he felt guilty and confused for years. In Hong Kong's last, pleasure-filled months of peace before the Japanese invasion, what seemed important was that she had great beauty and sophistication, and danced superbly. It was when war came that her other qualities emerged – courage, ingenuity and an inexhaustible capacity for love. Yet, despite her attractions, his underlying sadness did not lift. When he looked back on those six months before war broke out in December 1941, he confessed that he was 'not too happy', and the opening of his diary showed that it was intended to be the record of his actions rather than of his own gloomy feelings.

All those considerations were blown away by the dawn raid on Kai Tak airfield on Monday 8 December. Until that moment, Hong Kong had been the solid outpost of an empire which covered a third of the world's territory and contained a quarter of its population. Or so it seemed, for the reality was that its defence depended on Japan's fear of provoking such a formidable enemy. At the highest military level, the Committee of Imperial Defence in London, strategists had accepted that the colony lay too close to Japan to be defended. Thus British policy towards Japan was simply to avoid provoking her hostility unnecessarily. In 1940 Winston Churchill had bluntly written, 'If Japan goes to war with us, there is not the slightest chance of holding Hong Kong or relieving it. It is most unwise to increase the loss we shall suffer there. Instead of increasing the garrison, it ought to be reduced to a symbolic scale. We must avoid frittering away our resources on untenable positions.'

Nevertheless, among all the overseas postings that the empire offered, Hong Kong was the serviceman's favourite. The climate was almost tropical, steamily hot in summer, and merely cool in winter. Although nothing like the commercial power-house it became after the war, the colony was successful enough to maintain two luxury hotels, a range of superb restaurants and, closer to the military heart, pubs, beaches, brothels and dance halls without number. In the words of a 1930s tourist brochure, visitors would find there 'the exciting and the exotic, the breathtaking and the colourful – everything in fact that typifies the Wondrous East, hand in hand with the comfort of an up-to-date British Colony'.

As such it illustrated in graphic fashion the empire's strengths and prejudices. Its governor was invariably British, as were most of the members of its Executive Council, but commercially its mixture of races competed on equal terms. Apart from the great trading names, like Jardine Matheson and Swire, the richest families in the colony were Chinese, and several were appointed to the Council. Nevertheless, the underlying power structure could be deduced from where people lived. In Kowloon, all but the wealthiest Chinese had their homes at sea level; further inland and a little higher were the Japanese, then came the Indians, and after them the continental Europeans, beginning with the Portuguese and ending with the French. May Road in the foothills marked the crucial frontier and, in the only slightly ironic words of one Hong Kong history, 'from May Road upward to heaven was the exclusive preserve of those who gloried in the name of Briton'.

A similar form of unofficial racial segregation separated the working areas of prostitutes, courtesans and bar-girls. The Europeans operated furthest up the hill, mostly in Lyndhurst Terrace which was known from its string of brothels simply as 'The Line'. Their acknowledged leader, a beautiful Russian blonde with the impeccably anglicized name of Ethel Morrison, became so wealthy that she was accepted as readily in the cathedral as at the racetrack. This combination of administrative rectitude, social hypocrisy and commercial licence gave Hong Kong life an extraordinary intensity which mesmerized its inhabitants. Outside the frontier, the Japanese had occupied the neighbouring province of Kwangtung since 1938 and evidence of their tightening grip in China came from the steady stream of refugees coming into the colony. But, inside, the parties and the money-making only grew louder and more frenzied.

When it ended, it did so with a suddenness which took everyone by surprise. Little more than a fortnight after the first aircraft roared in over Kai Tak airfield, the empire's outpost had gone, and with it the mystique that had sustained the world's largest empire. Trying to convey the shock of it to her fellow countrymen and women, the American Emily Hahn wrote of the last peacetime party, 'Half the men I remember that night horsing around are dead, and the girls are standing in line at Stanley [detention camp], cup in hand waiting for a handout of thin rice stew. Does that sound banal? It isn't. It strikes me sometimes like a slap in the face.'

It was Donald Hill's tiny air force which took that first impact. At 8.00 a.m. Japanese fighters and bombers coming in low from the north headed straight for the airfield. While the bombers droned on towards the docks and strategic targets like oil depots and electrical power stations, the Zero fighters wheeled round in a tight turn low over the airfield, and began to machine-gun the aircraft below. Within minutes, one of the three Vildebeeste was in flames, and another badly damaged. Beside them in the bay were the two seaplanes. Again and again the waters were whipped up by lines of bullets which eventually smashed into the canvas-covered Walruses. The big seaplanes rocked with the impact, then quite quickly began to sink. The first lesson of the war was being demonstrated – it was not Japan that had been bluffing, it was Britain.

In the relative peace left by the departure of the attacking aircraft, it was the roar of flames from the burning Vildebeeste parked by the tennis court that attracted the airmen's attention. There was nothing to be done about the Walruses. One of the Vildebeestes had survived the raking fire untouched, while another had been damaged. It was the fire that caused most anxiety. The day before when Donald had taken the plane up on a reconnaissance flight he had loaded it with two bombs, and in anticipation perhaps of war breaking out he had left them on board after the flight. Now there was a good chance that they might explode in the intense heat produced by burning aviation fuel.

The danger was such that Ginger Sullivan asked for volunteers to help extinguish the fire. It was an awkward moment because the risk was so obvious and he was so new to his command. He never forgot that Donald was the first person to volunteer. Through most of the morning, they attempted to put out the flames. The heat made it impossible to bring the hoses near enough to douse the fire, and soon they could see the two 500-pound bombs glowing white in the heart of the inferno. Miraculously neither went off, but the plane was reduced to twisted metal spars and lumps of engine fused to the bombs.

Later that afternoon, the airmen watched helplessly as the Japanese bombed the docks on Hong Kong island, and the crowded tenements in Kowloon on the other side of the hills from the airfield. But by nightfall they had made one gain. The damaged Vildebeest was repaired.

The pilots made an oddly homogeneous group. Each had a nickname: Donald Samuel Hill became plain 'Sammy', Flying Officer Gray, the next most senior, was named 'Dolly' after an actress of that name, the Irish pilot Baugh was christened

'Wimpey' after the construction company which relied on Irish labourers; Crossley, the youngest, was simply 'Junior', but Hennessy, who had only just arrived, was still Frank. They favoured RAF moustaches, and the obligatory slang, and each was deeply envious of their counterparts back in Britain for the experience of flying in combat.

Now they too had an enemy, and two serviceable aircraft. In reality it was little enough. All the Japanese fighters could outfly them, but, with the courage of young men, Donald and Dolly Gray decided that the night offered them one small chance of using the ancient machines to some purpose. They had no night-flying equipment, but there was half a moon and the railway line between Hong Kong and Canton would reflect enough light to guide them there. A stocky man with an absurdly luxuriant RAF moustache, Gray had come up through the ranks. Like Donald, he was older than most pilots and felt somewhat apart from the others. What they shared above all was a passion for flying; indeed Gray had won fame five years earlier by taking part in a record-breaking flight from London to Sydney.

Looking at the two Vildebeeste, they came to the same conclusion. Japanese troops would be congregated by the railway station ready to reinforce the Hong Kong attackers, and presented a good target. Between them they would be able to drop just four 500-pound bombs, but the chance of striking back in any way at all made it worth the risk. As they argued forcefully to Sullivan, anything was better than sitting on the ground doing nothing.

Sullivan supported them, but standing orders required all air operations to be cleared by the General Officer Commanding Hong Kong Forces, Major-General C. M. Maltby. Fearing that a bombing raid might provoke reprisals against civilians in Hong Kong, Maltby curtly refused permission, and the two old bombers stood unused on the ground.

Hong Kong was not entirely defenceless. Six battalions of infantry were posted on its frontiers, and their composition reflected the empire's scope. They included Canadians, Punjabis, Rajputs, Scots and English. With almost 1,000 artillerymen, British and Indian, and 3,000 men of the Hong Kong Volunteer Defence Corps representing seventeen different nationalities, the garrison was multicultural to a fault. The naval defences consisted of two warships from the First World War, and a flotilla of six torpedo boats. Except for the loss of three aircraft, the colony's forces were still intact at the end of the first day.

For years, there had been plans to build a defensive line to separate the New Territories from the mainland. Stretching from Gin Drinkers' Bay on the south coast to Tide Cove on the north, it would consist of pillboxes, barbed wire and trenches, but there had never been a great sense of urgency about it. After three years only one short section by the Jubilee Reservoir had been completed. Nevertheless, the colony's defence required the enemy to be held up in the New Territories for perhaps a week, and only then would the front line start to withdraw through the hilly countryside where several commanding peaks offered the possibility of resolute defence. The next line of defence was in the crowded streets of Kowloon, and finally the defenders would fall back across the narrow strait and make their final stand on the island of Hong Kong itself. There they would hold out for as long as was needed for a British or American fleet to appear over the horizon, or a Chinese army to attack the invaders from the rear. It was hoped they might be able to keep the Japanese at bay for as long as three months.

On Tuesday the Japanese 23rd Army under General Sakai Takashi launched its attack on the Gin Drinkers' Line. The assault troops consisted of the 38th Division, that is, three regiments of infantry, numbering almost 9,000 men, with perhaps another 3,000 in artillery and other support units. The Hong Kong garrison was also about 12,000 strong, made up of about 5,200 infantry, with some 7,000 artillery and auxiliary units. But the raw numbers counted for little compared to morale and training. The Japanese had been fighting as a unit since October 1939, and had known nothing but success. They were battle-hardened and confident, supported by total air superiority and naval dominance, with around 27,000 troops in reserve.

Most of the regular troops among the defenders – two battalions of British infantry, and four of Indian artillery – had spent years on garrison duty. Two Canadian battalions which had arrived weeks earlier had little more experience than a recruit's basic training, and the members of the Hong Kong Volunteers were part-time soldiers ranging from young students to fifty-five-year-old businessmen.

The ground assault began on the New Territories, and within twenty-four hours the attackers had broken through Gin Drinkers' Line and were threatening Kowloon. There were pockets of individual resistance, often mounted by old soldiers, in one case a Boer War veteran, who already knew the shock of battle. The Indian battalions which had experienced real conflict in the North-West Frontier held their shape. For many of the others, the onslaught of Japanese forces, particularly at night, advancing silently in rubber-soled boots and under cover of heavy artillery and mortar bombardment, was simply over-whelming.

As the scale of the collapse emerged, the RAF detachment was among the first mainland units to be ordered to retreat to the island. No one among them was in any real doubt that their eventual fate was to be killed or captured. They still had two workable aircraft, and again the two Donalds, Hill and Gray, volunteered to put them to some use. This time they pleaded for the chance to bomb Japanese airfields at Canton. Once more Sullivan begged permission for the raid, pointing out that if they were not destroyed the planes could be flown on to Nationalist Chinese airfields, thus saving two pilots from captivity. Maltby, facing the worst nightmare of any commander, the certainty of defeat, forbade them to take off, and ordered the planes destroyed. Nothing must be done to inflame the temper of the eventual victors.

From day to day the fate of anyone caught up in the destructive machinery of war is so precarious that each moment might be regarded as decisive. But for Donald Hill, who had trained for years to perform this single task, this one order shaped quite crucially the subsequent course of his life. Maltby's consent would have allowed him a chance to put his unique skill to use, and possibly to escape capture and continue fighting. The refusal condemned him to captivity.

War alters more lives than it ends, but, for Gray, the second negative led to his death in extraordinarily brutal circumstances. Perhaps he would have died in the war anyway, but there was a particular poignancy in the courage with which he faced his terrible fate.

That day Donald Hill for the first time did not keep up his diary. Even for someone of his self-discipline it was a forgivable lapse. The evacuation of the airfield meant that every bit of machinery that could not be carried had to be destroyed in order to deny it to the enemy. The two serviceable planes, one undamaged, the other laboriously repaired, needed now to be sabotaged irreparably. There were huge quantities of papers to be burned, men to be sent across to the island, and final checks to ensure that obstacles scattered across the airfield had put it out of action. Finally Donald himself left Kai Tak with the last party of airmen carrying all the detachment's weapons and ammunition.

At the docks, the makings of a small Dunkirk armada was assembling to ferry troops to the island. Bent under the weight of kitbags and weapons, the first evacuees filed aboard an ancient destroyer, HMS *Thracian*, or one of innumerable ferries, launches and sampans. The group of airmen clambered on to a lighter, but, as the boat pushed out into the open water, a British artillery battery began shelling them. Quickly a Union Jack was hoisted and the shelling ceased, but the confusion of battle was growing. Eventually it enveloped everything so thickly that, when defeat came, its clarity was a relief. The RAF detachment had been sent to Aberdeen on the south side of the island, where a giant building for handicapped children, known as the Industrial School, had been requisitioned for their use. To reach it, they had to push their way through crowds of evacuated troops searching like them for food and accommodation. By the time Donald at last found a bed, he was too exhausted to do anything but fall on to it and sleep.

The news from the Far East was all bad. Pearl Harbor had been bombed and the Americans' Pacific Fleet crippled. The core of Britain's naval force in the region, the battleship HMS *Repulse* and battle-cruiser, HMS *Prince of Wales*, had been sunk. Japanese troops had landed in Malaya and were advancing on Singapore, and now it was evident that Hong Kong's defence was disintegrating. The BBC put the best face that it could on this last item. 'The evacuation of the mainland is now complete,' its announcer said in clipped, unemotional tones on 11 December. 'Hong Kong is now settling down to an old-fashioned siege.'

That 'old-fashioned' was masterly. In Tunbridge Wells, Pamela's alarm at the thought of what might have happened to Donald diminished immediately. Britain was good at old-fashioned things, and the suggestion of castles, and thick stone walls, and hunkering down until the siege was lifted, was distinctly reassuring. Then early the next morning, Friday 12 December, she received a cable from Hong Kong. It was from Donald, and told her simply that he was well and alive, and that he loved her. Relief drove out any lingering apprehension. Clearly the BBC had got it right again, he was 'settling down' to the siege.

There was indeed a lull in the fighting. Success bred its own problems and the Japanese needed to regroup before the assault on the island. Meanwhile, within the siege lines, fragments of peacetime life continued. The banks cashed cheques, the cable office sent out cables, and restaurants on the island still served European dishes like grilled steak.

The RAF detachment had brought over its own heavy machine-guns which could at a pinch be used against low-flying bombers. At first they were drafted in as makeshift anti-aircraft gunners on the roof of the Aberdeen Industrial School so that they could defend the nearby docks, which were certain to be a target for Japanese bombers.

Among the besieged troops rumours began to fly around. It was firmly reported that Chiang Kai-shek's Nationalist Chinese army was about to attack the Japanese from the rear. But it was also said that the Japanese success was due entirely to the work of Chinese collaborators. Then came news that not content with crippling the United States' Pacific Fleet and invading Hong Kong, the Japanese had attacked Malaya.

Waiting for the Japanese onslaught, the young airmen realized that the whole world was at war and that anything could happen. In the crowded surroundings of the Industrial School, they discussed their own part in the great conflagration. Soberly they accepted that in the short term they were doomed and that Hong Kong was no more than 'a small fry in a tremendous issue,' but with a last flicker of pre-war optimism they agreed that in the long term civilization would surely triumph. It was easier to think of that than of the more immediate reality.

A few hundred yards away on a small island just outside Aberdeen harbour, Michael Wright, a young architect who had joined the Hong Kong Volunteers, was arriving at a similar conclusion with his colleagues on the artillery battery which they manned.

'None of us was in any doubt that Hong Kong would be taken by the Japanese,' he said, recollecting the mood many years later. 'I don't think it was spelled out, but we knew that sooner or later, and probably very much sooner, we would either be captured or killed. There was no other outcome.'

So far no attempt had been made to land on Hong Kong island, but the fighting on the mainland had demonstrated the difference between a force trained in peacetime parades and one used to the ferocity of war. The defenders had seen the quality of Japanese soldiers, and understood how formidable they were individually and how effectively they co-ordinated massive artillely and mortar fire with infantry attacks. On the mainland, where the defence had been unprepared and over-confident, courage before the event came easily. Knowing exactly what the future held required a deeper, more complex response.

So confident of success were the Japanese that on 13 December they sent three officials across the water under a truce flag to offer terms of surrender. The offer was rejected out of hand. Then loudspeakers on the mainland began broadcasting Christmas carols and popular songs mixed in with appeals to the troops to give themselves up if they wanted to see their families again. Despite knowing what lay ahead, no one responded, and the next day the Japanese began to bombard the island from two sides. Patrolling the open sea to the south, their warships pounded the town of Aberdeen and the hilltops, while from the mainland heavy guns fired on the northern coast.

Running the length of the island from east to west was a line of steep hills, divided almost halfway by a pass called the Wong Nei Chong Gap. The main road connecting the north and south coasts of the island ran through the pass. West of it lay the island's two principal towns, Victoria on the north coast and Aberdeen on the south, while most of the reservoirs on which the inhabitants depended for their water were in the east. Both sides understood that whoever held the Gap would dominate the island. It was here that Brigadier Lawson, the commander of the Canadian forces, had his headquarters.

The problem for General Maltby was to decide from which direction the attack would come. An invasion from the north was the more likely. Here the victorious Japanese forces on the mainland were separated by barely 500 yards of water from the island, but on the south side the Japanese navy backed by waves of bombers continued to pound Aberdeen harbour as though they were preparing to make a surprise assault from the sea. With fatal indecision, Maltby chose to spread his forces thinly across the entire island instead of concentrating them on the most vulnerable sector opposite the mainland.

Most of the small RAF party under Donald Hill was sent up into the hills just above Aberdeen to hold a section of line measuring almost a mile from Bennet's Hill to Mount Nicholson, whose peak almost overlooked the strategic Wong Nei Chong Gap. This was controlled by a company of the nearest Canadian battalion, the Winnipeg Grenadiers. Its commander was a friendly, enthusiastic major called Baillie. Concrete pillboxes had been sited near the top of strategic hills, but elsewhere men who had been trained to fly and service aircraft had to become infantry soldiers, digging trenches as best they could on the rocky, scrub-covered slopes. It was, Donald's commanding officer later reported, 'a task that was utterly foreign to them'.

On 16 December a probing attack by a small force in sampans and junks was driven off, and the next day a surprising, second offer of a truce was made to Sir Mark Young, the Governor of Hong Kong. Japanese intelligence had many well-placed agents and fifth columnists on the island, and must have known that many civilians wanted the authorities to accept the reality of the situation and capitulate at once. Despite this pressure, his response was unequivocal. 'The Governor', he wrote, 'declines most absolutely to enter into any negotiations for the surrender of Hong Kong, and he takes this opportunity of saying that he is not prepared to receive any further communications on the subject.'

Its meaning could not have been plainer and, on the night of 18 December, the expected invasion began. It came at the most obvious point, on the north corner of the island nearest the mainland. Brushing past the thin line of defenders, the Japanese fanned out east and west, but with the main central force driving inland straight for the Wong Nei Chong Gap. Most of the defence was wrong-footed. Hastily the RAF machine-gunners, like others in the central mountains, improvised new lines to face an attack coming not from the west but from the north and east. At the same time, troops stationed on the southern coast were hurried up into the hills.

Among the latter was Major Robert Giles of the Royal Marines, who had been on duty at the naval dockyards in Aberdeen and was now sent with naval reinforcements to strengthen the defences round the Gap. A seasoned regular, with a strong, almost fussy belief in discipline, he took over Donald's part of the line and set about trying to strengthen their position. He had no illusions about the hopelessness of the task, but refused to acknowledge it except by ensuring that his section posts knew their job and remained where they were. In Donald he found a kindred soul, who despite his youth and lack of experience had the steadiness of a veteran.

'He kept completely calm under all circumstances,' Giles wrote later, 'acted with energy, and did all he could to help me. In fact he gave me what I valued most, an officer I could leave at HQ when I was out at the section posts, who I knew could be relied upon to carry out any instruction I had given, or to act on his own if a situation I had not foreseen arose.'

As the sounds of battle approached through the hills, steadiness became a diminishing quality. Reports of the Japanese tactics emphasized their skill at infiltrating enemy lines. Advancing stealthily under cover of night, they took up position as snipers so that in daylight they could pick off unsuspecting troops from vantage points in trees or behind rocks. Using any ground cover available, they crept up undetected on troops sheltering in concrete pillboxes from snipers or artillery attack, and several sections had been wiped out by grenades dropped down the ventilation shafts. None of the defenders had been prepared for fighting like this. Raw troops, as the Canadians were, became jumpy, and the strain of their sudden frights added to the unspoken anxieties of detecting the rustle of the enemy's approach against a constant background of crackling small-arms fire and thudding artillery exchanges.

Within twenty-four hours of the enemy's landing, they had come so close to taking the Gap that the nearest Canadian troops were sucked into the battle. Donald and his Royal Marine commander remained in position through the night listening to the firefight. No one could sleep. At midnight, an exhausted sergeant from the Canadian section stumbled back to the pillbox almost weeping from the impact of his first experience of the sudden slaughter of battle, the screams and hideous dismemberment of living bodies. Another followed him a few hours later in the same state. To add a final twist to the misery of living through what might be their final hours, the weather had changed, and a cold rain whipped on by a sharp wind chilled them to the bone. Throughout the night, a constant supply of tots of navy rum was all that kept the spirits of weary, frightened soldiers alive.

In the morning, the encircling Japanese were thought to be threatening the dockyards, and Giles together with his naval detachment and his naval rum was called back to help in their defence. Now there were only the main Canadian party and the dozen or so RAF men. A constant bombardment from warships and mainland artillery prevented them from sleeping or getting rations. The next night, starving and exhausted, they were suddenly ordered off the hill by the Canadian company commander, who was convinced that their position had been surrounded. At two in the morning, they were told to fall back on Aberdeen, about five miles away. They groped their way through the dark, and once they had reached the town fell asleep in makeshift barracks until a fresh artillery barrage crashed into the building the following morning.

There was nothing now but confusion. The Japanese had taken the strategic Gap, and repeated counter-attacks had failed to shift them or prevent their further advance. Each part of the island was isolated from the other. The nightmare that had been pushed to the back of the defenders' minds was coming true. Yet, even as the inevitable was becoming real, extraordinary acts of bravery were still performed.

As the invaders swarmed into his headquarters by the Gap, Brigadier John Lawson sent one brief but memorable message to General Maltby: 'They're all around us. I'm going outside to shoot it out.' No more was heard from him, but six days later a burial party found his body with two empty revolvers beside him, and eight enemy lying dead near by. On Mount Butler, another Canadian, Company Sergeant-Major John Osborn, made that same choice to confront danger head on. Leading a company reduced in strength from 200 to 30 men, he drove the Japanese off the hill, and held it for over eight hours before he himself was killed and the last five men alive were captured.

'The man who can most truly be accounted brave', said Pericles in his great funeral oration over the Athenian dead in the Peloponnesian War, 'is he who knows best the meaning of what is sweet in life and of what is terrible, and then goes out determined to meet what is to come.'

The reality was that everyone had a choice about how he would react to the violence of battle. Perhaps he had no more than a moment to make it, and in its form and extremeness the occasion might have been overwhelming, but, waiting for the attack to come, they had days to appreciate what might happen. At that point when the violence came – in the death, to use a good expression – a quality emerged that others called courage.

'Much talk about war with Japan but no one seems to think anything will happen,' Donald had written when he began his diary barely a fortnight earlier. At that moment, he still enjoyed a uniqely privileged existence: he was in love, he was an officer in a powerful, undefeated military force, and he was a servant of the greatest empire on earth. By Pericles' definition, he knew what was sweet in life. In the few days since the Japanese invaded, that had been swept away, and he had begun to taste what was terrible. When he was woken early on the morning of 24 December 1941 with news that the order to retreat had been a mistake, and that he was to return to Bennet's Hill, he could hardly have been ignorant of what was to come.

His RAF section, strengthened by a dozen Canadians, was still armed with machine-guns, together with as many grenades as each man could carry. They struggled up the steep slope, hauling their packs and weapons. As they reached the top, they were seen and the Japanese opened up with mortar fire from a neighbouring hill. Caught out in the open, they threw themselves flat, but the enemy had the range, and immediately shells landed among them. Several men were hit by splinters of metal, including the man lying next to Donald. He himself was showered with pebbles and dirt from the explosion, and some shrapnel clanged off his helmet. Out in the open, they were perfect targets for the mortars, but standing up they would be vulnerable to rifle fire. Between two bad options, one was certain, the other only potential. Shouting above the sound of explosions, Donald ordered his men to disperse and take cover lower down the hill.

Miraculously they all made it into the shelter of undergrowth out of sight of the Japanese, but at the top of the hill, just as the mortar shells were coming in, he had noticed further along the slope a little group of soldiers wearing the pale khaki of the Canadian forces. Clearly they had not received the order to retire given the night before. So far the Japanese had not spotted them, but it was only a matter of time before they did, and then the mortars would start exploding among them. They were not his responsibility, but he knew they had to be warned. Shouts would attract the enemy's attention. To reach the stranded party, someone would have to crawl out into the open.

Perhaps Donald felt that he had no choice: there were Canadians in his section, and he had been alongside the Winnipeg Grenadiers for almost a week. Perhaps he felt lucky: seconds after he had got up that morning, a bomb had landed on his makeshift bed in the Industrial School, blowing the room to pieces. Whatever he felt, the reality was that he could have left the outpost to its fate.

A Canadian, Corporal A. C. Blueman, volunteered to come with him. Crawling through the thickest undergrowth, they climbed out of the shelter they had found and wormed their way up towards the isolated troops. The movement of the bushes caught the attention of Japanese snipers, who repeatedly fired at them, but each time the bullets flew wide. When they were close to the concrete pillbox which the Canadians were defending, Blueman called to them. There was a hurried conference. They could take only what arms they could run with. Once they had been spotted, speed alone would save them. The heavier weapons and ammunition were piled inside the pillbox. A couple of grenades were tossed in on top of them, and everyone began to run back down the hill. Before they had gone more than a few yards, the grenades went off, and suddenly there were bullets flying everywhere. Donald found himself running with his head ducked down as though that would protect him, but the commotion distracted the enemy and they reached safety unscathed.

Unable to find out where they should go, Donald led his little band of twenty-two soldiers – ten RAF and twelve Canadians – back into Aberdeen, where a distracted Canadian command post admitted that they had no idea what was happening. The Japanese had taken the vital Wong Nei Chong Gap, but then their troops had spread out in all directions. In the east of the island they seemed to be everywhere. In the west, Aberdeen had so far escaped attack, and Victoria was still not taken. Perhaps a new line could be established between the two towns. In that case, the Aberdeen reservoir, the last supply of water in the area, would be strategically important. Wearily, the men marched up into the hills again, and in late evening took up position on a bridge which carried a road across the reservoir.

As night came an eerie silence fell. The artillery ceased firing once the light faded. Elsewhere on the island, the quietness made it seem as though the enemy had taken a rest. But, across the water, sounds carried clearly. Twigs snapped, pebbles rattled down rocks, branches suddenly rustled although there was no wind. They had experienced enough in the past week to know that the Japanese were far from asleep.

Suddenly, just after midnight, the dark night was split by flashes of yellow flame and the silence broken by the crack of small-arms fire and wild cries of 'Banzai! Banzai!' The attack seemed to happen on the further shore, and quite soon they could distinguish black shapes running across the bridge towards them. Warning shouts showed that they were Canadian. The Japs had broken through, they yelled, they had crept up on them and blasted them apart. There was an officer with them, trying to get them under control, but they were too demoralized to listen. The Japs were right behind them, they claimed, just the other side of the bridge. As though they could actually see the enemy's squat silhouettes, Donald's party opened up with every weapon they had, machine-guns, rifles, revolvers, shooting into the darkness down the road.

The firestorm provoked an immediate response, and once more Japanese mortar shells began to explode around them. It was too much for the jumpy Canadians. To Donald's horror, they began to run off down the road, but before they had gone far they were brought up short by Major Baillie, who drew his revolver and threatened to shoot anyone who retreated another step. With operatic timing, the shooting stopped everywhere, so that only Baillie's furious voice, cracking with emotion, could be heard swearing at his men.

It was not the voice of leadership. There was too much fear in it. Even when he called for volunteers to go back across the bridge, it was not with authority. In the silent night, the Japanese must have heard every word and known exactly where he was. None of his own men moved. Waving his pistol, Baillie went on himself, striding on into the dark, cursing the men who were supposed to be under his command.

Donald watched for a moment, then could not bear to watch the solitary figure any longer. Everything indicated that Baillie was walking into a Japanese ambush, but even so Donald could not let him die alone. Jumping to his feet, he ran after the Major. Together they reached the other side, unharmed, whereupon Baillie was violently sick. Only then did Donald smell the alcohol and realize that he had risked his life to accompany a man who was hopelessly drunk. Oddly enough, he found himself feeling sympathy rather than anger. The poor Major, it was clear, had simply been unable to cope with the intolerable stress of commanding untrained troops in battle.

A little foolishly they returned through the darkness to their own side, only to find that more of Baillie's men had taken the chance to slip away. Paradoxically, in the lottery of warfare, they might in fact have been safer staying, for in the stillness Donald could hear Japanese circling round the far side of the reservoir, evidently having decided not to attack the bridge. Instead of letting them go, Baillie decided that the sound of the enemy made a target too good to miss. A mortar was hauled into place on the road, aimed across the reservoir, and a shell dropped down the tube. Shaken by what they had gone through, no one had checked the positioning of the mortar tube with sufficient care. The shell was fired, but, instead of flying out across the water, it hit a branch of a nearby tree and fell back to the ground among the firing party. The explosion blew off the mortar operator's right arm and almost severed another man's leg, besides wounding several others.

The casualties were carried to a dugout, where the others made unavailing efforts to stop the bleeding. They had no painkillers, only bandages, but however tightly they ligatured the shattered limbs, the blood kept welling out. Above the cries of pain, Donald tried to call up an ambulance, but none arrived. By now the remainder of the force were totally demoralized. The bridge had been left unguarded, and there was no pretence at being other than frightened men. Although not the senior officer, Donald was evidently the only one left able to take command. For a long time, he laid into them. He must have told them about the need for self-discipline, the importance of hanging together, their duty to behave like soldiers, because they began to go back to their posts. 'His powers of leadership were outstanding,' his commanding officer Ginger Sullivan later observed, and the fact that he carried weight in a situation where rank no longer counted was proof of that judgment.

Before dawn, the ambulance came, and with it two young subalterns from the Winnipeg Grenadiers, who were so shocked by Baillie's inebriated state they wanted to arrest him on the spot. But there was no time left to restore order or normality. It was Christmas Day, and the surrender for which the previous fortnight had been a preparation was at last about to come. At ten o'clock, a rumour went round that a truce had been declared, but the Japanese artillery barrage that followed did not encourage belief. In his last act as a combatant, Donald decided to take his RAF platoon away from the reservoir and rejoin the main British force, which he thought must be further west. They trudged up the long slope of Mount Butler and at the summit came upon the main road between Victoria and Aberdeen. It was crammed with retreating troops.

They bore the unmistakable air of defeat, heads down, weary movement and above all no weapons. Beyond them, the sky was filled with columns of black smoke as ammunition and fuel dumps were torched. Shells whistled and screeched overhead and exploded into houses scattered along the peaks. Suddenly the barrage ceased, and from the windows of the battered buildings white flags began to appear. The time was 4.30 p.m. The surrender of Hong Kong had taken place one hour before.

CHAPTER 4

PRISONER OF WAR

Love seeketh not Itself to please,
Nor for itself hath any care,
But for another gives its ease,
And builds a Heaven in Hell's despair.

William Blake, *Songs of Experience*

The 'old-fashioned siege' had lasted a fortnight. In Tunbridge Wells, the news of Hong Kong's fall demolished the fragile confidence that Pamela had sustained on the reassurances of BBC news bulletins. In the next three months, the rest of Britain's Pacific possessions, from Malaya to Borneo and New Guinea, along with a string of island colonies, all surrendered – including most shatteringly, on 16 February 1942, Singapore, the rock on which the whole defence of the Far East rested, together with a garrison of 120,000 men.

At first it was impossible for Pamela to separate her own bitter anxiety from the mood of recrimination and doubt which settled on the country. She wept and blamed herself for not somehow having found a way out to Hong Kong so that she could have been with him. On a national level, *The Times* blamed the catastrophes on the 'easy-going routine of colonial administration', while censors noted that servicemen's letters were filled with criticism of Blimpish attitudes in government. Attempting to shore up morale, an MP, Captain Leonard Gammans, reminded the critics that 'We cannot expect Asiatics and Africans to believe in us as a colonial Power unless we believe in ourselves.'

That old imperial certainty never did recover, but quite soon the country's temper solidifed into a narrower conviction that in Europe at least it would not be defeated. In the stirring words used by Pamela's local newspaper, the *Courier*, in 1944 to sum up Kent's resistance to Hitler's onslaught: 'There was seldom a day that enemy planes were not overhead, but no note of terror was struck in the hearts of a people who had long since steeled themselves to these wanton attacks on the towns and villages of rural south-east England.'

In similar fashion, Pamela's own volatile feelings eventually settled into a stubborn faith that somehow Donald must have survived. It was difficult to explain why she should have been so certain. For over six months, she had no news of him. He had simply disappeared. The RAF's official notice was that he was 'missing, believed PoW [prisoner of war]', but no one knew for certain. Normally after a battle, each unit would find the time to call a roster; survivors would pool information about who had become casualties or been taken prisoner, and the news would be passed back to families. After a surrender, nothing could be known about the fate of individuals until the enemy chose to release the names of those it held in captivity. The Japanese did not begin this process until the summer of 1942.

Stoicism was not one of the qualities that Pamela's family associated with her, but she had started to learn it almost from the moment that she waved goodbye to Donald in July 1939. In the days after his departure, she took to her bed, and wept for the misery of life without him. When she got up, it was only to write him a long, tear-stained letter saying that it hardly seemed worth living if he was not there. His reply took weeks to arrive, but it transformed everything for it contained plans for a meeting in Singapore, where, he promised, they would be married. With their wedding on the horizon, her spirits soared as extravagantly as they had earlier plunged. Now she had something to live for. It was something strange, which her sisters remembered with startled clarity amid the explosive impact of the declaration of war, that Pamela – who had never cared about any of her other boyfriends enough to scribble a note –

now regularly sat down to cover pages of Basildon Bond writing paper with her open, looped handwriting.

'I missed him so bitterly,' she said. 'The letters were the one way that I still had of talking to him. So I did write to him, day after day, and I continued even after Hong Kong fell and he had disappeared. Everyone else thought I was mad.'

On 3 September 1939, much of the United Kingdom heard on the wireless the thin, beaky tones of Neville Chamberlain explaining that Germany had attacked Poland despite Britain's guarantee to protect the integrity of her borders. Hitler had been asked for an undertaking that his forces would be withdrawn, but no such undertaking had been given. 'As a result, I must tell you', Chamberlain declared in his plaintive voice, 'that we are now at war with Germany.' Almost at once, air-raid sirens began to wail in London, a false alarm as it happened, but appropriate response. To the general apprehension, Pamela added her own fear. A voyage to Singapore might no longer be possible, and the wedding would have to be postponed.

While the Far East remained at peace, Britain wearily braced itself for the second half of the conflict which had begun in 1914. The Kirrage girls responded to the outbreak of hostilities as most well-brought-up girls did, by taking up work of national importance. In Sheila's case, this was farmwork. Brigit organized files in the Ministry of Defence, but Pamela understandably aimed at something a little more elegant. She chose the Red Cross, expecting to become a nurse, but when she told her interviewer of her previous work in Bermondsey, she was briskly informed that the organization stood in far greater need of cooks. Her first job was at a convalescent hospital in Ascot called Winkfield Place.

In Donald's absence, her parents provided an emotional refuge, and it became a habit to spend every weekend with them. There was just time after lunch on Saturday to get a lift from the hospital into London, and then take the uncertain train from Charing Cross to Tunbridge Wells, to be in time for supper before going to bed in the same bedroom she had occupied since she was a child. At the centre of the drama and self-display, it might be seen as a small steady cry for security. When the real war finally burst on the country, she stubbornly persisted in her routine.

In Kent they had a grandstand seat at the cataclysm. They saw the defeated army which had been taken off the beaches at Dunkirk to be landed at Ramsgate and Dover. They heard the desperate whine and staccato gunfire beneath the vapour trails as the Brylcreem boys of the RAF's fighters countered the Luftwaffe in the Battle of Britain. In the night the drone of bombers had passed overheard carrying the Blitz to London and Coventry and the Midlands. The Kent coast was lined with anti-aircraft guns, observer posts and the mysterious radar stations, and every flat expanse of ground that might take a glider attack was peppered with concrete pillboxes. Sometimes the *Courier* would describe them as being 'in the front-line of the war', though by the middle of 1940 there was in truth no front to be lined in western Europe. Except for fascist Spain and Portugal, all the landmass from Brittany to Stalingrad was controlled by Nazi Germany.

Through it all, like Mrs Miniver refusing to let Hitler's bombs change her habits, Pamela insisted on travelling to and from Tunbridge Wells, so that she could walk up the hill from the Central Station to arrive at the peace of her parents' house in Queen's Road. But even there the effects of war were apparent. All but one of the servants had disappeared to join the forces or work in war production, and the great house, so full of life in peacetime, was almost empty. Her father had joined the Home Guard and cultivated an allotment. Her mother had become an air-raid warden responsible for ensuring that the blackout was observed. For a brief period the Road's closed doors and gleaming windows shielded by neat white net curtains, which in peacetime kept out prying eyes, were opened to her as she checked on the blackout arrangements. For Tunbridge Wells, giving up so much of its cherished privacy must have counted, next to the bombs as the ultimate hardship of the war. Nevertheless, it remained Pamela's home, and if she timed it right she could stay until Monday morning before catching an early commuter train back to London, and a connection out to Ascot to be in time to prepare lunch.

'I specialized in good English cooking,' she recalled. 'Once rationing came in, it became impossible to get the right ingredients, but I learned to stretch out whatever beef or lamb we could get, and I made sure that at least once a week the patients got a really delicious pudding.'

In the tattered pages of her menu book, shepherd's pie, mince and potatoes and whale-meat stew appear repeatedly, mixed in with 'Resurrection Pie' when all the previous week's scraps returned in a single dish. The strongest flavour they convey is one of austerity. It was not until the summer of 1942 that she found a setting better suited to her temperament.

The Political Warfare Executive was one of the war's more shadowy organizations. Nominally it was part of the Special Operations Executive, whose mission, in Winston Churchill's magical phrase, was to 'set Europe ablaze' by acts of sabotage. The PWE aimed to achieve the same end by feeding false information and sabotaging the news organizations of occupied Europe. Increasingly it developed its black arts independently of the SOE, but it shared the same smart headquarters in the Riding School at Woburn Abbey, the Duke of Bedford's ancestral home.

Apart from its size, the very beauty of the place served a propaganda purpose. Many of the men and women who arrived there were French, Polish, or Dutch nationals who had escaped from Nazi domination. In Woburn Abbey, once a medieval Cistercian abbey and finely restored as an eighteenth-century mansion surrounded by a 3,000-acre park, they had a picture of the civilization for which they were now fighting. It was a reminder that they stood for the good against the evil. Everything served the same end, even the food, which was good and largely exempt from rationing. The staff, including the cooks, were expected to be as stylish as their meals. A Polish member of SOE training for a sabotage operation in his native country was particularly struck by the women who looked after him and their effect on morale. 'You couldn't have found a finer type of Englishwoman anywhere,' he wrote. 'Cultured and friendly, hard-working and smiling, they created the relaxed, happy atmosphere so necessary before the coming adventure.'

When a friend suggested she come to work at Woburn, Pamela did not hesitate. It was the perfect setting, beautiful and glamorously secret. In fact it was so secret that officially she was still at Winkfield Place. That remained the address to which all her post was sent, and the return address she put on the letters which she continued to send for week after week to Flight Lieutenant Donald Hill.

Through those first ferocious years of the war, she had gradually accepted the postponement of their wedding until he could return to Britain. Time drags slowly for any twenty-three year-old who is waiting to hear from a lover. For one who was living through the sudden death of the Battle of Britain and the nightly destruction of the Blitz, the antlike progression of the days was interminable. Then came the battle for Hong Kong and silence.

'I don't know how I got through that time,' she recalled. 'I thought I would go insane with anxiety. It was as bad as when he first left.'

The surrender of the Hong Kong garrison took the Japanese by surprise. Although they had twice called on the island's inadequate forces to give themselves up, they had made no preparations for that eventuality. At 3.25 p.m. on Christmas Day, the Governor, Sir Mark Young, finally accepted the advice of General Maltby that further resistance was pointless, and ordered commanding officers in the field to cease fighting, 'it being abundantly clear any further resistance meant the useless slaughter of the remaining Hong Kong garrison'. Most troops, including Donald Hill's small party, stopped firing soon afterwards, but a few pockets of troops had still not heard the news twenty-four hours later. Even then, the Japanese were still not ready to deal with them.

On their outlying island, Michael Wright and his Hong Kong Volunteer battery did not know that any change had taken place until the night of Christmas Day, when they saw cars driving through the streets of Aberdeen with their headlights on. A party was sent ashore to find out the reason, and was told of the surrender at the Industrial School. Wright's feeling – like that of most soldiers, both amateur and professional – was predominantly one of relief that he had survived the ordeal. The choice had always been between death and captivity, and he was thankful to have arrived at the lesser of the two evils.

Elsewhere on Hong Kong island, the realization that they were still alive prompted many of the garrison to celebrate. There had never been any shortage of alcohol on the island, and those who did not fall asleep took the chance to drink themselves into oblivion.

'Discipline had vanished,' an anonymous private in the Middlesex Regiment recalled after the war. 'We scrounged, looted and stole, ignoring the respect we owed to each other. We fought and argued over trivial matters and behaved like untutored and inexperienced children.'

Donald Hill's reaction was different. After almost a week with only broken sleep and the constant tension of moving warfare, he was physically exhausted. However, his immediate instinct was to escape. With four burly RAF colleagues, he grabbed the first car that they could find, a tiny Austin Seven, determined to drive back down the hill to Aberdeen and find a boat with supplies to get them to the mainland of China. Night had fallen and the engine would not start, but unfazed they freewheeled down the steep narrow road, crashing through flimsy roadblocks on the way and eventually came to a halt in Aberdeen itself without having seen any of the enemy. They jumped out and ran to the Industrial School to get their kit. Inside the School, they found a Chinese man who promised to find them a boat and to provision it for them. It was late at night at the end of a long day, and evidently they were slowing down, or the conference with their helper had taken longer than they thought. When they finally assembled in the hall ready to leave, they found to their horror that the door was locked. The Japanese had arrived in Aberdeen, and orders had been given that no one was to leave the building. Their chance had gone.

Hong Kong was the first territory the Japanese captured, and the actual business of dealing with its defenders and inhabitants had to be improvised. Initially civilians were held in requisitioned hotels, until on the advice of the British Director of Medical Services, Dr Selwyn-Clark, they were interned in Stanley, a peninsula in the very south of Hong Kong island, the healthiest place in the colony, where existing large buildings made it possible to house a population of almost 2,500 men, women and children. More complex arrangements had to be made for the combatants. A week was to pass before they were ready.

When they awoke on Boxing Day in the badly damaged Industrial School, Donald and his companions tasted first the luxurious sense of being alive on the first sunny day since hostilities had begun. There was no artillery barrage, and no prickling tension of listening for the furtive sound of a bomber or sniper creeping up unobserved. Almost immediately afterwards came the realization that they were about to become prisoners of an enemy renowned for ill-treating their captives.

Throughout their campaign in China, some Japanese practised all the barbarities of war. From the notorious 'Rape of Nanking' in 1938, when the fall of the city had been followed by medieval scenes in which up to 300,000 male prisoners had been killed, many by being made targets for bayonet practice, others by beheading, while tens of thousands of women were raped and imprisoned in military brothels, it had been clear that the armed forces of Japan condoned behaviour which modern western nations regarded as criminal.

For fear that drunkenness might aggravate these murderous tendencies, the senior surviving officers decided to destroy all supplies of alcohol, and most of that sunny morning in Aberdeen Industrial School was spent smashing bottles of beer and spirits. Units which had lost men in battle sent out burial parties, while others were ordered to destroy weapons. The five RAF officers commandeered a car to drive over the hill to military headquarters in Victoria to find out what they should do next. In the bright sunshine they passed through groups of Chinese looters, but still the victors were not to be seen. Donald had been fighting them for a fortnight, he had been defeated by them, but still he had not seen them.

At headquarters, he learned of the terms of surrender. All units were to assemble by Victoria docks to be shipped to a camp on the mainland. Until then the men of the RAF detachment were to be held in detention barracks, while the officers were confined to headquarters.

His old life had effectively ended, but his new life as a prisoner had still not begun. The conquerors were not yet in command, the defeated not yet captive. On both sides, a drunken chaos reigned. Poised on the cusp, Donald had enough time to reflect on what he needed from the old, ordered, privileged existence if he was to survive in the new, uncertain impotence into which he was about to be delivered. Materially, he needed his kit, clothes, food, toothbrush and razor. At a deeper level, he needed something more important – mementoes of his old identity. The most precious of these were the presents that Pamela had given him during the brief three months they had known each other: the gold ring, her photograph and a cigarette case. Even when the bomb exploded in his room, he had rescued them from the rubble. To be deprived of them would have seemed like losing the last memory of happiness. But there was something else he needed – the diary.

Only he knew why it had to come with him. The evidence of Japanese atrocities was clear to everyone. At headquarters, numerous reports had already been made of prisoners who had been beheaded, and of wounded men beaten to death. When he and the other officers talked of what would happen to them as prisoners of war, one constant piece of information that entered every speculation was the knowledge that the Japanese regarded surrender as shameful, and prisoners as consequently expendable. Obviously, to continue keeping a diary while in Japanese hands was to run the risk of being killed. Yet, when he decided to go back to Aberdeen Industrial School to retrieve his belongings, that was one of the things for which he returned.

Once more he would have to make the absurdly beautiful journey over the spine of the island from Victoria to Aberdeen. He took with him two other pilots who wanted to collect their kit, the Australian, Frank Hennessy, and Wimpey Baugh. This time the only suitable vehicle he could find was an abandoned milk lorry. There was one other change: for the first time they encountered the enemy, thousands of Japanese soldiers plodding wearily down the road towards them. It was impossible to turn back, and so they drove on through the ranks of their conquerors. They were small, in some cases almost dwarfed by their rifles. Many wore wire-rimmed spectacles, and their uniforms were coarse and ill-fitting. Faces looked up, registering their strange blue uniforms and western appearance, but no one interfered until one officer more alert than the others stepped out and signalled them to stop. This was the moment when they would discover for themselves how the Japanese treated their prisoners.

The officer gestured at them to turn the lorry round, then loaded his men into the back. He seemed bemused by the uniforms, but more interested in having his soldiers carried to their destination in Victoria than in finding out why they were driving the lorry. Having unloaded the Japanese in town, the three pilots set out again. This time, by dint of turning a blind eye to the gestures of other officers, they made it through the lines of marching soldiers to Aberdeen. Hurriedly they picked up all the supplies of food and clothing they could carry, and

Donald carefully packed his diary and Pamela's gifts into his bags. One more journey would see them home. Hardly daring to believe that their luck would hold, they drove the ancient lorry back over the hill, and down again to headquarters in Victoria. Not until they piled out of the milk lorry did the tension lift. At that moment, a Japanese officer approached Donald and ordered him peremptorily back behind the wheel. Quietly, Frank and Wimpey let themselves out, taking the precious kitbags with them.

As much as at any time in the battle, he was now in the grip of forces beyond his control, and the way he reacted offered as good an insight into the depths of his personality as his response to the physical danger of bombs and bullets. For hour after hour, he and his lorry were passed from one inebriated Japanese to another to transport troops around the island. The streets were filled with soldiers, and the seriousness of their intentions was made obvious by the corpses of Chinese civilians they had executed which littered the road. In the immediate aftermath of victory, most of their officers were good-humoured, but not all, and there was never any room for misunderstanding. One jabbed a bayonet in his buttock when he reacted too slowly, another group began gesturing angrily at him, and when one pulled his long officer's sword out of its scabbard, Donald recognized the gesture. It was part of the samurai ethos to see whether one could decapitate an enemy with one blow. He resigned himself to what was to come. But, instead of execution, the officer produced a bottle of beer, and with the point of his sword neatly flicked the cap off, then handed Donald the bottle. He drank it showing neither fear nor relief.

Late at night he was still ferrying his dangerous and unpredictable enemies through the black streets. One officer gave him a loaf of bread, another shared a beer opened on the lorry's mudflaps, while others shouted and swore at him. In Aberdeen, two drunken Japanese volunteered to drive him in a car without headlights and crashed into a traffic island in the middle of the road. Bowing politely to his stunned fellow passengers, Donald walked quietly back over the hill to the safety of his bed in Victoria.

The cusp was not a comfortable place to be. For three more days, they waited for instructions from the Japanese about their future. In that time troops from other parts of the island were gradually assembled in Victoria, each of them bringing more news about the fighting, and increasingly detailed reports of atrocities. The worst came from Stanley, where the Japanese troops had entered St Stephen's hospital, murdered the doctors, bayoneted patients in their beds, then raped and killed the nurses. That was when the extent of the survivors' impotence first began to strike home. However dreadful the events, there was nothing they could do. Not even an officer whose wife was one of the nurses could be allowed to respond. When he attempted to assault the nearest Japanese, it was his brother officers who held him back. They were powerless. For Donald Hill, this was a new challenge. He had discovered that physical danger produced in him a response unlike most others around him. He became cool and clear-sighted, able to take effective action to counter the menace. Now there was nothing he could do physically. He had to learn how to be passive. And for someone of his size, the lesson was to be taught with particular harshness.

'He once said that he thought the Japanese disliked big men,' Barbara Hill, his daughter-in-law, remembered. 'Because they were so much smaller, they seemed to feel physically challenged and it made them particularly aggressive towards him.'

On 29 December the prisoners were told to be ready to leave at first light the following day. There was to be no transport for personal possessions. They would walk, and they could take with them only what they could carry. The rule held good for General Maltby and the youngest private. In a country where face and public appearance counted for so much, the signifi-cance of the arrangements could not be mistaken. They were to be publicly humiliated. There was nothing they could do about that either. Any resistance had to be on the inside. To himself,

Donald made one silent promise. Whatever happened, however much humiliation was heaped on him, he would bear it without a murmur. His captors would never have the satisfaction of knowing his inner fury and despair.

Donald had come to value the laconic humour of the Australian fighter pilot Frank Hennessy. Together they decided they could take more of their belongings if they shared the burden. They slung their kitbags from a pole which they carried on their shoulders, and tied blankets round their necks. There were 6,000 men on Hong Kong island, and all of them had to be taken across to the mainland. At dawn the next day, they marched through the streets of Victoria to the ferry, and the effect of their new status could be seen reflected in the outside world. Crowds of Chinese lined the streets to see those who had been rulers and were now prisoners pass by. Some jeered, but most were silent, as though the change were too momentous for immediate reaction, and Donald noticed that a few wept.

At the ferry they were forced to wait again until they could shuffle aboard, and then they were paraded up Kowloon's major street, Nathan Road, through a maze of roads, then down again. Either their guards were lost or they were trophies being put on display by the victors, much as a Roman general would have made a triumph of a vanquished army. Officers rode by on horseback, bands played and photographers ran beside them to record their downfall. The day was warm, the hills steep, and soon the shuffling columns were leaving a trail of discarded coats and blankets. The pole on which Donald and Frank Hennessy carried all their kit grew heavier and bit deeper into their shoulders. Neither dared discard items on which their lives might depend, and so they stumbled on until they could go no further. A Japanese guard came up, but, instead of shouting at them, compassionately let them transfer the burden to professional bearers. The incident almost passed unnoticed, yet, amid the crushing sense of shame, even that little kindness rubbed its own grain of salt into the wound.

Their eventual destination was Sham Shui Po Barracks.

Before the war it had been home to an infantry battalion, and much of the camp was occupied by parade grounds. The accommodation consisted of concrete huts and a large block of flats which had been the married officers' living quarters, all surrounded by a barbed-wire fence. The camp was built on land reclaimed from the harbour, with sea on two sides and a road on the other two. It had never been luxurious, but a brief occupation by the victors and subsequent looting by inhabitants from the neighbourhood had left it looking, as Donald remarked, 'as if a typhoon had hit it'. Only the shells of the huts were left. Their doors, windows, tables and beds had all been stolen, and among the ruins they found two members of the Middlesex Regiment who had been captured at the beginning of the battle. They had been stripped of their clothes, then tied up with wire, and after three days without food or water were barely alive.

There was a rush to find huts and anything at all that would make a bed. Donald discovered some hanks of horsehair which he used as stuffing inside a knotted blanket to make a thin mattress, and the first night of genuine captivity passed in numb discomfort. Over the next twenty-four hours, each one of them became miserably aware of the reality of their new existence. Almost 6,000 men were housed there with no sanitation, no power and no fuel. Their only food was watery rice served twice a day. And so ended 1941. The next year, Donald told himself, had to be better.

Donald shared his small hut with five others, including Frank Hennessy, their commanding officer Ginger Sullivan and the two young pilots Wimpey Baugh and Junior Crossley. Their first task was to patch up its windows and door with planks of wood and any kind of scrap material they could find. They had no cups or plates, and so had to improvise from empty tins or discarded bits of crockery. Around them in the huge camp, the first semblance of organization began to take shape.

Their twice-daily meal of rice was cooked in large oil drums with the tops cut off, which retained a lingering flavour of fuel. Latrines were dug, although the overcrowding and open sewage pits attracted swarms of flies which helped spread dysentery. The doctors set up a makeshift hospital in an empty hut and, despite the lack of medicines, attempted to treat gaping wounds and the first outbreaks of disease. But, when over a hundred Indian soldiers were brought in suffering from dysentery, lack of beds meant that they had to be placed on the hut's concrete floor where, unable to move, they were soon covered in faeces and blood. The prisoners' torment was compounded by the violent, seemingly haphazard punishments handed out by their captors. The offences might seem trivival − failure to salute a guard, walking too close to the wire − but they would be rewarded by punches to the face, or a rifle butt repeatedly slammed into the ribs.

Yet within a week every other tribulation paled into insignificance beside the lack of food. It was estimated that the two rice meals contained less than 900 calories, about one-third of the recommended daily intake for an adult male. One night as they were going to bed, a lorry roared into the camp, and the men heard the squealing of pigs. Those still up saw Japanese soldiers herd some thirty pigs out of the back of the lorry, and drive off. Within minutes the animals were rounded up and penned in an empty hut. The next day they were slaughtered and divided up among the camp's inhabitants. Donald found one small lump of fat in his rice.

As the diet took effect, their thoughts turned insistently to food. They began to shiver and constantly feel cold. Every hut had to provide buckets for use as night-time lavatories because the lack of vitamins and constant supply of polished rice produced bouts of diarrhoea. In the morning, columns of working parties went round the camp collecting the buckets to empty in the sewage pits. To add to their misery, when they were fed, the swarms of flies attracted to the open latrines settled on their food and buzzed round their mouths as they ate.

Compared with the prisoners who worked on the Burma

Railway – inspiration for *The Bridge on the River Kwai* – those in Hong Kong got off lightly. Although work parties had to be provided for labour on the extension to the Kai Tak airport, the conditions were not as hard as those in the jungle. It was simply that, lacking almost any medicine or food supplement, they were being slowly starved to death. In the first six months, over a hundred of them died as the result of poor feeding. Many of those who survived owed their lives to the courage of the Chinese, and in Donald's case to the courage of his girlfriend Florrie in particular.

'That girl probably saved my life,' Donald admitted many years later. 'My God, she smggled food into me. It's something I'll never forget. I think she saved my life.'

During his lifetime, it was the only direct reference he ever made to what she had done for him, and it was no more than the sober truth. At the end of the first week of captivity, Florrie arrived outside the barbed wire surrounding the camp, accompanied by her amah or maid and carrying a basket of food. Already some market traders were selling food across the wire to the hungry prisoners, but the unpredictable attitude of the guards made it a risky business. On some days they seemed to regard it as a useful and cheap way of feeding the inmates. On other occasions, and even in the course of an afternoon, the mood changed and they would charge into the crowd flailing their rifle butts. At those times, if they caught anyone, man or woman, the victim was stripped and beaten in full view of the camp. Yet the traders not only returned but were joined in growing numbers by the Chinese wives and girlfriends of men in camp.

'It was surprising to me how many came,' observed David Bosanquet, a sergeant in the Hong Kong Volunteers. 'It was wonderful how loyal some of these girls proved to be. After all, there was no need for them to run the risk of being beaten up by the Japanese for a boyfriend who was no longer able to be with them. Food and money were very short outside.'

On that first occasion, Florrie and the others were chased

away by the guards because a Japanese general was expected to inspect the camp, but a few days later she was back with a parcel of bread, butter, milk and tomatoes. No nutritionist could have chosen more carefully the foods he needed, and for the next fortnight she brought more every few days. To find supplies in a city where the normal markets had broken down must have taken hours of effort. The food was shared with the others in his hut, and even with the extra rations he felt cold and listless. Without them, he would have been in a serious state. Then for several weeks Florrie was interned in the civilian camp at Stanley, and although his hut pooled their money to buy from traders he immediately felt the loss of her parcels.

Even in the first few weeks of Sham Shui Po, it was clear that some would not survive. Malnutrition was only part of the cause. In the formless but high-anxiety environment of the camp, each individual had to find his own way of resisting the corrosive effects of helplessness. Remembering his own experience, the architect Michael Wright saw it in stark terms.

'If you wanted to survive you had to take a positive attitude, to assert yourself in some way, however small,' he said. 'Even in the first few months, you could see the people who were not going to make it, because they had given up and lost the will to live.'

It was now that prison character began to form. Small things counted disproportionately towards survival. In the damp atmosphere, for example, clothes and shoes rapidly began to disintegrate, but when a man had so little resistance against coldness and wounds, it was important to protect both body and feet. Utterly undomestic though he always had been, Donald methodically taught himself both to sew and to cobble, and in time became so adept as a cobbler and clog-maker that he could earn cigarettes by repairing other prisoners' footwear. He was careful to get his hair cut short. He was conscientious about distributing the hut's precious supply of cigarettes so that no one could complain. He took pains to make his provocative size as inconspicuous as possible, so that fifty years later those who still remembered him as a prisoner also remembered how quiet and withdrawn he seemed. Above all he made sure that his feelings were thrust so far out of sight that no one could even guess at his profound sense of humiliation.

The weak spot in his defences was his love for Pamela. He thought about her constantly, and fretted bitterly that he could not tell her that he was still alive. Images from their brief time together kept returning, yet he dared not dwell too much on it for fear that the emotion would break him up altogether. The more powerful the feelings, the more dangerous they were.

Next to their hunger for food, the POW's sharpest need was for news, and just as they imagined fantastic feasts to satisfy their empty bellies, so they began to conjure up extraordinary rumours to fill the void in their minds. The most persistent was that Chiang Kai-shek's Nationalist Chinese army was massed near by and could be expected to attack at any moment. The Pope, it was said, had gone to negotiate peace in Berlin, and an equally definite account held that Hitler had in fact committed suicide. No less encouraging were the reports from Malaya about massive British victories over the Japanese. Quite soon they could expect to be liberated, ran the unspoken message, and each man would again be needed by his unit to help in the war against Japan. Donald appreciated that they were only rumours, and wild ones at that, but he could not help observing that their news was always good. Cautiously he allowed himself to conclude that things must be going well.

'A senior officer in the Royal Signals told me quite categorically that we had defeated the Japanese in Malaya,' Michael Wright said. 'It was a flat lie, and silly because it caused a great drop in morale when we found out the truth.'

The reality began to emerge by the end of January. There were enough radio experts in the camp to assemble sets, and gradually it became apparent from the BBC, despite the brave face put upon it, that the Malayan campaign was a disaster. The news had a devastating effect on spirits already battered by personal defeat and constant lack of food. In camp tempers were lost for little or no reason, and on one occasion a full-scale fight between British and Indian soldiers flared up. In many units discipline was in danger of breaking down completely, and, perhaps most seriously of all, the rules on sanitation and hygiene began to be ignored. The latrines were often not emptied and the few lavatories that functioned were not repaired, increasing the risk of a dysentery epidemic. Early in February Maltby felt obliged to issue the ultimate threat – unless men obeyed their own officers he would hand over direct control of them to the Japanese. It was a confession of his own incapacity to give a lead in those difficult circumstances, and since it implied a final betrayal of those under his command, it made the task of creating internal discipline harder than ever. Only the sudden relief from overcrowding, as first the Indian troops, then the Canadians were moved to different camps, prevented the camp descending into chaos.

'I think Maltby was pretty well a broken man by then,' Wright judged. 'The surrender was a terrible blow and he did not lead well as a prisoner.'

Once the early hopes of victory evaporated, prisoners started to think of escape. With only a wire fence to penetrate, the real problem was not so much getting out as getting away. Europeans were conspicuous and, unless they spoke Chinese or had contacts outside the wire, they were not likely to get far. But perhaps the biggest obstacle was the psychological sense of not knowing where safety lay in the immense space of China. The first man to go over the wire was Lindsay Ride, who had taken the precaution of bringing a map into camp. Yet even he, who as a university professor had twenty years' experience of Hong Kong and was accompanied by one of his Chinese students, reckoned the odds were ten to one against success. As it turned out, the presence of communist guerrillas operating in the countryside shortened the odds considerably, and many escapers, including Ride, were led to safety with their help. Nevertheless, when two of Donald's young pilot officers, Junior Crossley and Wimpey Baugh, decided separately at the end of

January to try to get out, they were venturing into what continued to be unknown and dangerous territory.

Japanese sentries were concentrating on the landward side of the camp to keep trading across the wire in check. As a result an increasing number of Chinese traders had taken to sailing up at night in junks and sending small boats to sell food through the wire along the sea-wall. It was from this side that the RAF men hoped to go. The two would-be escapers were in different parties, Junior with a group which had bribed a trading junk to take them across the bay, and Wimpey with two others who proposed swimming with a makeshift raft from the shore.

Independently each group had planned to go on the same night, since they needed a full moon in order to travel. The remaining RAF officers stayed up late to give them a last meal before they made the attempt. On their first effort, the moon was so bright that Donald and the others were able to pass the time playing cards. Both attempts were frustrated, one by the junk failing to turn up, the other by the collapse of the precarious raft made up of firewood scrounged or given by friends. Undeterred, they tried again two nights later, and this time slipped away. A little later, bursts of rifle-fire left their friends fearing the worst. Though no one in camp knew the outcome, both pilots did succeed in reaching freedom. Each flew again in combat, although Baugh was killed before the end of the war.

All of those left behind were prey to regrets – and to relief that they were still within the relative safety of the camp. Something of their confused feelings could be found in a comment from Major J. N. Crawford, a doctor who had been a colleague of Lindsay Ride's and refused the chance to escape with him. 'First my duty seemed to be to remain with the men,' he explained. 'Secondly I felt that anyone of my unusual height would minimize the chances of anyone getting through; and third I was damned scared and preferred to remain with the devil I knew. I deeply regretted my decision on many occasions subsequently.'

Although no doctor, Donald's sense of reponsibility for the men in his unit was unmistakable, and was one of the reasons why he was later decorated. Like Crawford, he must have felt that his conspicuous size was a handicap. On the other hand, as he was to make plain, he was desperate to be free, to see Pamela again and to fly. Since his courage was not in question, his preference for the devil he knew to the unknown beyond the wire must have been a matter of psychology. As their accounts unconsciously reveal, each of the escapers had a streak of self-belief amounting almost to arrogance. It was not a quality that Donald possessed, and without it no one was likely to launch himself into the hostile void of China.

The Japanese, so contemptuous of their prisoners, at first seemed almost oblivious to the escapes. There were extra parades, and long confused counts of their numbers, but although the sentries shot at junks that approached by day, they seemed to notice nothing amiss at night. Discussing their apparent indifference, Donald and his companions concluded that their captors must regard escape as somehow despicable, like deserting. What they failed to appreciate was that for Colonel Isao Tokunaga, the camp commandant, the prisoners' disappearance entailed a loss of face.

A week after the two escapes, every RAF officer except one was ordered to pack his kit. At dawn on 6 February they were put on a lorry and transported to Saigon, to be held for six weeks in a French colonial prison. The one left behind was Donald. Suddenly he was on his own, responsible for the welfare of sixty men in a situation which could hardly have been worse.

For the only time in camp, his composure almost cracked. Perhaps there was an echo of that sense of being abandoned which he must have experienced at his father's sudden death, for not even battle had provoked such anxiety. He recorded his despair in his diary, then buried the words in the crude letters-to-numbers code he still employed. Over time the secret was to be concealed more and more deeply, and what he felt at his crisis, the gut emotion that emerged from the inner core of his being, was to remain a mystery for half a century.

After six weeks in a Saigon prison, the RAF officers emerged gaunt and starving and so badly diseased that the worst affected spent months recovering in hospital. But none died. Many of those left behind in Sham Shui Po did not fare so well. Barely a month after the RAF escapers, another party of four led by Lieutenant Douglas Clague also got away. This time Tokunaga was furious. He demanded that every prisoner sign an oath not to escape, and as punishment the rice ration, which had gradually increased, was cut back to its original starvation level and all trade through the wire was forbidden. For men hovering on the verge of malnutrition, the consequences were immediate and catastrophic. Donald noticed in himself the preliminary signs of beriberi, which was caused by a lack of vitamin B. Oedema swelled his ankles and legs like balloons, but the residual effects of Florrie's parcels saved him from the next stage, agonizing shooting pains in the feet that sufferers called 'electric feet'. The agony could reduce victims to tears, and to escape it they would sit for hours with their feet soaking in water until the sodden skin split across the soles.

But everyone's skin was erupting and suppurating as the vitamin deficiencies returned with renewed violence. Diphtheria made the throat swollen and septic. Pellagra left the skin roughened and itching as uncontrollably as eczema, usually round the groin. Sufferers' inflamed genitals swelled to the size of tennis balls, a condition known as 'strawberry balls', and were so itchy that one man literally scratched himself to death. The deadliest consequence of the malnutrition, however, was dysentery, which affected almost half the camp that April.

A few days after his friends were removed, Donald himself was taken out of camp for questioning. It was not a reassuring prospect. Escorted by an unusually large guard, a Formosan sergeant known simply as George, who stood over six feet tall and was notorious for the beatings he gave with his sword, Donald was marched in front of the commandant Lieutenant

Hideo Wada, whose protuberant teeth and character earned him the nickname 'Ratface'. Instead of a beating, however, he was offered a cigarette, and George asked him how the Japanese air force compared with the RAF. Donald took the opportunity to steal a handful of cigarettes, and offer his forthright, and largely mistaken, opinions about the slowness of the Zero fighter.

Although he did not know it, he had failed a little test. The Japanese had decided that the number of escapes would be reduced if the officers were transferred to a more secure camp. Some, however, would have to remain at Sham Shui Po to be in charge of the servicemen still there, and one would be appointed to be in overall command, and thus directly responsible to the Japanese. Donald was only one of several officers surveyed, before they found their ideal candidate in Major Cecil Boon. Notoriously inept and soon christened Major Disaster, Boon proved himself so ready to do anything to ingratiate himself with his superiors that after the war he was court-martialled on a charge of treason. Yet, even before his appointment, the starving camp had produced a flock of informers ready to sell their friends' secrets for extra rations.

The exception to this rule was the RAF unit, and much of the credit for its high morale was due to Donald's work during these weeks. From the start, he had ensured in his meticulous way that they were able to cope with the trials of prison life. He lectured them on the need for discipline, but singled them out for praise because unlike other troops they had kept up their standards. When the existence of the camp's clandestine radio was betrayed to the Japanese by informers, Donald took the RAF signals specialists aside, warning them that they would be questioned but that they were to deny all knowledge of the set. As it happened, a total of three radios had been constructed, of which the guards discovered two – the third having been dismantled before it could be found. Although they had certainly been involved with at least one of them, Donald's men

admitted nothing and escaped punishment. Amid the debilita-
tion of malnutrition and the universal news of military defeat,
this tiny triumph helped to keep their spirits up.

Among so many demoralized units, the example of the RAF
was sufficiently striking for Maltby to remark on it when
Sullivan returned from his prison cell. Five years later Sullivan
reminded Maltby that he had 'complimented me on the high
morale and good behaviour of the Unit, a state of affairs for
which Flight Lieutenant Hill was largely responsible'. Taken
with Hill's courage in battle and his attempt to save the burning
Vildebeeste, he suggested that it warranted a decoration, and
Maltby's decisive scribble of 'Recommended' indicated how
vividly he recalled what Donald achieved in camp.

In April, he was forced to leave the men he had cared for
when all but about twenty officers were transferred to a camp
on Argyle Street. It had been built for internees before the war,
and its relative security could be measured by the fact that only
one person successfully escaped from it. There was no furniture,
and nothing in the long wooden huts but their concrete floors,
but the compensations made up for the renewed discomforts.
Ginger Sullivan, Frank Hennessy and all Donald's other friends
were sent there too. They had space. But most miraculous of all
the Japanese had at last responded to Red Cross pressure to
allow prisoners to write home. They were allowed just 200
words, which had to be printed out.

Very carefully, as though any mistake might prevent it being
sent, he wrote:

To Miss Pamela Kirrage, 2 Queens Road, Tunbridge Wells,
England.
From: D. S. Hill.

Then came the date, '3rd June 1942', and after that a large gap.

My darling,
    The Japanese authorities are allowing us to write and this is to

assure you that I am safe and well. Would you communicate with mother telling her you have heard from me. I shall be writing to her soon.

Well my darling perhaps by now you have given me up as dead. I dont know. But through all these months you have been always in my thoughts. Whatever happens I shall always love you. When you write darling please stick to the rules I have set out below.

All my love darling. I love you. Always have and always will. Don

The rules, designed to help Japanese censors, required the correspondent to write in capitals, use only simple words, omit political or military information, and restrict herself to one side of the paper. In addition there was rule five: 'Do not use code or secret marks.' For someone who was keeping a coded diary, that must have caused at least the ghost of a smile.

CHAPTER 5

DISGUISING THE TRUTH

It is impossible to obtain real privacy in the information age without good cryptography.

Philip Zimmerman, author of PGP (Pretty Good Privacy) software for email encryption

Early in March, it occurred to Philip Aston that, although Donald Hill had neither a computer, nor privacy, nor security, he possessed one priceless advantage that his decoder lacked. He had an abundance of spare time. Philip had begun to ransack the university library for books on prisoner-of-war camps in the Far East, and the more he read, the better he understood the conditions under which Donald must have been working. For Donald the problem would have been how to spend time rather than how to find it.

There were fewer people and a greater degree of organization at Argyle Street than at Sham Shui Po. On the other hand, there were the same huts filled with long lines of beds, and a parade ground with the same long-drawn-out inspections. When they arrived, the huts contained nothing, and so there was the same hunt for material which could be fashioned into everyday objects like furniture and crockery. As before, their bunks quickly became infested with bedbugs. Their clothes and shoes disintegrated equally quickly in the heat and humidity, and, to save the remains of their uniforms, in hot weather they wore only a rag pulled between the legs and looped round a string belt. And, what clearly grated hardest, they were forced to follow the same humiliating regulations requiring prisoners to bow to every guard, regulations which were enforced with the routine resort to face-slapping and body-punching.

Against that sort of background, the careful boxes and minute numerals by which Donald had diguised his diary seemed impossibly ordered. Suddenly Philip realized that it would have been impossible to code the entries directly into this form. There must have been at least one intermediate stage. The entries would have been written first in normal English. This was the plaintext. Presumably he would have immediately disguised this in some simple cipher. Later he would have translated it with another cipher, and then added one more layer of complexity, before the final transformation into numbers and its neat entry into the diary. Philip had uncovered two of the layers and was facing a third in the blocks of meaningless letters. Beyond that there might lie more.

Yet, even as he struggled to find a key to the puzzle that Donald had set, Philip's thoughts kept returning to the circumstances in which it had been composed. From the calm and order of his small study on the fourth floor of Building AA, an anonymous brick rectangle on a modern university campus whose landscaped lawns and functional buildings looked down on the prosperous, ribboned streets of Guildford, it was an unimaginable distance to the prisoner-of-war camp with its gnawing hunger, heat and constant threat of physical punishment. The immediate challenge was to find a solution to the code, but half consciously he was aware of the deeper impulse to get through to that world, and to learn what it was that had happened there.

As the days lengthened and the code deepened its hold on him, he found it harder to regard it as the amusing diversion it had at first seemed. Linda, his wife, began to recognize the pages of numbers and jumbled letters that he took home two or three evenings a week. In the midst of family discussions, she grew familiar with a vacant look indicating that his attention had wandered away, and, whatever else he was thinking about, it was not what was happening in the Aston family.

'That was a really stressful time,' she said ruefully. 'Matthew, our youngest, was only eighteen months old and he wouldn't sleep at night. Philip was thinking about the code and he wouldn't sleep at night. And when I wasn't listening out for Matt, I could hear Philip moving restlessly about in bed, and that meant I couldn't sleep at night. One way or the other we all spent most of our nights awake.'

After one such restless night, Philip woke with a pain beneath his ribs, and when he got out of bed he found it hard to stretch his arms. With a stoical wince, he recognized the symptoms.

The first time it had happened was just before Matthew was born, and he had gone to work hoping the pain would go away because he could not afford to be ill with the baby due. In the afternoon, when the pain finally forced him to go to the doctor, he learned that his lung had collapsed, and he needed immediate treatment. A tube had to be inserted under his left arm to remove the air from his chest, which was pressing in on the lung and preventing it from expanding. Characteristically, he insisted the doctors discharge him immediately. He arrived home just in time to drive back to the hospital, this time with Linda about to give birth.

Now, knowing what was involved, he decided to finish some pressing work. He spent a morning editing the proceedings of a conference on chaos, then interviewed an applicant for a university job whose speciality happened to be lungs, then took himself to hospital. He allowed himself just two days, enough time for the lung to be reinflated and sealed to his ribs so that it could not collapse again, then went back home. Reluctantly obeying orders to remain in bed for a few days, he took up some pressing university work to occupy him. A few minutes later Linda heard him call out, 'Could you bring me up the diary?' Yet, however he examined them, the medley of words which had taken the place of numbers – *ascg utyt ttce ashs lion tlrh mnee pfnm* – defied every attempt he made, whether in bed or in his office, to produce any sort of sense.

The limitation of a computer was that it could only look for regular patterns. A cipher which rearranged the pairing *th* or *he* in the same way each time the letters appeared would produce a pattern which a computer program could detect immediately. What he had to accept now was that Donald had used a key which jumbled up the letters in an apparently random fashion. If there were sometimes five spaces between the *t* and the *h*, and sometimes two, then seven, the machine would be defeated. In that case, only the human intelligence would be able to understand how chaos had been created out of order. Yet he still remained convinced that he would eventually see into Donald's secret. Chaos and complexity were Philip's speciality: his most recent paper had the apposite title 'Analysis of the Control of Chaos – Rate of Convergence'. And so, while he convalesced, the sleepless nights in the Aston household continued.

'The great thing about Philip is that he's dogged,' Linda acknowledged, and it was impossible to tell whether exasperation or appreciation dominated in her voice. 'He will always keep going whatever happens. He doesn't like anything to defeat him.'

Philip imagined the problem being worked on by some half-conscious part of his brain. 'It's ticking over, it's on the back-burner' was how he liked to put it. The process was a constant, almost visual probing at the code, as though he were mentally feeling its shape. Only when he sensed something significant would he bring it sharply into focus. The more he worried away at the problem the more convinced he became that there had to be an independent key, a word or phrase which would suggest a way of rearranging the letters. The difficulty was that a key need not have much connection with the message itself.

On 3 August 1822 the Duke of Wellington was summoned urgently to the house of the Foreign Secretary, Lord Castlereagh. The Iron Duke listened while his former colleague in the Cabinet poured out a garbled tale of being blackmailed for some unspeakable crime. None of it made sense, and when Castlereagh at last fell silent, Wellington said in his customary plain way, 'I am bound to warn you that you cannot be in your right mind.'

Later, he told all this to his friend Charles Arbuthnot, who naturally enough asked what kind of crime it was that Castlereagh felt he had committed. This was a difficult question because it was, in the words of Arbuthnot's wife Harriet, 'a crime which could not be named'. But, as a young officer, Wellington had been accustomed to number-substitution codes, and so he replied 'It is a story of 1 9.' Since the standard military cipher was $B = 1$, $C = 2$, and so on, it was easy to work out his meaning – 'It is a story of BJ' – but what that meant was another matter. Arbuthnot, who was up to date with London gossip, got the answer quickly enough, but others might have been puzzled because the key to deciphering the meaning of the letters depended on local knowledge, which was entirely independent of the military cipher.

In fact, the letters referred to the notorious case of Percy Jocelyn, the Bishop of Clogher, who had been discovered having sex with a guardsman in a private room in the White Hart Inn at Westminster. Thus BJ was Bishop Jocelyn, and Wellington's message meant that the Foreign Secretary thought he was being blackmailed for a homosexual act, which was then a crime punishable by death. Deciphering his secret was no help. Such a belief could only end in suicide. Ten days later in a state of severe depression, the Foreign Secretary killed himself by cutting his throat.

What Philip suspected was that Donald's key depended on some equally specialized knowledge. It might not be related to the text, but such keys were rarely selected entirely at random. During the Reformation, both Catholic and Protestant agents would build ciphers round quotations from the Bible which suited their spiritual leanings. Later code-makers have taken a particular passage from a favourite book to indicate how letters should be rearranged. Since Donald's key needed only to be known to himself, it might come from anywhere. But it was a

reasonable inference he would have taken it from the circumstances of his imprisonment. Time was not one of Philip's
luxuries. He should have been preparing a paper for the
International Journal of Bifurcation and Chaos, but instead he
snatched some hours to read more about the camps.

In some way, the encryption of his diary was almost a
reflection of what Donald must have been going through
himself. His past would have bred in him the normal human
expectations of love and hope, of personal security and
predictable events. That was the plaintext, the original pattern of
his life, and somewhere inside him it must still have existed. But
round it he must also have evolved a way of existing which
concealed its fragile coherence from the madness of the prison
world. To be effective, the disguise had to be as impenetrable as
the code itself.

Those who best survived Sham Shui Po and Argyle Street took
the robust view that the life in the camps was not too bad. In
September 1942 Brigadier Cecil Templer moved to Argyle
Street from hospital after recovering from wounds received in
the battle for Hong Kong, and found the contrast with the
boredom of convalescence stimulating.

'There were activities of all kinds under way,' he wrote.
'Lectures, courses of instruction, rehearsals for plays. There were
courses in German, accounting, a debating group and a very
interesting series of talks on English literature and composition
every Sunday.'

Other parts of the experience were, he acknowledged, less
educational. Overall command of the camps was in the hands of
Colonel Tokunaga, whose gross appearance gave rise to the
nickname 'White Pig'. After the war he was found guilty both
of systematically looting the Red Cross parcels which were sent
to the prisoners and of being responsible for the camps' regime
of random violence. In this, however, Hong Kong was no
worse than other Japanese camps. David Piper, who was in
Changi prison in Singapore, described a beating given to four

prisoners there, catching in sharp focus both its routine nature and the curiously distanced reaction of those who had already been through it themselves. 'There they were, four lean figures lined up,' he wrote.

> One of the guards, about half their height, walked down the line beating their faces. He swung his arm straight from the shoulder, leaning into the blow, and each time he struck, the bayonet on the rifle in his other hand swung and caught the sunlight. At the end of the row he changed hands and worked back on the other cheek. The sound of the blows reached me late, sounding small and remote. It was as though I was watching a rather crude film that had failed to grip me.

It was not only the guards who beat them up. Every encounter with the camp authorities was made through interpreters, and the names of two in particular aroused real hatred. There was the half-Canadian Inouye Kanao, nicknamed 'Slap Happy' for his tendency to hit the defenceless people he was talking to, or 'Shat in Pants' for the deep hang of his trousers, and the equally sadistic Niimori Genichiro, who had spent twenty years in the American mid-West and addressed his victims as 'Youse guys' or 'Baby'. Yet most prisoners also recognized that such personal violence was endemic in the Japanese army: officers punched NCOs, and NCOs slapped private soldiers. And with utter unpredictability some of those in power, like the interpreter Kyoshi Watanabe, who was a Lutheran, or another who had lived in Wales and was known as 'Cardiff Joe', treated them with unwavering courtesy. Like David Piper, everyone learned to wall themselves off from what was being done to them.

Their diet still consisted largely of three meals of boiled rice, but even this had to be picked over to remove clumps of weevils and their eggs. Periodic issues of vegetables did provide some vitamins, occasionally supplemented in summer by chrysanthemum leaves, and once a fortnight two ounces of grilled fish appeared with the rice. Later they were allowed to make a garden on some disused ground where tomatoes and other vegetables could be grown. Nevertheless, men lost up to 80 pounds of their body weight on this regimen. Once more Donald was shielded from the worst of the food shortage by Florrie, who had again found out where he was kept.

In Sham Shui Po, she had not only brought him food but clothes, and once even a *mingtoia*, a warm, quilted Chinese blanket, and during the winter nights Donald was as grateful for that as for any of the life-saving food. Arrangements in Argyle Street were more formal. Food could be brought in and left in the guardhouse, but civilians were not allowed to stand in the road outside, and prisoners were forbidden to attempt to communicate with passers-by. The clandestine whispers that took place could lead to misunderstandings, and for several weeks one hungry prisoner kept receiving packets of needles from his Chinese wife. Finally in exasperation he ran to the wire and defying the guards bellowed, 'I said noodles not needles!' According to witnesses, the mordant humour of it was best appreciated on an empty stomach.

The Chinese, however, were suffering just as badly from lack of food, and Florrie was visibly less healthy. Even at Sham Shui Po, Donald had repeatedly told her that she should leave the colony for mainland China, where food might be more plentiful, but she refused to abandon him. When he persisted, she told him to mind his own business. The Japanese stole her jewellery, and before long she was turned out of the comfortable flat where she lived. But she continued to bring him what she could. Her affection overwhelmed him, and he was filled with admiration for the ingenuity and persistence with which she found a way past the guards. Yet it was not an easy feeling. Her very effectiveness reminded him of his helplessness. She was spending money she desperately needed for herself to keep him alive, and he could not hope to repay her. And there was something more. What he felt for her did not balance what she so clearly felt for him. It was only Pamela that he loved.

'I had a terrible conscience about her,' he admitted in old age. 'She probably saved my life and I couldn't repay her.'

Every month he wrote to Pamela, and as time passed without word from her he began to grow anxious. Before the invasion, they had written weekly to each other. They were often mundane communications about the weather and parties, but they gave him assurance that their love was a real, shared emotion, not something he had imagined. Six months without any communication revived his deep-seated apprehension that whatever he most valued would again be taken from him. When the camp authorities announced in June 1942 that each prisoner would be allowed to send one letter a month, his hopes and fears soared equally.

The sharpest fear was that she might have been killed or wounded in a bombing raid, but beneath that came a dull foreboding that her feelings for him might have changed. She loved attention, she was fun and she was beautiful. In wartime, when life was so short that it had to be lived to the limit, those were an electric mixture of qualities, and he knew how young men in uniform behaved. At times he almost clung to the hope that she had not yet heard from him.

The prisoners never knew what happened to their letters. They were collected for censoring and then supposedly for onward transmission by way of the Red Cross, but the same procedure was followed every month, and their communications simply disappeared into a void. No reply arrived, nothing happened. The letters might never have been written, except for the sense of having spent so much emotion composing them.

In fact many of those fervent messages never got beyond Japan. Few enough Japanese could read English, and most of those were employed in strategically important jobs. Censoring prisoners' letters could not have had a lower priority, and, with ill-trained translators stumbling painfully through the mountain of post, the backlog reached such numbing proportions that frequently they were simply burned. When there was no response, everyone who had opened up his heart to some distant person he loved suffered his own particular torment.

Within the Argyle Street camp, there were extraverts and introverts, pernickety lawyers and diffident architects, professional soldiers and amateur musicians, cross-dressers and straight men, cardsharps, king rats, officers, gentlemen, cowards, conformists and the courageous. And most were several of these mixed together.

'What I learned from my time in camp was that there was good and bad in everyone,' said Michael Wright. 'You couldn't separate it out, the line went right down through each of us. There was good in the worst, and bad in the best. But on the whole I found there was more good than bad.'

The absence of news from home was one of the stresses that kept the level of anxiety high. Fights broke out between prisoners over apparent trifles. The way someone talked or dressed might be enough. And all the time there was the constant, nagging inability to escape from other people. Round each crowded bed ran a boundary invisible to an outsider but as obvious as a brick wall to a prisoner, and it could not be passed without the permission of the occupant. It was possible to retreat there, but it was impossible to seal off the other forty-nine people in the hut, and the other 600-odd who filled the spaces round the huts.

'What we resented most during our imprisonment was not the bad food, or the cold, or the domineering attitude of the Japanese, although all these were unpleasant,' wrote Brigadier Crawford, the Canadian doctor who had refused to escape, 'but what bothered most of us more than anything else was the overcrowding, the complete lack of privacy. In camp, we lived cheek by jowl with the same little group, year after year. And under such circumstances, the dearest friend can become hateful.'

That was what it meant to be a prisoner. Like children they were helpless to exercise control over their existence. All they could do was learn how to control the show of feeling. Even five decades later, that careful wall remained apparent to an outsider. It was neither hostile nor self-protective, just an instinctive piece of behaviour required for survival.

As at Sham Shui Po, Donald shared his hut with other RAF officers. They were all in Hut Eight, which held almost fifty people. Of the original seven, only Ginger Sullivan, Frank Hennessy, Dolly Gray and he remained, and they were exceptionally close. To fill the time, Donald went with them to lectures on philosophy or deer-stalking or training to be a Church of Scotland minister or any other area of expertise that someone was prepared to talk about. The most popular was one on wine-making, and when a Red Cross parcel filled with South African fruit arrived in November, Hut Eight attempted to make their own wine from the raisins. He went to German classes given by someone who happened to possess a German grammar. The camp had acquired a supply of books from the public library which he read voraciously. With Ginger he began to learn how to play bridge, and when volunteers were required to help dig a garden beyond the road, he gladly took part. He would do anything to fill the time.

In September the Japanese ordered an RAF officer to transfer to Sham Shui Po to be in charge of the RAF troops there. It could not have been easy to decide who should leave the circle of friends, but events were to make the selection a matter of life and death. In effect, the choice lay between just two of them. Because Ginger had to remain at Argyle Street as commanding officer, and Frank had barely got to know the men before the fighting began, it could only be Donald or Dolly Gray, the pilot with whom he had volunteered for a suicidal bombing mission in the old Vildebeestes. Donald had been an excellent commander in Sham Shui Po while the others were in Saigon prison, but in the end it was decided that he had done his stint there. Early in September Gray was sent to Sham Shui Po. The choice was to save Donald's life.

Quite probably it was at this period that he began to devise another, safer cipher for the contents of his diary. All his classes and pastimes showed how desperate he was to keep his mind busy, and everyone understood how dangerous it was to keep any kind of record of events. One officer who took notes on camp life used to bury his journal in the ground. Another used minute scraps of paper which he concealed in his clothes. Donald chose to bury his in the numbers he had loved in childhood. Presumably he first made a rough copy, but it was at about this time too that he acquired a stiff-backed, parchment-coloured notebook. At first all he wrote in it were the rules for German grammar. Any activity helped occupy his mind and dull the growing anxiety at receiving no reply from Pamela. In November, several officers received letters from their families, and more came in December, but not for him.

Disappointment was a corrosive emotion and it was second nature for Donald to conceal it. When he came to write his Christmas letter to Pamela, he tried not to let her guess at the running sores which the loss of freedom caused.

'My darling,' he wrote,

This is the sixth letter I have written to you; and so far I have received none in reply, but I am sure that it is not that you have not written.

As for me, darling, I am fighting fit, basking in the sun all day. Nearly a year as a prisoner of war, and the time just flies. Our lives our [sic] made up with lectures, classes and Bridge, with a spot of gardening to supply the exercise.

I wrote to my Bank some time ago instructing them to send you a hundred pounds. I hope you have received it by now.

I live for the day when I will receive my first letter from you. On that day I shall drink a toast to you in home-made raisin-wine.

All my thoughts are with you, darling. Je vous aime; Always have and always will.

Donald.

It was impossible to tell the truth, not just because the letter would have been censored, but because to acknowledge that his bones pushed through like tent-poles, that his skin itched from scabies and bed-bugs and pellagra, and that time dragged by like a snail, would have been to destroy what kept him going.

Although he could not know it, the letter was to lie for two years in a Japanese censor's office. And so the silence continued and the tension of waiting banked up. It was not something he could afford to acknowledge. Like almost every other prisoner of war, he concentrated on survival, and that meant not thinking of anything more than the detail of each day's activities. German, bridge, gardening, lecture, then German, bridge and gardening again. Early in 1943, that narrow tunnel vision was blown apart by a message from the outside world.

Lindsay Ride, one of the first men to escape from Sham Shui Po, accused the Hong Kong prisoners he left behind of not being sufficiently 'escape-minded'. Australian by birth and adamantly independent in temper, he later wrote of his own break-out that it had been inspired by a classic escape book of the First World War called *The Road to En-Dor* by E. H. Jones, describing his escape from a Turkish prison. One of the book's underlying themes was that simply thinking of escape had a psychological value in transforming a prisoner's outlook on his condition. As in Argyle Street, Jones's fellow inmates had made an effort to occupy themselves in captivity. 'But in spite of the outward cheerfulness,' he wrote, 'the brave attempts at industry, and the gallant struggle against the deterioration that a prison environment brings, an atmosphere of hopelessness pervaded the whole camp. At heart we were all unhappy, for we had created for ourselves an "Inevitable".' In other words, the prisoners had accepted that escape was impossible. From his own experience, Jones believed that whatever punishments were meted out for trying to escape, the gain in pride and self-esteem justified it. 'Prisoners most of us would have remained,' he argued, 'but not beaten captives, the victims of misfortune, but not its slaves.'

The moment he reached freedom, Ride set out to make the same opportunity available to those still in camp. To help them he set up an organization with a deliberately vague title, the British Army Aid Group (BAAG), whose purpose was to make contact with the camps and set up escape routes through occupied China to the independent city of Chungking.

Soon after Dolly Gray arrived in Sham Shui Po in September 1942, the first BAAG message reached that camp. It came through the work parties which were still going out to work on the extension to Kai Tak airport. Chinese labour gangs already on the site soon began talking to Cantonese-speaking prisoners, among whom was an RAF flight sergeant, Ralph Hardy. In October, one of them gave him a cigarette packet, and when he opened it he found two scraps of paper with messages on them. They contained news about the North African campaign, and offered prisoners help with medicine or in organizing escapes. One was signed mysteriously 'Agent 68', but the other purported to come from a familiar figure, Douglas Clague, who had escaped from the camp in April 1942. 'Keep chin up. Help in Waichow' ran the one from Agent 68. The other asked the senior British officer to send information about the camp to Major Clague.

As senior British officer, the message should have been delivered to Major Boon, but his eagerness to collaborate with the Japanese made him untrustworthy. Hardy decided to show the notes to a captain in the Royal Scots, Douglas Ford. In a camp where morale was low, partly because of malnutrition and partly because over 1,800 of the fittest men had been shipped to Japan on board a freighter, the *Lisbon Maru*, everyone who met him recognized the exceptional quality of Ford's solidity and strength of purpose.

There was every chance that the messages were a trick, but Ford decided that the risk was worth taking. He consulted two other officers who shared his outlook, and with their advice formulated a measured reply to be sent to Clague. Because Hardy was in the RAF, Ford judged that his senior officer should also be told what was happening. Thus the newly

Above Bridget Ferguson (née Kirrage) Pamela's sister, taken in 1937 prior to her burns accident.

Left Maggie Rouf's summer collection of 1938 modelled by Pamela Kirrage.

The golden summer of 1939. Donald photographed by Pamela in a village on the South Downs.

Hong Kong's front-line air defence, the obsolete Vildebeeste torpedo-bomber.

Above
The dispirited survivors of the battle for Hong Kong on their way to Sham Shui Po prisoner-of-war camp, 30 December 1941.

Right
A gaunt, withdrawn Donald in April 1945, sketched by a fellow prisoner.

To: Miss P.S.Kirrage,
    Winkfield Place,
      Windsor Forest, Berks.

From: Donald. S.Hill,
     Prisoner of War Camp N,
      HongKong.

Date: 17th. April 1943.

My Darling One,
          Last week a miracle happened, I received a letter from you, dated 11/7/42. My first letter Darling and what a difference it made. I was so excited that I started reading it upside down. To know after all these months that you are safe and well. Darling what more could I ask.
          Ginger and I were delighted to hear that you had met Beryl. We have started to plan the reunion party when this is all over Incidentally it's the first time I knew that you had a passion for red heads darling. He's in great form and has been absolutely grand.
          Nearly four years of separation darling and I love you as much, if not more, than ever. I remember so well how the prospect of three years away from you seemed a lifetime. It has been an eternity Darling. But having stood that test we can be sure of the future. I just live for the day when I shall see you again my darling. I shall probably be struck completely dumb.
          I have just about used up my 200 words. I would need another 200 to tell you how much I love you darling. You are for ever in my thoughts.
          Take great care of yourself my Darling.

                I love you,

                      Always have and always will.

                         DON.

Rules For Correspondence.
1. Use one side of the paper only.
2. Letters must be typed or written in Block Capitals.
3. English language only to be used.
4. Use simple words and phrases.
5. Do not use code or secret marks.
6. News about Military, Political, Commercial and Industrial affairs is not allowed.

Scorched and fragile from much reading, the letter that told Pamela that she was at last in touch with Donald.

Above
Eric Maschwitz,
secret agent,
eternal romantic
and Pamela's
dancing partner.

Below Donald at
ease on the lawn
in 1946. A moment
of peace before
his experiences
in camp returned
to haunt him.

Above 13 January 1946. The end of six and a half years
of waiting.

Top Pamela (second right) and Donald (third left) in 1947 with friends in Tunbridge Wells. His pensive look hides the inner turmoil that overcame him that winter.

Above The growing family: Pamela with (from left) Joanna, Christopher and Carolyn in Kirkuk, Iraq, 1952.

Left The code cracked at last: Philip Aston, the man who provided Pamela with the story that Donald had hidden for 50 years.

香港停虜枚

Letters from prison. Separated by over
forty years, two of the impassioned
messages Donald sent to Pamela.

To: Miss Pamela Kirrage,
    Winkfield Place,
        Windsor Forest, Berks.

From: Donald S Hill,
        Prisoner of War Camp N. HONGKONG.

Date: 12th July 1943.

Darling One,
                    Yesterday I received my second letter from you, written
on the 2nd Oct. 1942, in which you say you had just received my first letter.
My Darling it was like water to a man dying of thirst. Ginger had three from
Beryl written a little later than yours. He was very disappointed as she
had'nt heard from him-officially. So far I have'nt heard from Mother.
                    My own sweet Darling to know that you are well and still
love me after four years of waiting is almost too much to believe. Often at
night I lie awake thinking of you, wondering when I shall see you again. I
know fully all the sacrifices you have made because of me, and I'm overwhelmed
with love for you. Heaven knows it's going to be a crazy world when this war
is over; families broken up and everyone seeking new ideals. But you are all
ideals rolled into one sweetheart, to work and to live for, and to try to make
up to you everything that you have sacrificed for me. I live for two things;
to be free, and to hold you in my arms again. Four years ago today we were
together for the last time. Those few days and nights we spent together have
been with me all these years darling.
                    I'm very fit; have'nt had a days's illness since I left
England. I read a lot and take plenty of exercise. I miss my flying terribly
and, when I'm not thinking of you, my thoughts turn skyward. I'm very proud
of the Service and regret deeply not being an active member of it. How's
Mac? and I often wonder where Ralph is. I dont suppose you have met Douglas.
                    My alloted space is up darling. Your letter has given
me added strength to face things cheerfully. Please give my love to the Family.
                    Here's to our future my darling and until then I shall
just have to dream about you. I love you so much that it hurts.

                    All my love darling one,
                            I love you now and always,

                            DON.

RULES FOR CORRESPONDENCE
 a. Use one side of the paper only.
 b. Use block capitals or type.
 c. Use simple phrases only.
 d. Do not use code or secret marks.
 e. News about Commercial Industrial or Military matters is forbidden.

Pamela Kirrage aged 22, photographed by Angus McBean.
'I don't think I had ever seen a more beautiful girl', Donald Hill recalled.

returned Dolly Gray was recruited to join the tiny core making up the contact group at Sham Shui Po.

Although Ride had set up headquarters in the city of Chungking, over 150 miles away in south China, he had sent a forward group under Clague to operate from Waichow, a scant 40 miles from the camps. As a former prisoner of war himself, Clague might have been expected to sympathize with conditions in the camp, but his response to Ford's cautious message took an abrasive tone. All officers in the camps had to regard themselves as being under orders to make preparations for escape, he wrote on a scrap of silk cloth. 'A much more offensive spirit must be worked up,' he added. 'To hell with this defeatist attitude. There will be risks but I am ordered by the authorities to tell you all, especially officers, that your duty is obvious.'

Much of this was implictly directed at Maltby, who discouraged all attempts at escape, but its hectoring tone took little account of conditions, either in Sham Shui Po or in Argyle Street. The swingeing cut in an already meagre ration following his group's successful break-out had shattered many inmates both physically and psychologically. Less rice, no extra food from beyond the wire, fewer vitamins, all had a direct result in the number of swollen legs, itching scabs, aching guts and sudden explosions of diarrhoea. These physical illnesses produced in their turn a further loss of vitality and confidence. By Ford's estimate, only 20 per cent of the once fit young men 'have the staying power to carry out any real job of work'.

In truth, however, there was no attractive option. An escaper who was caught would certainly be executed, but the alternative was hardly better. Word was seeping into camp of the fate of the men who had been sent to Japan on the *Lisbon Maru*. A total of 1,816 prisoners had been battened down in the hold, and when the ship was torpedoed by an American submarine on 1 October 1942 just 724 survived. Further drafts were due to be sent to Japan, and even if they arrived safely the future of underfed men doing forced labour in steel-mills and coal-mines was not inviting.

In clear, sensible fashion Ford steered a course between the two. No escape was possible while malnutrition was so prevalent, he insisted. Their physical state would quickly improve with more Red Cross food parcels and medicine, and then they would be prepared to co-operate with any plans that BAAG put forward. By chance, a Red Cross food delivery was made that November, and BAAG's Chinese agents found ways of delivering medicine to the camp, including thousands of tablets of nicotinic acid, which was the recommended treatment for pellagra. So rapid was the physical improvement of the prisoners that from the end of 1942 Sham Shui Po's contact group started planning for escape.

It was not until the spring of 1943 that BAAG's agents made contact with Argyle Street. Four times a week a ration truck came into the camp with sacks of rice and vegetables. Agent 68, a resourceful Chinese named Li Fong, bribed the Formosan driver to deliver the message either in a discarded cigarette packet or simply as a crumpled piece of paper pushed into a prisoner's hand.

Since there was always an armed guard on the truck, and guards on duty at the camp entrance a dozen yards away, with sentries patrolling the perimeter fence and others overlooking the scene from watchtowers, this operation was fraught with danger. The first unexpected note was transferred almost in open view, with only the crowd of prisoners milling round as they unloaded the rice serving as a distraction. The immediate priority was to devise a safer method of transmitting future messages.

The note was addressed to Colonel Newnham, Maltby's senior staff officer, since he, unlike the General, was known to be sympathetic to escape attempts. A quiet, narrow-faced man with deep-set eyes, Newnham possessed an intense and private character. Almost too readily he tried to take on his own shoulders the whole responsibility for communicating with

BAAG. Initially he detailed just two officers, John Harris and Godfrey Bird, to pick up messages from the food truck. But this impulse to keep to a minimum the number who knew about the contact soon proved impractical. Camp duties, such as emptying garbage pails, or peeling lily roots, were rotated between the different huts on a daily basis. In the tiny village of Argyle Street, it was quickly noticed that, whichever hut was on duty for unloading food trucks, Harris and Bird were always present. Once suspicions were aroused, they would become the subject of gossip – the latrines were a favourite spot to discuss the camp's events, even though an English-speaking guard was usually lurking near by – and the secret would soon be out. Reluctantly Newnham decided that the contact group needed to be enlarged.

The one essential quality was coolness. It was not easy to know how the message would come, whether handed over directly or stuffed among the vegetables or left on the floor at the back of the truck. Nor could they afford to make a mistake or attract the attention of the guards. Every prisoner had seen and experienced enough of the punches and clubbings that greeted the smallest infraction of the rules to be able to imagine the punishment for communicating with British forces and Chinese guerrillas if they were detected. They could expect no mercy. Godfrey Bird, whose refusal to talk under torture was to earn him the George Medal, observed wryly that just before his arrest he had been reading a book about Torquemada, the legendary examiner of the Spanish Inquisition, and that the Japanese employed every one of the many tortures listed there.

Among those that Newnham approached were Ralph Goodwin, who later broke out of camp and made his way alone to freedom. And from Hut Eight, he asked Donald Hill to help. Quite typically, before letting any of them agree, Newnham went to great lengths to detail the dangers and offer each one the opportunity to think the proposition over and to withdraw if he thought the risk too high. From what is known about the contact group, it seems probable that Newnham was drawn to private, self-reliant people, not unlike himself. If so, his judgment was good, for none of them backed out.

It is doubtful whether Donald seriously considered refusing Newnham's offer. He had shown that in response to danger he became cold and clear-minded. But the continued denial of the things he yearned for most in the world must have made the prospect irresistible whatever the risk. Ride was right in estimating how much the prospect of freedom altered a prisoner's outlook. Being part of a scheme which might lead to escape blew away his narrow focus on the camp's daily rituals. He still played bridge, continued to write out tedious rules for conjugating German irregular verbs, but they were no longer what they appeared to be. Now they became like Russels Mathematical Tables, an appearance of something mundane which disguised the importance of the secret within.

It was harrowing work. Each man was responsible for collecting every scrap of paper from the food truck so that no message would be overlooked, and for delivering it to Bird, who took it on to Newnham. It was also their job to see that the driver's attention was attracted so that outgoing messages could be planted either directly with him or on the truck where he could find it later. Not only were they being watched by the guards on duty around the camp, but they became aware that from elevated points outside the wire there were other watchers studying their movements through binoculars. If Donald ever wondered why he was running the risk, a play which the entire camp attended on 5 March 1943 would have reminded him. Written by one of the prisoners, it was called *The Golden Road*, and played upon their deepest fears. It was set after the end of the war, a time they all looked forward to, and its story of a prisoner of war hurrying home to be reunited with his fiancée was one that most of them imagined nightly. It was the ending that came out wrong. The man discovers that the girl has married someone else. Her explanation that 'two years is a long time' was greeted by the audience with the tense silence of men who recognized in it a horrible truth.

Then amazingly on 10 April the long silence was broken. For the first time in sixteen months a letter arrived from Pamela. In his excitement, he could hardly read it. The words jumped off the page – 'My darling' – 'an eternity' – 'with all my love'. The miracle had happened. He was still loved.

CHAPTER 6

A NIGHTINGALE SANG

'Gardenia perfume lingering on a pillow,
Wild strawberries, only seven francs a kilo,
And still my heart has wings,
These foolish things Remind me of you . . .'

Eric Maschwitz, 'These Foolish Things Remind Me of You'

Writing to him had been an act of faith. Months had passed since the news of the colony's surrender, and Pamela still had no indication whether Donald was alive or dead. Although a Red Cross representative had been allowed into the camp in July 1942, no authoritative list of prisoners had been issued. Yet every week she continued to write into the silence.

The letters had become a kind of confessional in which she told him the things that meant most to her, how much she missed him, how slowly the time passed, and the horrible sense that her life was slipping away. 'An eternity' was how she described the waiting. She had been twenty-three when she last saw him. In war, life speeded up to keep pace with death's acceleration, and in the years since she had said goodbye, her girlfriends had seen their men off to war, and welcomed them back, had fallen in love and out again, had got married and given birth, had boasted of their babies' accomplishments, and some were pregnant again. In February 1943 she would be twenty-seven, but for her nothing had changed. All she had was the certainty that three years earlier she had been touched by a happiness which seemed unmatchable with any other man. So she continued to tell him what she could nor properly tell anyone else, that she loved him as she had loved no one else, but that the waiting was a sacrifice. It was her choice, but a sacrifice all the same.

What made her constancy more astonishing still was that everything else seemed to have been transformed since she had last heard from him. The relentless advance of German and Japanese forces had been halted, and after Allied success at Midway in the Pacific, and then at El Alamein and Stalingrad, the pendulum was swinging back. As eventual victory began to seem possible, the mood of the country altered dramatically from dogged duty to an aggressive optimism. The bombers still passed over Kent, but now more of them were heading in the opposite direction towards Germany. The *Courier* allowed itself a congratulatory leader on what the world owed to its readership: 'Kent, Sussex and Surrey stood between the enemy and his objective. It was a solid bulwark of wonderful endurance, of courage and fortitude, of thrilling deeds, of daring which will never be surpassed.' Even in Tunbridge Wells, where it had always seemed rather implausible that the foreigners might actually win, there was relief that the threat of invasion should have passed into history.

Surveying the town on one of his returns from military service, the historian Richard Cobb noted that the only scars it bore were some bomb damage to a few prosperous houses in Lansdowne Road, but he acknowledged, 'it would have been hard not to have hit a middle-class target in a town such as the Royal Borough'. Fortunately its only industry, a factory which made water-biscuits, had escaped the onslaught.

It was more complicated to reach home from Woburn Abbey than from Windsor, but Pamela continued to make the journey as often as she could. At least the train service had begun to improve in the absence of bombs and aerial gunfire, and she could still stay over the entire weekend. One Monday morning early in July 1942, she was about to step out of the door to get the London train when the phone in the hallway rang.

Automatically she picked it up. 'Tunbridge Wells 744.'

She did not recognize the woman's voice at the other end.

Her name was Beryl Sullivan, and she said her husband was Wing Commander Sullivan. The names meant nothing, but she was saying it as though they should. Then she explained that Ginger Sullivan was Donald's commanding officer, and suddenly Pamela was having to listen very hard to pick out the news that threatened to be swamped by her excitement. Mrs Sullivan had heard from her husband, who was a prisoner of war. It was not clear how she had heard, but somehow her husband had told her that he had a friend with him in the camp called Donald Hill. He had given Miss Kirrage's name as the person to be called with the news that he was safe and well. That was all she could tell her, that Donald was alive and well.

Pamela gabbled her thanks, and hurtled out of the house. She had to race now or she would miss her train, but tears of happiness blinded her so that she could hardly see. As she rushed down the hill, her wedge heels seemed absurdly high. They caught on pavements and bumps in the road, and she kept stumbling into people who were only smudged outlines. To each of them she called out through the blur of weeping the same wonderful words, 'My fiancé's safe – Donald's alive – he's alive.' The train was still at the platform, and jumping aboard she shouted out her good news to everyone in the carriage. Even the normally silent commuters were moved, and out of the teary haze complete strangers came up to her and shook her hand. When she reached Woburn, the polyglot collection of Poles and Czechs who were its inhabitants wept with her, and hugged and kissed her.

The timing of the message might almost have been fated. On 12 July it would be exactly three years since they had parted, and the anniversary had been looming grimly ahead. When she wrote to him, her letter was alight with relief and happiness. The waiting was no easier, but now at least it was for a real Donald rather than his memory. She told him too that she had been to see Beryl, and Ginger's wife had been jolly and optimistic about getting the men home soon. It was cheering talk. She had beautiful red hair, and Pamela said how much she had liked her. But she kept to herself the thought that Beryl did not really need her man as much as she needed Donald.

It was late in September before Donald's first letter finally arrived, and the sadness of it undid her completely. Reading that phrase 'Perhaps by now you have given me up as dead, I don't know' printed in careful schoolboy capitals, she knew that – compared with what he had to endure – her ordeal was nothing. She put the folded sheet of paper back in its envelope. Her clothes were strewn around the room where she had dropped them, but, with great care, as though she were handling the Crown Jewels, she placed the letter in the top drawer of her dressing table. More than a year passed before a second letter joined it.

Then, borrowing a typewriter from the secretarial office, she poured out her heart, telling him how much she loved him, how she thought of him day after day, and how sure she was that one day they would be together again. Sooner or later this war had to stop, and then they could begin to build a new life and a new world. The future is ours, my darling, she wrote, and we shall spend all of it together.

For some reason, but perhaps it was loneliness, she wrote to Brigit early in 1943 asking her to come and join her at Woburn. They had worked together before. In one of their periods of sibling solidarity, she and Brigit had teamed up in the kitchen of Winkfield Place. Officially classified as disabled as a result of her accident, Brigit had only been able to find work too tedious for her keen intelligence. Under Pamela's guidance, she became an efficient cook and a merciless catering manager, but at the next outbreak of sisterly rivalry she had moved off to supervise the canteen of a munitions factory. Even without the clatter of canteen trays in the background, the glamour of Woburn sounded irresistibly attractive. With minimum notice, she abandoned the factory to team up again with her sister.

Neither of them was entirely sure what happened at Woburn Abbey. At first, Pamela did not even know where it was, because she had been taken there in a van with the windows blacked out. 'It was a police Black Maria,' she would tell her friends, 'just as though I were a dangerous criminal.' Security police checked all vehicles coming into or leaving the Abbey, and kept constant surveillance on the grounds. The phones were tapped, and outgoing calls were forbidden. Inside the gates they met and fed representatives of almost all the occupied countries of Europe, as well as a cross-section of professors, psychologists, journalists and broadcasters.

In fact several secret organizations were based there, including Admiralty signals intelligence, whose work by coincidence involved code-breaking, the planning section of the Special Operations Executive, and the Political Warfare Executive. Although still nominally part of SOE, the Political Warfare Executive had acquired a new head in the abrasive Oxford don and soon-to-be Labour MP, Richard Crossman, who was in the process of making it into a virtually independent body. Its remit had several labels which changed in the course of the war – 'political warfare' to describe its aggressive intent, and 'information subversion' to indicate the area in which it worked, but the commonest was 'black propaganda', which conveyed the sense of its illicit purpose. White propaganda set out to sway its audience using straightforward information and argument; the black version was prepared to use deceit, trickery, lies, but rarely, if ever, the unvarnished truth – tactics which seemed more shocking then than now. The PWE broadcast in forty different languages, and published newspapers, leaflets and cartoons, but its radio stations frequently purported to be coming from within the country they were broadcasting to, and even took on the identity and wavelength of official stations. Its newspapers were often forgeries of real ones but containing demoralizing news about diseased troops or debauched Nazi leaders.

One of the PWE's most elegant coups was to point out that the opening four notes of Beethoven's Fifth Symphony – three shorts and a long – were the Morse equivalent of the Allies' 'V for victory' sign. The results were a propagandist's dream. The

BBC began to use the notes to announce news broadcasts to Occupied Europe. Fearing that it might be thought subversive, German concert halls became increasingly reluctant to perform one of the finest symphonies of Germany's finest composer, and in every other part of Europe the Fifth became the unofficial anthem of resistance.

The SOE had ensured certain privileges for its agents – stately homes were requisitioned for training, the finest instructors were recruited and the food was the best that could be obtained – and the PWE inherited their outlook. Outside the gates, the rigours of wartime rationing had made the population familiar with powdered egg, milk powder, whale meat and a butter ration of two ounces a week. At Woburn, the cook had almost unlimited rations available. There was farm produce on the doorstep, as well as the results of bloody encounters between army trucks and the Père David's deer which were bred in the Duke of Bedford's park. Pamela's plain English recipe book began to bristle with beef stews and roast venison and rack of lamb in season, puddings made with fresh eggs, and newly baked cakes.

No matter how secret the place was, this was not the sort of food that could be kept to oneself. To her embarrassment, her mother would ring in on the tapped telephone. 'Darling, we have some people coming to supper,' she said. 'Could you possibly bring down some extra butter with you next weekend?' But however carefully the security police were listening and however much Turnbridge Wells had changed, it always remained home, and she duly smuggled the butter out.

She was not the only inhabitant of Tunbridge Wells to notice the change that war had brought to what had always seemed a changeless place. Richard Cobb was struck by the lowering of the age range as military camps were set up in the area and fit young men began to populate its streets, which had always been the preserve of the middle-aged. But he was less prepared for another, more personal difference, and one for which Pamela was almost entirely responsible. The distant, despairing admiration he had had for her and Brigit in peacetime suddenly became more hopeful once war arrived and he appeared in the classless, patriotic garb of khaki serge.

It was Brigit with her sharp tongue and quick intelligence to whom he now felt most attracted. Meeting her in a tea-room in the fashionable Pantiles, he let drop a hint of his acerbic amusement at the town's more bizarre social conventions, and found an instant response in her ironic commentary on the absurd exclusiveness of its bridge-playing circles and golf clubs. Whenever he had leave, he sought her out, each of them enjoying the other's shrewd humour.

He could not have known that, like her sister, she was nursing an impossible passion, in her case for a fighter pilot killed in the Battle of Britain, but he evidently understood that, where romance was concerned, girls as beautiful as the Kirrages belonged to the aristocracy. Rashly he attempted to pass himself off as one. He could not be a pilot, but he could pretend to be a hero.

One moonlit night, as they walked past the town's memorial to the dead of an earlier war – it portrays in silver granite a particularly heroic infantryman with rifle and bayonet in hand – he let drop his desire to play a more active part in the war than his current job of teaching English to Czech soldiers. She knew that he was clever, that he spoke French fluently, and by the time he had finished she also knew, though this did not have to be spelled out directly, that he was physically brave and wanted to experience some real danger. It was a line that young men were spinning in one form or another to girls up and down the country, and few, if any, expected it to be acted on.

'Richard was brilliant, quite mad of course but brilliant,' Brigit recalled. 'It was such a glorious moonlit night, and he was so insistent, that I said that I would have a word with Eric.'

Eric, it seemed, had something to do with the BBC, which did not seem entirely relevant. Nevertheless, a little later, Cobb received a vaguely official invitation to attend an interview at the Inter-Services Research Bureau in Baker Street in London. To his growing alarm, he discovered that an idle boast had been taken literally and he was being interviewed for his suitability for hazardous service in occupied territory. Colonel Jephson, who interviewed most recruits for the French service of the SOE, had a habit of switching to French halfway through the first session, and the majority of applicants were weeded out there and then. Cobb passed with flying colours, and it was a measure of his passion for Brigit that he did not confess to the misunderstanding immediately. Not until he was well into a follow-up session which involved a slightly fuller job description about the need to learn how to set off explosives and to withstand the rigours of capture and torture, did he admit that he was not really the sort of person they were looking for.

At the end of the war, he attempted to re-establish himself in Brigit's eyes. The army and his languages landed him in Brussels, where, as he observed, one could obtain anything, and he bought her a pair of wildly expensive silk stockings. 'She had not yet been demobilised,' he wrote in his autobiography, 'and was working as manageress of a canteen in Eastbourne. I went over there with the stockings, and we walked up and down the Front for an afternoon.' But it was too late and he had fallen too far. At the end of the afternoon, he was left to find his way back to Tunbridge Wells alone. He took the rejection badly. Almost forty years later, clearly still feeling the sting, he gloated in his autobiography that since their last encounter she had taken to bridge and lost her good looks. (Where the Kirrage girls were concerned, love's pangs and passions never seemed to fade.) But the astonishment at having his bluff called also persisted. 'She must have had influence well beyond the limits of the canteen in Eastbourne,' he commented in undisguised bewilderment.

It was Eric who was responsible. And he was the only man who ever threatened Pamela's commitment to Donald.

It was hardly surprising that an attractive young cook who dressed with a sense of style and had a weakness for emotional drama should make a mark among PWE's susceptible males. She

had always found it easy to make friends, and all that she asked
of her boyfriends was that they should be exceptional and
physically attractive. Now she was in her element. At Woburn,
the men were special almost by definition.

Brigit used to remark sharply of her sister that 'She always
wanted to be the centre of attention,' and there was some truth
in the gibe. She liked men and loved going to the pub outside
Woburn's gates with a group of friends or travelling up to
London at weekends to see a show, or better still to go dancing.
But she was adamant that their feelings should not go beyond
friendship. In old age, Pamela was inclined to think that the
men must have behaved gallantly, recognizing that her heart was
engaged elsewhere. 'I thought about Donald the whole time,'
she remarked. 'I had no idea where he was or what sort of
conditions he was living in. Perhaps I should have forgotten
about him, and got on with my life, but I couldn't. He was the
man I loved, and only him.'

She may have been right about the men she met. The Pole
who was so impressed by the type of Englishwoman staffing
SOE's training establishments described how they cooked or
chauffeured by day, and how in the evening 'in exquisite long
dresses' they partnered the men in waltzes, foxtrots and Polish
obereks and *kujawiaks*. 'Though they were young and attractive,
not to say beautiful,' he concluded, 'we had no heart-pangs over
them.' But not everyone behaved with such well-bred restraint.

By the time Brigit arrived in 1943, the United States was
sending over selected personnel under the aegis of William
Paley, the chief of Columbia Broadcasting Services, to be
trained by the PWE in the arts of black propaganda. Brigit
recalled the excitement of so many unattached, intriguing men,
and the need for sisters to stick together. The British and varied
European males at Woburn tended to accept the boundary that
governed Pamela's friendships, but the Americans, armed with
nylons, lipsticks and higher wages than other servicemen, had
learned never to take no for an answer. To keep them at bay
required fast repartee, faster hands and female solidarity. But

Brigit appreciated how important Donald was to her sister. Together they put up such an effective defence that they became known, not completely unadmiringly, as Kelvinator and Westinghouse, the United States' two leading brands of refrigerator. What was strange, and half a century later Pamela remarked on it herself, was that, with one exception, she did not find any of these men physically attractive. As she put it, 'I remained awfully pure, I wasn't even tempted.'

The exception was Eric, an intelligence officer who was employed as an instructor at Woburn. Had that been all there was to him, she might have remained untempted. But Pamela's description showed that, for the first time, she had met a man who caught her imagination. He was older than she, but tall, handsome, beguiling in his charm, witty, wealthy and hardly less famous than Laurence Olivier. As if that were not enough he had just composed a song so romantic that it was entering the repertoire of every dance-band and singer in the country. In short, to be wooed by Eric Maschwitz, writer of 'A Nightingale Sang in Berkeley Square', was not a disagreeable experience.

There were so many mysteries in Maschwitz's life that even after his death much of it remains blurred, as though the camera had been jogged at the crucial moment. On the surface, he was constantly in the public eye. He was one of the BBC's earliest and most golden recruits, becoming editor in 1927 of the *Radio Times*, then Director of Variety until he resigned in 1937 to write for the theatre. His hit musical *Balalaika* ran for over 500 performances at the West End, and even before 'A Nightingale Sang in Berkeley Square' came out, everyone knew songs of his like 'Good Night Vienna' and 'These Foolish Things Remind Me of You'. His affairs with fashionable actresses were the stuff of gossip columns, as was his short-lived marriage to the theatrical personality, Hermione Gingold. In short, his life seemed to be open for all to see, and to envy.

Behind the eye-catching glitter, there lurked another career as an intelligence officer with considerable power. In 1940, when invasion by the Germans was a possibility, he was one of

MI5's recruiters, selecting what he called 'local citizens likely to prove daring and close as an oyster' to be trained in sabotage should the country be occupied. Then he was recruited by the Intelligence Corps with the rank of lieutenant-colonel, and transferred to the SOE. For them he did a perfect piece of black propaganda, discrediting German organizations in the United States before it entered the war with the help of forged information carefully leaked to newspapers and radio. This success led to a job in 1943 as an instructor at Woburn. It was there that he met Pamela, and through her Brigit, and thus fished the astonished Richard Cobb up for interview as a candidate for SOE's operations. For this sort of work, he always used his showbiz career as cover, justifying his questions and his travels as research for a new show. Nor was it merely pretence. *New Faces*, with its show-stopping song of the nightingale in Berkeley Square, was written during a mail-interception operation, and the American black propaganda coup gave rise to a successful musical play, *Waltz without End*.

The girls at Woburn were taught not to ask questions about people's jobs and so Pamela never really understood what he was doing there. In any case, like everyone else who knew Eric Maschwitz, she found it impossible to believe that there was more to him than the easygoing charm that met the eye. He was simply too nice and too romantic to be engaged in skullduggery. He stood six feet two inches tall, had high cheekbones and dancing black eyes, and from her point of view possessed one particular talent that was irresistible. He danced beautifully.

She had waltzed and tangoed with PWE's operatives before and enjoyed it, but the experience was dimmed to invisibility by the incandescent pleasure of whirling in his arms to the hiss and crackle of records played in the great hall of Woburn Abbey. The Victorians attempted to ban the waltz because when a man held a woman close and swirled her and swayed her to that tripleting, hypnotic rhythm, it enflamed passions beyond the control of even the best intentioned. By the 1940s, those nineteenth-century prohibitions had long since been forgotten, but the premise was not necessarily mistaken.

On the verge of the twenty-first century, the recollection of his dancing still triggered a faraway smile. 'He was the only one I was attracted to physically,' she mused. 'And he thought he was in love with me.'

This was certainly true, for it was his charm and habit always to love whatever woman he was with. Frank Muir, who knew him at the BBC, observed that he was invariably 'festooned with girls' and usually in love with at least three of them at once. Nevertheless, in one entirely serious way, his love for Pamela was unlike any of the others.

When she told Eric about Donald, he reacted quite differently from other men, who regarded the distant presence of an imprisoned lover either as a challenge or as a passion-killer. Eric adored the romance of it. In his eyes, it added to her attraction. Although he had been born in England and educated at public school, his parents were Polish immigrants, and beneath the English self-deprecation and easy humour which he wore as stylishly as his cricket blazer, his temperament was as passionate as any Pole's.

All his songs and musicals were about love, he himself was forever falling in love, but the real thing, the constancy of love, was something that always escaped him. In his autobiography, he offered a stern self-assessment in the third person: 'he thinks too quickly and words come to him too easily . . . his reactions are too quick and too superficial'. Now here was love, a beautiful woman unswervingly and steadfastly yearning for an airman imprisoned on the other side of the world, and he was bowled over. Everything he did showed that he must have wanted the emotion for himself, and everything he did made her feel that he was someone who understood her fully. It was a dangerous combination.

She learned that he liked Carol Gibbons, her favourite band-leader, who played at the Savoy, and the next time they danced it was beneath the chandelier in the Savoy ballroom. She had been taken there before, by her father, but then she had been anonymous. Now she was in the company of the king of romantic lyrics, and when they walked on to the dancefloor the band struck up his hit 'These Foolish Things Remind Me of You'.

> A cigarette that bears a lipstick's traces
> An airline ticket to romantic places
> And still my heart has wings
> These foolish things remind me of you

The next letter to Donald was unusually sunny in tone. She could not help herself. Everything was going so well, she told him: it was undeniable, the war, the work, her whole feeling about the world, but it was impossible to explain why. Censorship rules prevented her mentioning the war or her work, and good sense censored any mention of Eric, so she restricted herslf to writing about the fine weather and their bright future, and even added that she and Brigit were getting along together very well.

At Woburn the sisters had to share a bedroom, and the simmering rivalry which marked their relationship frequently boiled over into argument. Yet, despite the quarrels, the similarities in their demanding and beguiling temperaments went deeper. Pamela might be the more emotional and more intuitive, Brigit the better read and less conventional in outlook, but they were utterly alike in manner, alternately imperious and seductive, slow to tolerate fools, and as quick to freeze with annoyance as to smile when amused.

When Eric was away on clandestine missions, he would let the girls stay in his Mayfair flat. It had white walls, white carpets and white furniture and, slightly to their alarm, black satin sheets on the bed. The sheets looked better than they slept. Staying overnight on their way to Tunbridge Wells, they found them so hot and slithery that they lay awake for hours. Still, as they told each other, it was Mayfair and they were Eric Maschwitz's sheets.

When he returned, he took Pamela to West End shows and to glamorous parties enlivened by Noël Coward's dangerous wit and spring-heeled consonants, and Judy Campbell's spectacular beauty and husky voice. They went dancing, and one night he took her to the Mirabelle nightclub, and there in Berkeley Square, he sang his song just for her:

> That certain night, the night we met,
> There was magic abroad in the air,
> There were angels dining at the Ritz
> And a nightingale sang in Berkeley Square.
>
> I may be right, I may be wrong,
> But I'm perfectly willing to swear
> That when you turned and smiled at me,
> A nightingale sang in Berkeley Square.

She never forgot the moment. It was a warm night and she was wearing a dress made from delicate pre-war silk. To have succumbed in such circumstances might almost have been forgivable. But, had she done so, they would both have lost what they loved most. At the last moment, he drew back and, as she gratefully acknowledged, 'He was decent enough to realize how much I loved Donald, and that I would not want to be unfaithful to him.'

Curiously, once the prospect of his slippery satin sheets faded, a genuinely warm friendship emerged. Each provided the other with the partner they needed: she gave him proof of the reality of romantic love, he gave her glamour and a dancing partner. She took him down to Tunbridge Wells to meet her parents. Her mother was immediately won over, but then she often gave the impression that she was grateful to find any man interested in one of her daughters. When Sheila rang before dawn one morning to say that the farmer she worked for had just asked her to marry him, Marjorie offered her a distinctly backhanded blessing. 'Far be it from me,' she sighed down the phone, 'to interfere in any way in a romance that takes place in a cowshed at six o'clock in the morning.'

Pamela's father, on the other hand, was far more suspicious of a man of such overpowering charm. However, his brusque behaviour and pointed references to the impropriety of his daughter associating with a man twice her age failed in any way to deter Eric. 'Dear Krusty Kirrage,' he purred, 'how deliciously traditional you are.'

Brigit once asked him where the inspiration for the Berkeley Square nightingale had sprung from.

'Oh, I was in love with such a beautiful girl,' he began.

'No, no, Eric,' she interrupted briskly, 'that's what you always say about all your songs. I want a proper answer this time.'

But that was the only one he would give, so perhaps it was true. No such song appears to have come from his time with Pamela, but the example of her constancy clearly had its influence. He decided to marry Phyllis Gordon, who had fallen in love with him before the war and remained faithful to him through all his wartime affairs. The marriage was not a great success. As he acknowledged in his autobiography, 'he has had great happiness from women, and made several good women unhappy'.

When she next wrote to Donald, she dropped in a reference to Eric, but only as the family friend which he had become. It would have been impossible to explain how close she had come to betraying the man she loved.

In any case, very few of her letters got through the maze of different channels that had to be negotiated. The quickest took nine months to reach him, and his almost as long to come back. The appearance in early 1944 of a strange typewritten envelope with the red stamp 'Service des Prisonniers de Guerre' and a little block of Japanese characters was the first indication she had that any of her hundreds of letters had got through at all, but when she opened it the emotion leaped off the page. It was dated 17 April 1943.

'My Darling One,' he had written, 'Last week a miracle happened. I received a letter from you, dated 11/7/42. My first letter Darling and what a difference it made. I was so excited that I started reading it upside down. To know after all these months that you are safe and well. Darling what more could I ask.'

It had taken a year and a half, but finally they were in communication. Each of them knew what the other was feeling. Yet when he should have gone on, he suddenly resorted to banality, as though he had let his guard down.

'Ginger and I were delighted to hear that you had met Beryl. We have started to plan the reunion party when this is all over. Incidentally it's the first time I knew you had a passion for red heads darling. He's in great form and has been absolutely grand.'

From the safety of Britain, she could not guess how ingrained the habit of concealing feelings had become. But it was only a momentary lapse. Again he wrote of what concerned them both:

Nearly four years of separation darling and I love you as much, if not more, than ever. I remember so well how the prospect of three years away from you seemed a lifetime. It has been an eternity Darling. But having stood that test we can be sure of the future. I just live for the day when I shall see you again my darling. I shall probably be struck completely dumb.

I have just about used up my 200 words. I would need another 200 to tell you how much I love you my darling. You are for ever in my thoughts.

Take great care of yourself my Darling.

I love you,

Always have and always will.

Don

She read it through over and over again as though she could

hear his excited voice in the typed words. It moved her more deeply than the most seductive of Eric Maschwitz's enchanting lines. 'Nearly four years of separation', he had written, and now reading the words it was nearly five. The endless waiting only made sense if he felt, as she did, that when the future came they would always be together. And here was the proof: 'having stood that test we can be sure of the future'.

For a few moments, she could almost drink the happiness created by those words. She put the letter with the other two that she had, then took them all out to read again trying to catch more of him. Those three sheets were all she had to stretch across the empty years. They contained barely 600 words, less than one a day in all that time. However hard she tried to squeeze him from each mark on the page, there was less of him than before. Suddenly the happiness went and she began to weep from the emptiness of it.

Throughout the rest of 1944, the PWE's activities accelerated as broadcasts to occupied countries were stepped up and radio stations were established in newly liberated areas. Then Allied armies crossed into Germany and all at once the purpose for which it had been brought into being was more or less achieved. Very quickly its operations were wound down, the staff at Woburn dispersed, and Pamela moved on to cook at a hospital in Nottingham. She did not mind. For her, the smallest cog in the PWE's engine, the advance meant only one thing, the restoration of her whole purpose in life. A mighty gulf existed between love and grand strategy, but the least emotional planner could see that, once Germany fell, the focus would turn on Japan. Then the most important battle of the war, at least as seen from Queen's Road, Tunbridge Wells, would be fought.

As peace in Europe approached, people's thoughts turned from war's grand objectives to the smaller, more insistent goals of peace – education, employment and the welfare stare promised in the 1944 Beveridge Report. Divorce rates soared as men and women who had married in the expectation that life was too short to wait discovered the prospects lengthening and repented. 'Heaven knows it's going to be a crazy world when this war is over,' Donald wrote in a letter which Pamela received in 1945; 'families broken up and everyone seeking new ideals.'

The envelope, forwarded from Winkfield, bore a new address, Epperstone Manor Convalescent Home, near Nottingham. It was there that Pamela moved from Woburn in the last months of the European war. Everything was ending, PWE, the war and eventually their separation. His letter emerged from the prisoner-of-war camp like an archaeological specimen from an earlier age. It was dated 9 June 1943.

My Darling One,
    I wrote to you last month saying I had received my first letter from you. I must have read it well over a hundred times and every time it thrills me. I have your ring, your photograph and your letter as my inspiration darling.

Each of them was engaged in the same frustrating task – trying to absorb a person from a letter. They shared that too. His tone swung from the passionate to the commonplace. 'This kind of life makes one frightfully domesticated,' he wrote in one paragraph. 'I am rapidly becoming a master of the needle and thread as well as being adept at the arts of culinary. I've even learnt how to bake bread. I hope to be a distinct asset around the house darling when we are married.' He made her smile. It was almost like a parody of normal life. 'Time passes fairly quickly. I'm learning German, Japanese and polishing up my French. Ginger and I play bridge most nights and I think I've learnt just about all the card games in existence. We spend many pleasant hours planning our reunion parties when this is all over.'

Then abruptly the tone changed. 'I can endure anything darling with the thought of seeing you again,' he burst out, 'holding you in my arms and being able to tell you all that is in my heart, things that have been stored up all these years.' Those were the phrases that made her loneliness bearable.

Yet the contrast in tone offered a clue that something was wrong. She could hardly have guessed, but the letter had been written at a moment of crisis. The petty rituals of the camp continued, but behind them loomed a monstrous fear. On 9 June, at the very moment he was writing, everyone involved in communicating with BAAG and the Chinese guerrillas had just become aware that the organization had been penetrated by the Japanese police. A few days earlier Agent 68 had sent in a terse signal on the food truck: '71 detained by gendarmerie. Suspend operations.' After that single message there was silence. The terrified Chinese drivers who had acted as their go-betweens would no longer even look at them, far less pass messages. The civilian Japanese gendarmerie was backed by the dreaded Kempeitai, or military police, who had a ferocious reputation for their use of torture. If the agent passed into their hands, it could only be a matter of time before his mind and body and all resistance were destroyed. The trail would lead from him into the camp, and to the contact group. There were a dozen or so prisoners who were part of it, and Donald was one of them.

All Pamela could detect was that he still loved her, and like her yearned for the freedom to be together again. 'And so my Darling our reward is not so very far away,' he ended, 'until then I can take anything that comes along.' He meant more than she could possibly have known.

CHAPTER 7

ENTERING DARKNESS

Who then devised the torment? Love.
Love is the unfamiliar Name
Behind the hands that wove
The intolerable shirt of flame
Which human power cannot remove.

T. S. Eliot, 'Little Gidding'

There had been evil omens. Agent 71's carelessness had seemed to be tempting fate. Then, towards the end of May 1943, the guards became more aggressive. Day after day they would march into huts to conduct searches. With deliberate violence, they turned over the beds that were the prisoners' homes, ripped open carefully sewn-up mattresses, tore apart patched cushions, and broke into neatly made boxes. The destruction caused so much anger that Maltby had to warn the prisoners against the danger of being provoked into retaliation.

When Agent 68 sent his emergency message into both Argyle Street and Sham Shui Po, informing them of 71's arrest and ordering the operation to cease at once, there was a chill realization in both camps that they had allowed themselves to become over-confident. What had started simply as an attempt to help people escape had changed direction to become an intelligence-gathering ring. Its ramifications had spread far beyond the prison wire. Agents had recruited other agents, and not all of them could be relied upon. In Argyle Street, Newnham told his contact group of the message. It was possible, he suggested, that 71 had been arrested at random, and there was no direct connection with what was happening in camp.

There was a strong risk, however, that it was as a result of his work for BAAG. They would just have to wait and see.

That threat was still hanging over Donald when he wrote to Pamela four days later. It was in this letter that he started to count over the incidents of the golden summer in which they first fell in love. There was the dance at Gosport where they met, and he reminded her that he had gone back later to photograph the secluded place behind the officers' mess where they had first kissed. The picture of that sacred spot was one of his talismans. He recalled the accident with the Whitlock, the highballs, the early-morning coffee at a snack bar, the loss of his hat in a tea-room, and their last poignant days together. 'These are just a few of the things about you that I remember so well,' he concluded. 'They are all for ever coming back to me and reminding me that the future holds so much in store for us darling.'

For the few minutes it took to write, he must have been able to hold at bay the unthinkable present, but they were the emotions of a man on the lip of the abyss. When he assured her that 'I can take anything that may come along', the phrase included every apprehension of the brutality that might await him. If the worst happened, the letter would serve as a testament to what had meant most to him in his short life.

In retrospect the conspirators knew they should have taken more precautions, but even with the omens gathering they were more aware of the value of what they were doing. In the course of three months, their fragile contact with the outside world had developed into a successful information-gathering operation, and the groundwork was being laid for a mass break-out from all Hong Kong's prison camps. To have stopped all that simply out of suspicion that they were going too fast would have been to admit another defeat.

The connnection with BAAG had been prickly from the start, with Clague on the outside accusing the inmates of being too supine to escape, and Newnham angrily retorting that 'you are in ignorance of the greatly worsened conditions' imposed as

retribution for his escape. The details of this angry correspondence did not go beyond Bird and Newnham, but the gist of it
seeped out to the contact group. To them, it was plain that the
escape of a single group of prisoners would condemn the rest to
starvation rations again, meaning death for all but the fittest.
Thus the escape of perhaps six men might result in over a
hundred of their companions dying. Under pressure from
BAAG, they agreed to consider a plan for escape, but with the
condition that it comprised everyone in camp.

Whenever there was an air-raid, the Japanese called out all
reinforcements to guard the camp, and Ride proposed that it
would be possible to co-ordinate a bombing raid with an
ambush by a guerrilla army. With the Japanese garrison wiped
out, the occupants of all three military camps – Argyle Street,
Sham Shui Po and Ma Tau Chung, where the Indian troops
were held – and the civilian camp at Stanley would be free, and
could be rescued by a shuttle of aircraft flying into Kai Tak. The
size of the operation would have presented formidable problems
even if all the prisoners had been healthy. One competent
military historian has described the plan flatly as 'suicidal'.
Nevertheless, for some prisoners the risk was worth while.
Ralph Goodwin, who later got away by himself, pointed out
the basic flaw that all it needed was some artillery on the hills or
a naval vessel offshore to prevent a single aircraft landing at Kai
Tak. Yet, compared to the possible gain of releasing several
thousand prisoners, he decided it was a danger worth facing.

Donald too was prepared to take the gamble. In his next
letter to Pamela, written almost as retribution was being dealt
out, he revealed how much he missed flying, and how deeply
he yearned to be with her. There would have been casualties in
a mass escape, but in any military operation casualties were
inevitable, and so long as there was a reasonable chance of
success they were acceptable. He ended the letter, 'I live for
only two things to be free and to hold you in my arms again.'

In the event Newnham took the same decision as Ford in
Sham Shui Po, deferring plans for escape until the prisoners'

health had improved. As at the other camp, BAAG's agent began smuggling in medicines and the vitamins needed to supplement their diet. What was different about Argyle Street was its proximity to the Indian soldiers' prison camp at Ma Tau Chung, and Newnham's realization that they had links with civilians in Hong Kong which could be exploited. He decided that it was worth collating all the information they could gather about Japanese activities so that it could be passed on to Allied forces. In the short term the operation was infinitely more realistic than escape, but in the long run proved no less dangerous.

The information was gathered initially by Indian civilians and soldiers employed by the Japanese on guard duties at docks and depots. Their reports on shipping and troop movements went to Indian officers in Ma Tau Chung before being relayed across the garden separating the two camps to Argyle Street. There the information was written down in an invisible ink made from rice water, and then sent out of the camp by way of the contact group and the food truck. Its eventual destination was British military headquarters in Delhi for distribution to the United States Air Force in China. In an assessment of BAAG's operations towards the end of 1943, American intelligence rated as 'excellent' its information on shipping and transport movements. The report did not reveal, and the unwitting prisoners would never know, that American intelligence also believed BAAG to be a political nuisance which aimed to serve British colonial interests at the expense of their client, Chiang Kai-shek. That judgment meant that no American planes would be available for BAAG's escape plan, and without their resources the project could never take place.

Nevertheless, for over three months after the first prickly exchange with BAAG, medicine and news were smuggled into Argyle Street and information flowed out. The contact group found that the medicines were too bulky to be transferred by hand or left in the rubbish at the bottom of the food truck. Instead they devised a scheme to attach them to the underside of the truck's chassis with rubber bands which could be quickly twisted off. Donald and the other members of the contact group practised feeling blindly under the floor of the truck, until they could find and remove the message or package and slip it into a pocket in seconds. The timing had to be perfect, and the operator's nerves cool enough to do the job without attracting attention even from the rest of the hut party milling round the truck or onlookers watching the food being taken out. Their nerves would often be stretched more tightly because the agents outside had been too ambitious about the size of object which could be fitted into the space. Donald or whichever operator was on duty would find himself desperately attempting to tug free a package jammed into a corner of the chassis, and hoping that his efforts would not arouse the onlookers' attention or be spotted by a suspicious guard through the scrum of prisoners.

The improvement in the prisoners' health and morale must have been very noticeable, although the guards did not usually pay much attention to such matters. By June, BAAG had recruited a network of civilian informants outside the camps from among sympathetic Chinese, Indians and Portuguese, and in the Indian camp the exceptionally courageous Captain Mateen Ahmed Ansari had begun supplying information directly to BAAG. The very success of the operation had bred a dangerous over-confidence, and the sheer number of agents increased the chance that one would fall into Japanese hands. When news about the arrest of agent 71 came in, the danger was suddenly obvious, but by then it was too late.

At first nothing happened. The morning parade took place with no one called out. At eleven o'clock the ration truck came in, with the drivers staring rigidly ahead, obviously frightened. Yet no arrests were made. As the days passed, the strain on Newnham was plain to those around him. Even among the skeletal features of the prisoners, his face appeared gaunt, the dark eyes sunk deep in their sockets. When Michael Wright walked unexpectedly into his hut one day, his outburst of anger was that of a man living on his nerves. The continuing appearance of normality forced them towards the same secret calculation: somewhere outside the camp, the Kempeitai had found out what they needed to know. Either the danger was receding or it was about to burst upon them.

For Donald, like the others involved, it was a peculiarly solitary ordeal. Officially his work had to be kept secret so that if he were arrested no one else would be involved. He could say nothing even to Ginger Sullivan, who must have known what he had been doing. Even with other members of the group, contact had to be kept to the minimum in case the now ever present guards were watching. He had never known Bird and Harris, the original pair, especially well, but there were two members of the Hong Kong Volunteers whom he liked, a young naval officer whose name, Haddock, gave rise to bad jokes and worse nicknames (of which 'Kipper' was the kindest), and a middle-aged schoolmaster in his forties called Gordon Ferguson, known as Fergie, who had been commissioned into the artillery, and liked to boast that he was the oldest lieutenant in the British army. Yet it was no more possible to discuss with them than with strangers the one topic of overwhelming concern, what would happen next?

Almost three weeks after Agent 68's warning, Newnham decided to break the silence. The resourceful Goodwin devised a hollow bolt which could be substituted for the real one in the truck's chassis, and a message was rolled up in it and sent out. There was no reply.

Then on the morning of 1 July the ration truck appeared unexpectedly. The moment its two guards got out, the driver stretched his hand through the open window waving a piece of paper. The duty operator for the day was not in sight, but by chance Haddock was near by and took the paper. Immediately he felt that it was a set-up and, instead of taking it to Bird, left the scrap of paper in a lavatory. The safety measure was useless. Guards arrested him as he returned to his hut, and took him away. On the same day in Sham Shui Po, the two airmen, Dolly Gray and Ralph Hardy, together with Sergeant Routledge, a

Canadian member of the contact group, were arrested. A week earlier Captain Ansari had been taken from Ma Tau Chung camp, and from Stanley civilian camp and elsewhere in Hong Kong, over forty others – Indian, Chinese and European – were detained. Finally on 10 July Newnham and Ford were taken away.

In camp the anxiety was palpable. Outside the circle of the contact group, prisoners suddenly realized that a conspiracy had been going on of which most were utterly unaware. Any who had not heard of the arrests learned through the aggravation of the guards. As before, rations were cut and food supplies which had become almost dependable arrived irregularly or often not at all. New rules were introduced which became apparent only when a nearby guard abruptly halted a prisoner, and punched him in the face or slammed a rifle butt into his unprotected ribs or kidneys. It might be because he was walking too close to the wire or because he was smoking where he should not be, but mostly because the evidence of communication with people beyond the wire reflected badly on the guards and they were taking out their irritation on the prisoners.

'One thing all we prisoners have learned during our captivity,' Goodwin wrote in his diary during that period, 'and that is how to hate.'

The intelligence-gathering remained a secret, but news of the escape plans leaked out, and prisoners like Cecil Templer directed their fury less at the guards than at BAAG. 'The British Mission at Chung King hatched up a *crazy* plot for a mass escape from our camps under cover of a bombing raid,' he commented in a note added later to his journal.

The arrest of Newnham and Haddock brought the threat of the Kempeitai very close, but in Donald the reality of danger induced a clarity of mind which was a long way from the venom that Goodwin expressed or the confused anger and apprehension in the camp. Since there was nothing he could do to change the situation, he had to handle it as competently as possible. He had to assume that under torture Newnham would reveal the full extent of what they had been doing in camp. Once the Kempeitai had the names of the contact group, he would be taken in for questioning. What was important then was to separate the safe knowledge from the dangerous. He could say what he knew about the passing of messages, since the Japanese would know about it anyway. But what the messages contained, who else was involved, all that had to be pushed to some deep irretrievable pocket of his mind.

In the midst of this, on 11 July, Donald received another letter from Pamela, and for a brief moment it swept all other considerations aside. 'My Darling it was like water to a man dying of thirst,' he exclaimed. What made it especially welcome was that it came as a reply to the very first letter he had written to her thirteen months earlier. In it she told him of her delight at hearing from him at last, but also of the slowness of the long empty years without him. What sort of world would it be, she asked, when they were finally reunited? He had been about to write to her in any case, because 12 July would be the fourth anniversary of their parting. Now the dislocation between his present danger and the spontaneous joy of hearing from her produced some strange leaps in his reply.

My own sweet Darling to know that you are well and still love me after four years of waiting is almost too much to believe. Often at night I lie awake thinking of you, wondering when I shall see you again. I know fully all the sacrifices you have made because of me, and I'm overwhelmed with love for you. Heaven knows it's going to be a crazy world when this war is over; families broken up and everyone seeking new ideals. But you are all my ideals rolled into one sweetheart, to work and to live for, and to try to make up to you everything that you have sacrificed for me. I live for two things; to be free, and to hold you in my arms again. Four years ago today we were together for the last time. Those few days and nights we spent together have been with me all these years darling.

As with her first letter, his deepest feelings came to the surface in response, but at such a moment they were a weakness. Thoughts of Pamela and of freedom could only be a distraction from the threat he might shortly have to face. Abruptly he turned to the safety of concealment.

'I'm very fit,' he said with unconvincing briskness; 'haven't had a days's [*sic*] illness since I left England.' He was reading a lot, he added, and took plenty of exercise. But there was one other distraction that caught at his mind. 'I miss my flying terribly,' he confessed, 'and when I'm not thinking of you, my thoughts turn skywards. I'm very proud of the Service and regret deeply not being an active member of it.' Then once more he drew down the blind: 'My allotted space is up darling. Your letter has given me added strength to face things cheerfully. Please give my love to the Family.'

The cloud hanging over him lent poignancy to his farewell.

Here's to our future my darling and until then I shall just have to dream about you. I love you so much that it hurts.

All my love my darling one.

I love you now and always,

DON

Although she knew nothing of the particular circumstances in which it was written, Pamela herself recognized that it was a letter designed to keep her from worrying. But the quandary Donald faced went beyond the usual prisoner's problem of finding something to say without mentioning the terrible reality in which he lived. To withstand whatever lay ahead, his mind needed to be utterly clear, and the delight and optimism and dreams which Pamela's letter aroused diverted his attention. They were as dangerous as his knowledge of the messages. Everything about life in camp drove a man to conceal his vulnerability, but at this moment survival must have seemed to depend upon it.

It was probably during these tense, empty days that the final transformation of his coded diary took place. The searches were growing more frequent, and the diary might be used against him. In its rough form it would have appeared as blocks of numbers, but any guard who saw it would want to know what they signified. Donald might have destroyed it, but that would have given a victory to his captors. Instead he chose to hide it in a guise which appeared utterly innocent. Like every schoolchild in the days before computers, he was familiar with the long columns of figures which appeared in multiplication and logarithm tables. So many educational classes were taking place in camp that one more mathematical aid would not seem out of place.

On the back cover of the parchment-coloured notebook used for his German lessons, he wrote out the words 'Russels Mathematical Tables'. Then, on the inside back page, he ruled a grid of tiny boxes, but, before he entered the numbers in this new form, he added one final twist to his code. Using a secret keyword, he jumbled up the order in which they appeared. It was an intricate, time-consuming process to translate the order in which the numbers were to be read and then to enter them on the page. But that must have been a great part of its attraction. While his attention was focused on the code, he had no opportunity to brood on what might be coming.

The blow never fell.

With a degree of courage which defies imagination, Newnham and his fellow principals from Sham Shui Po, Ford and Gray, resisted every attempt to break them. For seven weeks they were kept in solitary confinement without bed or blankets. They were taken out only for interrogation, and the sound of their screams and the blows as they were beaten with leather whips and clubbed with bats penetrated through to the cells where the others were kept. Their wrists were lashed behind their back, and, with the other end of the rope looped round a beam, they were hoisted off the floor. Bird, who later fell into the hands of the same torturers and survived, told of the horror of the water torture. Strapped in a coffin so that he could not move, he saw a silk cloth draped over his face, then felt the coffin slid beneath a dripping tap. As the cloth became saturated, the air was gradually blocked off so that he had to draw in larger breaths. The tap was turned on harder, and each breath sucked in water which filled his mouth and nostrils. With the next gasp his lungs were flooded. Choking and struggling for air, he pulled in more water so that he was suffocating and drowning with each breath. His body convulsed uncontrollably inside his bonds until he fell unconscious or the cloth was removed. If he did not speak, the procedure was repeated.

Captain Ansari, arrested at the same time, endured similar treatment. Forty-eight civilians had also been seized. Several died in the course of their torture and, of the remainder, thirty-three were sentenced to death at a brief trial. Ansari was beheaded on 20 October, and the others were executed in the same way nine days later. Newnham, Ford and Gray, together with their subordinates, Haddock, Hardy and Routledge, appeared before a military court on 1 December. Despite beatings and torture which had crippled them so severely that only Ford could walk unaided, the three senior officers refused to admit anything other than that they alone bore responsibility for what had happened. The others, they insisted, were acting under orders. Not one of the six gave the name of any other member of the contact group at either camp. As Goodwin commented in his account of what happened, *Passport to Eternity*, 'Theirs was an almost incredible feat of fortitude.'

The three senior officers were sentenced to death, while their subordinates received prison sentences of fifteen years. In the midst of the brutality occurred a moment of almost unbearable pathos. Overcome by pity for the prisoners, the Japanese soldier in charge of the escort party taking them back to their cells burst into tears. To comfort him Newnham mumbled through swollen lips, 'Cheer up, we aren't dead yet.' On 19 December, he and Ford and Gray were taken down to the beach and shot.

Their fate was not known until after the war, although it was assumed in camp that the worst had happened. But prison life dislocated feelings from experience. Beatings happened to other people, or, if they happened to you, they were endured until they were in the past and could be moved away from. The problem was to survive mentally and physically, and that daily struggle kept attention concentrated on the immediate present. In August every officer over the rank of lieutenant-colonel was transferred from camp to Taiwan, and some weeks later a series of spectacular air-raids culminating in the destruction of the oil tanks in a blaze lasting for three days and nights began to build hopes that victory might be in sight. For most prisoners, memory of the break-up of BAAG's information-gathering system soon passed out of mind.

Even members of the contact group moved on to other concerns. Bird tried to re-establish contact with Agent 68, but was soon arrested. Attempting to find another way of getting news into the camp, a new group was set up and successfully operated a clandestine radio for months until its hiding-place in a flowerbed was discovered. Donald continued to write to Pamela telling her of his love, and of the small distractions that hid the reality of camp life. But the lure of escape had gone.

Given the inmates' enfeebled physical state and the Americans' hostility to BAAG, the mass break-out envisaged by Ride was never feasible, but Donald had believed the risk worthwhile and had been ready to support it. Years later, in July 1976, when he heard of the Israelis' airborne raid to free hostages held captive in Entebbe, he took an almost personal pride in their success, as though they had achieved what he had set out to do himself. Without that lure he relapsed into the easier, narrower pastimes of prison life.

From his early days of mending clogs in Sham Shui Po, he had become a self-taught cobbler, and like several others occupied much of his morning making and heeling prisoners' clogs, when his hut was not on garden duty. During the afternoon, he ploughed through the camp's supply of books, or took part in marathon card games, a bridge competition that lasted for months, a picquet challenge over 150 games, and a rolling poker game involving Ginger and his friend from the contact group, Fergie Ferguson, which continued into the spring of 1944. The scores and amounts of money owed were meticulously entered in the journal. Next to them was a list of the 285 books which he had read together with his judgments on each. His favourites were romantic sagas like Hugh Walpole's *Rogue Herries* chronicles and John Galsworthy's *Forsyte Saga*, and it is easy to understand why such tales of family rivalries and triumphant love in a green and distant land each received five stars of approval.

In May 1944 the Argyle Street camp was moved back to Sham Shui Po, where numbers had been hugely reduced by drafts of men to Japan. A few weeks later, Ralph Goodwin, taking advantage of a torrential downpour, climbed over the electrified fence topped with barbed wire and made the most audacious escape achieved from Hong Kong. He had deliberately chosen to go by himself so that no one would be punished by association with him, but the response was serious enough. The prisoners were paraded and told that in future each hut would be held responsible for ensuring that its inhabitants did not break out. If one person escaped all the others would be executed. At the same time their rations were severely reduced. This might have been intended as punishment, but it was also true that Allied attacks on Japanese shipping were beginning to have their effect. Japanese soldiers also had their food supplies cut. The effect on the prisoners, always hovering near the brink of starvation, was far more dramatic.

Until then Donald had survived better than at any period of his imprisonment. A breakfast of boiled rice supplemented by some bran and beans would be followed at midday by a soup of rice and boiled vegetables with a pinch of salt fish and soya sauce. An evening meal consisting of a pint of boiled rice with two or three shallots from the garden completed the basic nutrition. But approximately twice a year Red Cross deliveries of bully beef, peanut oil and milk powder provided essential protein and fats. BAAG had also sent in vitamin tablets. The last food parcel arrived in November 1943, but it had been severely depleted by the prison guards, and there were no more illicit supplies of vitamins. When the supplements of fish and soya sauce were cut, it quickly pushed Donald over the edge. And this time Florrie was not there to save him. Almost certainly she herself died that year, probably as a result of the hardships she had suffered under the Japanese occupation.

By the summer of 1944, Donald was suffering from pellagra as a result of vitamin deficiency. It not only produced its most characteristic symptom, a rough, intolerably itchy kind of eczema, but most disturbingly a deterioration in his vision, which became so dim and blurred that he could no longer read or play cards. His friends tried to help by scrounging fresh food or vitamin supplements through the guards, but there was too little to make any real difference. At this literally darkest moment, he always remembered with gratitude Fergie Ferguson offering to read to him. Ginger Sullivan had no taste for books, but the middle-aged schoolteacher was happy to sit by him in the camp hospital working his way through Arnold Bennett and J. B. Priestley.

The prisoners' state had grown so desperate by August that, when the Red Cross representative made his hurried round of the camp, one prisoner, Captain Barnett, ran up to him crying, 'We are dying of hunger.' The beating he received for this infraction of the rules put him in hospital for weeks, but the protest evidently had some effect on the guards, because some days later they distributed 200 gamebirds apparently discovered in a cold store. Later in the year a few bulk supplies of corned beef and dried milk eked out over the months helped provide their basic nutritional needs. Gradually Donald's eyesight recovered, and by the end of 1944 he had returned to the life of the camp.

What he focused on now was surviving. He had boasted of his good health in his letters, and if that had been partly to spare Pamela, it was at least true that he had never been in hospital. This time he had suffered severely, and was slow to recover. And accustomed as he was to being a dependable rock for others, he must have been shaken by the helplessness of being blind. Physical weakness and the real fear that he might not see again narrowed his ambition down to making it through to the end. And the news that filtered into camp through whispers from sympathetic Chinese made the end increasingly certain.

The Allies were advancing through France, the Americans island-hopping across the Pacific, and even in Burma the Japanese invasion was at last being turned back. Everywhere the tide was flowing one way. Through the spring and summer of 1945, once dominating landmarks crumbled and were submerged by the flood – Mussolini was executed, Hitler killed himself, and Germany surrendered. Even the pro-Japanese newspapers which were sometimes allowed into camp could not conceal such events from their readers. The news that Russia had entered the war against Japan made the outcome certain, but the inmates knew only too well how their enemy regarded the ignominy of surrender, and rumours began to circulate that there would be a holocaust of the prisoners before that point was reached.

It was not until 12 August that the first rumour of a Japanese surrender came through the wire. Through alternating delight and gloom they tried to read the truth of it in the behaviour of the guards, but nothing changed until the evening of the 15th when Lieutenant Wada, the camp commandant, placed a large wireless on a table ceremonially covered with a white cloth. The guards came down from their watchtowers and filed in from the gate to line up in front of the table. A strange thin voice emerged from the loudspeaker, and they all bowed. To the watching prisoners, it was utterly incomprehensible, then someone guessed and the word raced round the camp: Emperor Hirohito had announced his country's surrender. The war was over.

The next morning no change was apparent, and two officers received the customary full-armed slap in the face for not saluting their guards. That, however, was the last of the humiliation. On the same afternoon, a week after the second atom bomb had dropped on Nagasaki, the camp commandant acknowledged that the Emperor had 'granted peace to the world'. On 17 August a service of thanksgiving was held, and for the first time since Christmas 1941 the national anthem was sung. 'It was the most impressive ceremony I have ever attended,' Captain White, a Canadian prisoner, wrote in his journal. 'Hell of a feeling in one's chest, we kind of choked up. Hearts were too full for much singing, many tears in evidence, I couldn't keep them back. We all realized more than ever before the meaning of Freedom. Some wives with their children arrived from Stanley to meet their husbands. It was so moving I couldn't watch.'

Yet, for another agonizing ten days, the prisoners had to remain in camp. The delay was partly for their own safety – Hong Kong was full of Japanese troops and armed Chinese guerrillas eager for battle – but mostly because no one knew whether the colony would return to the British or be handed over by the Americans to Chiang Kai-shek and the Nationalist Chinese. Behind the scenes, American, British and Chinese politicians negotiated for advantage while the prisoners fumed. 'Complete amazement and fury among all here,' Templer wrote, 'why no British troops have come or even dropped messages let alone supplies on us – quite incredible.'

It was Franklin Gimson, the pre-war Colonial Secretary who in 1941 had called Donald to warn him that war was coming, who broke the deadlock. Although interned in Stanley civilian camp, he arbitrarily set up a provisional government re-establishing British rule on 20 August, and thus cut short the international card-shuffling. Recognizing the changed situation, the Americans released the nearest British naval squadron, and on 29 August it sailed into the colony's harbour formally re-establishing British control.

One day later, Royal Marine commandos hoisted the Union Jack over the regained airfield of Kai Tak. There were hardly any RAF representatives available, but to their credit the Royal Navy had ferried over to the airfield two cadaverous figures.

They walked on stick-like legs, their eyes were dull and sunken and their skull-like heads seemed too large for their narrow bony shoulders. They wore their own RAF caps, but their borrowed shirts and shorts had been made for better-filled bodies than theirs. They were there because they symbolized continuity with what had gone before. Now the British were back, and what had happened in between would be wiped away. Normal service was being restored. The flag rose, the band played and Flight Lieutenant Donald Hill and Pilot Officer Frank Hennessy saluted. Perhaps just for that moment it was possible to imagine that the events between 8 December 1941 and 30 August 1945 could indeed be erased.

CHAPTER 8

TOGETHER AT LAST

Every farthing of the cost,
All the dreaded cards foretell,
Shall be paid, but from this night
Not a whisper, not a thought,
Not a kiss nor look be lost.

W. H. Auden, 'Lay your Sleeping Head'

Infuriating though the last days of prison were for inmates, for at least one outsider the added delay was almost unendurable. After the news of Japan's surrender, Pamela expected to hear from Donald at any moment. Even if she had known how to reach him, communication from Britain to Hong Kong was almost impossible for a civilian. Most telephones were out of order, most cable offices closed, and military and government calls had top priority on the few long-distance lines still working. She would have to wait for Donald to call her. With an intensity of longing that recalled the long silence after she first met him, she waited by the telephone in her parents' house willing it to ring. Only after 2.00 p.m., when it was 10.00 p.m. in Hong Kong would she give up hope for the day, and allow herself to go out.

It was not until the day he shuffled out of the gates of the Sham Shui Po camp to attend the flag-raising ceremony in Kai Tak that Donald was able to arrange a long-distance call to the United Kingdom. The ceremony almost overtaxed his feeble strength, but he was determined to tell her he had survived. Using a line from the airport, he booked his call to Tunbridge Wells 744 through the operator and waited to be connected. The phone had barely rung twice before Pamela snatched it off the receiver. Hearing the slow, hoarse voice on the other end, she could not recognize it for a few seconds. Then she knew who it was, and the sense of relief was so overwhelming she could hardly answer.

'I can't believe it's you,' she said at last. 'When will I see you?'

There was a little pause. 'I don't think you'd want to see me as I am,' he answered carefully. 'But we'll get married the moment I get back. It's been long enough.'

Many years later, after his death, she did see him as he had been then. A television documentary about the victims of Japanese prisoner-of-war camps showed some film taken of the Hong Kong survivors as they left the camp. Among the emaciated men, Pamela immediately spotted the tall figure of Donald Hill. Far from being 'fighting fit' or 'very fit' or any of the other comforting labels he had used in his letters, the reality was that he had been reduced to a skeleton whose sharp bones were almost pushing through his skin. His head, thrust forward, seemed too big for the emaciated torso beneath, and the hollow-cheeked face was drawn and wide-eyed with the experience he had been through.

As a result of their treatment, barely 60 per cent of the prisoners taken by the Japanese survived the war. The majority of these were shipped first to the Philippines and then on through the United States and Canada to Britain, but those who had suffered most severely were sent to recuperate in Australia and New Zealand. Donald was among them. It meant that he and Pamela were to be parted for another six months until he had recovered physically. 'It was terrible news. We had been apart for over six years, and now this,' Pamela exclaimed, as though the memory still hurt. 'But there was nothing to be done about it. However desperately I wanted him back, he needed treatment for what had been done to him. But I could have wept when he told me.'

Apart from one raid on Darwin, Australia and New Zealand had escaped being bombed, and their farms had developed into a cornucopia of food production providing for consumption at home and for much of the war-ravaged northern hemisphere. Physically, what the former prisoners needed was a good diet, and in convalescent homes near Sydney and Christchurch they quickly put on weight. In appearance at least, Donald had returned to a semblance of the man he had been before Christmas 1941. But prolonged malnutrition produced other effects than thinness.

By a painful irony, during the last months of the war while the inmates of prisoner-of-war camps in Japan and Germany were experiencing unavoidable hunger, thirty-two well-fed volunteers at the University of Minnesota became guineapigs in an experiment to discover what these effects might be. For six months they were fed just 1,570 calories a day, exactly half of their normal daily requirements, while a battery of medical and psychological tests monitored their response. All necessary vitamins and mineral-trace elements were provided, and it was only in its lack of calories that the diet was comparable with what Donald and his fellow prisoners had to eat. Equally important, they had space, clean clothes and washing facilities. Even so, the consequences were marked.

'How does it feel to starve?' one of the volunteers wrote afterwards.

It is something like this. I'm hungry, always hungry – not like the hunger that comes when you miss lunch, but a continual cry from the body for food. At times I can almost forget about it but there is nothing that can hold my interest for long . . . I'm cold. In July I walk downtown on a sunny day with a shirt and sweater on to keep me warm. At night my well-fed room mate who is not in the experiment sleeps on top of his sheets but I crawl under two blankets wondering why [he] isn't freezing to death . . . I'm weak. I can walk miles at my own pace in order to satisfy laboratory requirements but often I trip on cracks in the sidewalk. To open a heavy door it is necessary to brace myself and push or pull with all my might . . . Social graces, interests, spontaneous activity and responsibility take second place to concerns of food. I lick my plate unashamedly at each meal even when guests are present.

He went to see films, but was interested only 'in scenes where people are eating. I couldn't laugh at the funniest picture in the world, and love scenes are completely dull.' He could talk and think normally, but had no wish to do so. 'My talk is of food and past memories, or future ambitions mostly in the cooking or eating line.'

That an intelligent, independent-minded student living in a stimulating environment with every comfort available except sufficient food could so quickly be reduced to that ineffectual state gives a useful yardstick to measure Donald's achievements in camp, the long list of books, the painstaking attempt to teach himself German, and the prolonged concentration required to encode his diary. Evidently he possessed enormous self-discipline, well beyond the norm, if he was capable of pushing his energy-depleted mind into completing such mentally demanding projects.

But the chief interest of the Minnesota experiment lay less in the actual period of starvation than in the after-effects. Three months after returning to a normal diet the gauntness had disappeared and their weight was climbing to its original level, although muscle tone remained flabby. They still felt hungry even after a huge meal, and were subject to food bingeing, consuming over 6,000 calories in some cases. 'The men continued to want more than they received,' the report ran, with just an undercurrent of alarm; 'their appetites were insatiable. The men continued to be concerned with food and their rations above all else.' Nevertheless, in physical terms most subjects had returned to something close to normality six months after the experiment ended. Psychologically, however, they were still affected by the experience. They were prone to depression. They found it difficult to concentrate. They were moody and listless and irritable. One monitor concluded from their behaviour that they showed all the symptoms of having suffered 'an experimental neurosis'.

Given the brevity of the experiment and the cosseting that the Minnesota volunteers received, it suggests the extent of the invisible damage that the Hong Kong prisoners took home with them after what Donald scornfully called 'our so-called recuperation'. Perhaps he could have stayed longer in New Zealand and recovered further, but he had told Pamela that he lived for just two things, and, so long as he remained in a Christchurch nursing home, the purpose of surviving prison was only half achieved. The effort he made to get home demonstrated how determined he was to get there. In December he seized the chance of a seat in a cargo-carrying Dakota that ultimately took him to Sydney. After waiting a week, he hitched a lift in an American troop-carrying plane to Colombo in Ceylon. Several abortive efforts at onward flights left him stranded over Christmas near Allahabad. Eventually he picked up a flight in the tail-gunner's seat of a Lancaster bomber which carried him as far as Aden, where he caught a civilian flight on to Britain. He arrived there on 7 January 1946. It had taken him almost six weeks and over 120 hours of flying.

The details of every flight, its duration, the points of departure and arrival, and aircraft type were entered meticulously into a fresh page of his pilot's logbook. The last entry had been made on 8 December 1941. 'War with Japan. Aircraft destroyed by enemy fighters.' On this new page, all the running totals were carried forward. He remained a pilot with 884 hours' flying time, and the expectation of adding to them.

When the war in Europe ended, Pamela continued to work for the Red Cross, until she fell ill with appendicitis and was sent home to recover. Even if Donald had not minded, she could not have returned to modelling. She was approaching her thirties now, too old for that sort of work. It was not just the passage of years; the experience of war had changed her too. At Woburn there had been an intensity of emotion which suited her. The pre-war attentions of lounge lizards and eager curates might have been welcome enough to a teenager, but they could not compare to those from a young man about to risk his life to blow up a bridge or join a guerrilla gang, still less to those from a sophisticated, successful song-writer. But while others grew so addicted to the storms of passion and intrigue in the SOE that they found it difficult to adapt to the mild weather of peace, she had sailed through dreaming of the day when hostilities would cease and she could be reunited with Donald.

On the threshold of her thirties, there was an extraordinary certainty about her. It was a matter of being with one man. And he was coming home. That was all that counted. Looking back from the wrong end of the century, she acknowledged that her outlook might no longer appear so obvious.

'I know today it must seem so silly being in love like that,' she said as she tried to push his letters back into a large brown envelope. 'People have lovers all over the place. People find it so easy to fall in love. But that wasn't how I felt.' She had her head down so that her face could not be seen. 'There was just this one person. He was the only one who made me feel complete.' The letters refused to go back in. She put them down on the table. 'I don't know why I was so sure. Seven years is such a long time to wait, and when you love someone, being apart is such a *waste* of time. Time you could have spent together.'

There was a brief silence while she gathered herself. Then she took up the letters again. This time they slid neatly into the envelope. She laid her thin hand on it gently. 'At least we knew that we both felt the same way about each other. But it was still a long, long time.' Her sigh was barely audible.

On 8 January 1946 she received the telephone call which brought the waiting to an end. After the first delighted greeting, it was an awkward conversation. Caught by the sense of being lovers yet strangers, they stiltedly made arrangements over the telephone for their meeting the next day. He was staying in his mother's flat in Swiss Cottage in north London. It was more convenient because he had to report to RAF Hendon, which was not far away. Could they meet at the flat? They could. The address was 36 College Crescent. And would tomorrow evening be convenient? In that case she was to ring the bell in the hall, and he would come down. It was the top flat. He had to come down three flights of stairs, so she was not to go away before he arrived.

He spoke with the careful precision of an invalid.

When she put down the phone, she realized she had nothing to wear. Her pre-war clothes were out of date, and her post-war clothes were made of ugly, coarse utility material he would hate to see her in. She had been waiting almost seven years for this moment and when it came she had nothing to wear for it. Frantically she burrowed through her cupboards and found some pre-war material in navy blue and raced round with it to her dressmaker. An artist to her fingertips, the dressmaker understood the supreme urgency of the situation and dropped all other work. For the best part of twenty-four hours she cut and sewed and tacked and hemmed. The next evening when Pamela stood in the hallway of the block of flats where he was staying, she was wearing an exquisite navy suit with a flared skirt, and a great big navy hat. She thought that she must at least look better than she felt.

A fearful happiness gripped her so tightly she could hardly breathe deeply enough to feed air to her pounding heart. She pressed the top bell, and moments later heard his footsteps running down the stairs, leather on stone, round and round the stairwell. She was struck by sudden panic. What will he be like? she wondered. Will I even recognize him? Then suddenly her fiancé was before her at the foot of the stairs. He was Donald and not Donald. Older, strained and tense, but otherwise the man she had loved for all those empty years. She tried to speak but could only cling to him, too overcome to do anything but weep. She had waited for 2,435 days to hold him again.

Of all that they talked about, she recalled nothing except the memory of feeling and hearing and seeing him. Fifty years later that had lost none of its intensity.

They must, however, have discussed the wedding, for that weekend he came down to discuss it with her parents. In a formal, old-fashioned way, Donald explained that he and Pamela were finally going to get married and that he hoped they both still approved of him as a potential son-in-law. Her parents, having had to postpone their approval for so long, gave it with spontaneous affection, but Brigit who was there also remembered their unspoken reservation when he said they wanted the wedding as soon as possible. Pamela had found out they could get married by special licence in ten days' time. The wedding could take place as early as 23 January.

'You could see from Donald's face what sort of ordeal he had been through. He looked awful,' Brigit said. 'My father was convinced they should put the wedding off until Donald was better.'

It was not something that could easily be put into words to a couple who had waited through the entire war. In effect it acknowledged that continuity was impossible, that the war had made an irreparable break with the past, and things had to begin anew. Discreetly her parents voiced their doubts: perhaps Donald had changed, certainly their daughter had; were they sure they still felt the same way about each other?

This was a perfectly reasonable reservation, but it missed the point. They had both undeniably changed. The war had shattered them, just as it had the country at large. Everything about them was different, just as it was in the country. But, whatever its form, life imposed certain constants. Men and women had to eat and drink and they had to love. What Auden had written in 'September 1 1939' on the eve of war was still true in the dawn of peace:

> There is no such thing as the State
> And no one exists alone;
> Hunger allows no choice
> To the citizen or the police;
> We must love one another or die.

And if there was only one other person to love, then all else was swept aside.

'How could we have waited any longer?' Pamela demanded. 'We only wanted each other. That was everything we wanted. And we had wanted it for all those years.'

Among the casualties of war was Donald's younger brother Ralph. A slighter version of Donald, he had joined the army in 1939 and been sent to India. Having spent his entire life under his mother's thumb, except for five years at public school, he was singularly unfit to deal with the world, still less the atmosphere of the remote garrison town on the Burmese border to which he was posted. Early in 1942 he had shot himself. It was not clear why. His mother believed it might have been because he was depressed by a rumour that his adored elder brother had been killed in the battle for Hong Kong, but it was also said that there had been a love affair which went wrong, and he had not been able to handle being rejected.

'He had been domineered and overshadowed by Mother,' Donald told his own son. 'It was a very sad thing. He had never been brought up to the rough side of life – she completely protected him – and I think the life out there undermined him until he couldn't stand any more.'

Whatever the circumstances, Ralph reacted as his father did when he lost what he loved. For Donald, the connection was too close to be ignored. Where his family was concerned, at the foot of despair lay death. It was one more reason for loving the woman who had helped him survive the humiliations of the camp.

Almost equally poignant was the loss of Derry McConnell. He had made it through the war, having been awarded not one but two Distinguished Flying Crosses for his gallantry in Coastal Command. The flying which he loved had claimed him in the end. When the new Meteor jet was being developed in the months after the war, he had grabbed the chance to act as test pilot, but on an early proving flight the plane had suddenly plunged into the ground, killing him instantly. As Donald and

Pamela walked and talked together, and ran through the little roll of honour of their friends, it was not difficult to feel that they were survivors, the ones who had come through. Small wonder that they felt destined for each other.

For his best man, Donald chose Frank Hennessy, who had shared the burden of carrying their kit to Sham Shui Po, but events conspired against the choice, and by the time the wedding day arrived the man standing beside him with the ring turned out to be another of the little RAF group, Fergie Ferguson, who had helped him in what had been literally his darkest hour. It was the romance of the occasion that was to blame. The news quickly spread among their friends – that Pamela, who had waited through all those years of war, and Donald, who had suffered so badly as a prisoner, were getting married after being kept apart for so long. Even the least susceptible were touched by the evidence that love could indeed conquer all. Now in his late forties and so shy he was almost in the confirmed-bachelor class, Fergie was one who succumbed to the power of love, and Brigit, whose acid wit might in other circumstances have dissolved Cupid to pink mush, was another. She was in bed recovering from jaundice when Fergie came to the house. He saw her in her jaundice and her night-dress, and was instantly smitten.

'Can you imagine the colour scheme!' she exclaimed. 'I was wearing a green night-dress, pea-green, and inside was me, the colour of a banana. Heavens, I must have looked a sight, but dear Fergie never blinked an eye. And that was the beginning of it.'

One person who steadfastly resisted romance was Maud Hill. Pamela had always found it difficult to fit Donald's mother within the circle of adoration which enclosed Donald. It would have been hard for any mother to live up to her expectations, but Maud failed spectacularly. Years of widowhood had taught her to follow her own road, and she had developed a particular style which was the reverse of romantic. Having grown up in the last years of Victoria's reign when the old queen had been in perpetual mourning for Prince Albert, she had a clear idea of how a widow should appear. Layers of black bombazine were piled up in skirts and bodices and blouses and jackets and bonnets until they shimmered shapelessly round her. Her manner, by contrast, was definite. What she wanted she got, partly because she was shameless in asking for it, and partly because there was an undeniable force about her which had bent her husband and both her sons to her will. When her deep-set eyes started to flicker acquisitively around the room, it made people uneasy as though they might not be able to resist if she arbitrarily demanded one of their possessions.

Her eyes and her hair were her most noticeable features. She was proud of her hair, which was thick and lustrous and was sometimes allowed to fall about her shoulders when it was not piled up under her black bonnet. But Pamela preferred not to think too much about her hair.

'I'll tell you the secret of keeping your hair looking nice, my dear,' Maud said to her at one of their early meetings. 'You should wash it in your own urine. That's what I do with mine. Have done for years. And just you look at it.'

It was difficult to know which image was the more revolting – the one of a black bombazine mountain squatting over a chamber pot, or that of the contents being poured over her head. Eager to win fresh converts, Maud confided her secret to Brigit and to anyone else she could find. Soon all Pamela's friends knew of her about-to-be mother-in-law's peculiarity.

As the wedding approached, Pamela found it easier to think of Fergie and Brigit. They were spending enough time together to make her parents feel that the most dangerous and vulnerable of their daughters might have found her own match. At the last moment they announced their engagement. It was too late for a double wedding, but Frank stepped aside so that at least Fergie went up the aisle as best man. Amid the mounting anxiety of preparing for the wedding, it was one arrangement that was easy to make. With only ten days to go, there was a rush to get everything in place, the decisions about announcements and invitations, fittings for the wedding-dress, flowers for the bouquet, discussions with the vicar, and a reception to prepare with all the complications of ration cards and austerity restrictions on light and heat. Everything was in short supply, especially the luxuries of food and drink which a wedding demands, and the reception had to be held in the doctor's house, which had a particularly large drawing-room. Post-war reality took no account of romance.

The 23rd was a Wednesday, a half-day in Turnbridge Wells, and, despite the short notice, the number of acceptances made it clear that Holy Trinity church would be full. By this stage there was only the bride's last and most demanding test to be taken. The greatest day of her life demanded only that she wear the sort of dress that made her as beautiful as she had ever dreamed, and the morning was devoted to putting it on. It was white taffeta, a classic 1930s style, cut square in front with a neat waist and full-length skirt, but with its simplicity offset by clouds of white veil drifting from head to ankle. The head part of the veil was the problem, for it had to be pinned in place with a garland of flowers. At just that moment when the bride and her best friend and her mother were staring tremulously into the mirror where three pairs of hands were holding hair and veil and garland in place, they heard the unmistakable rustle of black bombazine coming into the room behind them.

'I've been told you can get wonderful vegetables in Tunbridge Wells,' Maud announced in her most definite voice, 'so I've come early to buy some potatoes. Now can someone show me the best place for really good potatoes?'

It was a wonder, Pamela thought, that such a creature could have produced Donald.

Someone was hastily deputed to shepherd Maud to the market before it closed, and only then could they finally pin the veil as it should be. The trouble was worth it. Even with a former model's critical eye, it was an exquisite dress, and wearing it she felt as beautiful as a bride should.

The photographs of the wedding were some of the few that

she always kept with her. They helped bring back the details of the day. Of the ceremony she recalled most clearly the emotion of it, the smiling faces turned towards her as she came down the aisle as though each of them had been hoping for this moment as long as she had, and the sense of peace when she said 'I do'. It felt as if she had at last reached harbour. Looking at the picture of them taken afterwards on the steps of Holy Trinity reminded her of the details, the prettiness of the winter bouquet of maidenhair fern, lilies and white carnations, and the veil which threatened to catch on every car door and flower stem. They reminded her too of the look in Donald's eyes, tender and quizzical and strained. For him too it was an arrival, but the journey had been infinitely harder.

The hardship was brought closer by the presence of others who had come through it. 'Four ex-POWs at wedding' ran the headline in the *Courier*'s report of the occasion. In addition to Donald and Fergie, Frank Hennessy and Ginger Sullivan had turned up, and for them in particular the marriage must have seemed a small miracle, an unmistakable sign that the horror was over.

The bouquet went to Brigit, and the magic worked because she and Fergie were married within the year. Then Donald and Pamela got the train to Charing Cross. There might have been more romantic means of departure, but it was only a step from the London station to the Savoy Hotel, where they had promised each other so long ago that they would spend the first night of their honeymoon.

As they waited for the train, the sight of a black tent-shaped dress on the platform made Pamela bury her face in Donald's shoulder for fear that Maud might want to share a compartment with them. Fortunately she walked past, but it was not until after the train had pulled out that Pamela realized that somehow her going-away suitcase had been left behind in Queens Road. As a result she learned that one immediate advantage of having a husband was that he could be left to deal with the crisis. At Charing Cross he telephoned her home to have the case put on the next train so that it could be delivered to the Savoy. To her mortification, however, while he was still on the telephone at Charing Cross asking her parents to make the arrangements, Maud appeared once more.

'Will you ask them to send on my potatoes too?' she said. 'I must have left them behind in all the excitement.' And with Maud-like obstinacy she insisted that her wretched potatoes be sent to the Savoy Hotel as well. Imagining the hotel porter's thoughts as he collected one suitcase and a sack of potatoes in the name of Flight Lieutenant and Mrs Hill in the Bridal Suite made Pamela so embarrassed she could not bring herself to utter another word to her new mother-in-law.

Nevertheless the ration-free, black-market luxury of the Savoy was designed to soothe the most savage breast, and soon Maud and her potatoes took their proper place as low comedy. Being with Donald reduced everything else to its true proportion. They had come through. That was the only thing that mattered.

In the dining-room, she noticed him looking round at all the luxury with an incredulous lift of his black eyebrows.

'Was it very hard in the camp?' she asked.

'Oh, it wasn't bad,' he said off-handedly. 'Other people had it much worse.' Then he added, 'I kept a diary for some of the time. I'll show it to you one day. That'll tell you.'

She could feel that there were secrets that had to be told, and, more than that, that she was the only one he could tell them to. But at that moment she did not want to know more. It was enough that he himself did not feel scarred by it. When the time was right, she would ask him more, and the diary would be there to answer her questions. That evening, the past and with it all the accumulated tension of waiting was finished. They could plan their future together. Donald had three months' leave owing to him. They had so much time they could squander it like millionaires.

They spent their honeymoon beside the sea in a flat she had taken in the little town of Bexhill. The only reminder of the past came in March with the arrival of a letter from Buckingham Palace to tell him that he had been awarded a military MBE for his services in Hong Kong. Unlike gallantry awards such as the Distinguished Flying Cross, which were awarded for specific actions, the MBE recognized service over a period of time. The citation's turgid language effectively muffled the high pitch of endeavour demanded by battle and prison, but it was wording that the service understood.

> This short service officer displayed before, during and after the operations all those qualities associated with the best traditions of the R.A.F. He was at all times ready to carry out any duty allotted to him with calmness, efficiency and determination. His powers of leadership were outstanding and his invariable cheerfulness was of particular value when he and his party were holding a part of the line, a task that was utterly foreign to them. As a prisoner of war, his conduct was exemplary, and at a time when he was left in charge of the R.A.F. unit, he was largely responsible for the high morale and good behaviour of the Unit.

Donald was pleased because he hoped that it might persuade the RAF to put him back on flying duties when his leave was over, and because he knew it must have come at Ginger Sullivan's recommendation. Otherwise, it was not an honour that he made much of.

It was one of a batch of decorations for service in the Far East, and among them was a remarkable quartet of George Crosses, the highest recognition for courage outside battle. These were awarded to the four prisoners executed for their roles in the collaboration with BAAG, Colonel Newnham, Captain Ansari, Captain Ford and Flight Lieutenant Gray. From his present happiness, the agony they had all endured must already have begun to retreat into the infinite distance. It simply had no part in the present day. The gap that had opened up made it impossible for him to put into words what he felt on seeing the newspapers' picture of Dolly Gray with his cap on the side of his head, and his luxuriant winged moustache. They might both have done something worthwhile had Maltby not forbidden their bombing raid. He might have gone in Gray's place to Sham Shui Po. Instead he had lived and his friend had suffered unimaginable torture and execution. It was pointless to speculate, it was pointless too to bring back memories.

'I don't live in the past,' he once told his son. 'I've suffered a lot of humiliation, but I've learned the most important thing life can teach you, which is how to enjoy life and get the best out of it.'

That summer he and Ginger held the great reunion they had planned in camp. Familiar faces, once skeletal but now half hidden by the return of muscle and fat, appeared, and they talked so glancingly of the camp that to their wives and girlfriends it sounded more like an eccentric boarding school than a prison. The future was what they discussed in detail. Most were out of the services and back in civvy street, and loudly complaining of the Labour government's penal rates of tax. Donald was the rarity.

The RAF might be discarding personnel as quickly as possible, but for him the future could hardly have been brighter. In March he had been given a permanent commission. Two months later he had been appointed station commander at RAF Hendon, one of the largest training and administrative establishments in the service, and in July he was promoted to squadron leader with seniority dating back to 1 December 1941, a week before the outbreak of war. He more than anyone, with the possible exception of Fergie, had cause to look forward to the post-war years with confidence. Fergie could be optimistic for another reason. He was about to take his new wife back with him to Hong Kong, where he had a job in the Education Department.

Altogether the reunion was a curious event. They were noisily pleased to see each other, but then it seemed that no one was quite sure why he had come. They could say nothing to each other about the great event that bound them all together.

Among themselves, Donald and Pamela behaved in the same way. He told her what the camps looked like, and gave a thumbnail sketch of a typical day, and the boredom of it. Sometime in the future they would talk in detail about what had happened to him in the war, but now was never quite the right moment. When they were settled, they would go through it all, and Donald would decode the diary. Meanwhile, Pamela told stories about her cooking, and about London in the Blitz, and about meeting Eric Maschwitz who was such a good friend. That was as much of the war as either of them wanted to discuss. They went dancing wherever there was music being played, even if Benny Goodman was no longer the dance bands' favourite. She discovered how much he loved her, and how little she knew about him, on the day she went up to London to meet him wearing her latest, sauciest little hat, a boater tilted to one side with a flower in front. Donald kissed her and said, 'Darling, I love everything about you, but would it be dreadful to say I don't like your hat? In fact I don't like hats at all.'

In May he took up his job at Hendon as station administration officer, a plum job which demonstrated the value that the RAF placed upon the qualities listed in his MBE citation. The one drawback was that for some intolerable weeks Pamela had to share Maud's flat in Swiss Cottage until she could find a place of her own. The saga of the potatoes had permanently soured their relations, for it had not ended with their delivery to the Savoy. With what seemed like positive malice, Maud had telephoned at 7.00 a.m. on the first morning of their married life to ask whether the sack had actually arrived. Except for breakfast, Pamela succeeded in avoiding her almost completely during these weeks, but it was the one area of married life which was, she felt, less than perfect.

In the bitterly cold spring of 1947, Donald was posted to Nottinghamshire, but later that year she found a flat for them back in Tunbridge Wells. It overlooked the Common, a wild expanse of parkland decorated with tall trees and unexpected rock escarpments. Here she felt they could be utterly happy, and

by then she was pregnant. Part of her knew that he was not as
he had been before he went to war. The camp had damaged
him deeply. He was less certain of himself, and more irritable.
He complained that he could not concentrate, and the huge
competence that she had been accustomed to would often break
down into petulance. Yet he was still the man she loved. She
felt sure that she could repair the damage. It would take time
and it would take love, but there was enough of those to heal
anyone.

CHAPTER 9

BREAK-UP AND RECONCILIATION

I hate and love. You may ask why I do so,
I do not know, but I feel it and am in torment

Catullus, *Carmina*, lxxxv

Donald and Pamela's first child, Joanna, was born on 15 October 1947. The arrival of this beautiful child with blue eyes and dark hair should have been the completion of what they had waited so long for, life together and the beginnings of a family. Instead she came just as her parents were made brutally aware of the legacy left by Donald's years in the prison camps.

In the months immediately after their marriage, Donald and Pamela might have discovered a way of approaching the problem. However hard he would have found it, he was prepared to try to tell her about what had happened to him, and the very act of talking would have countered the prisoner's instinct to conceal whatever meant most to him. The diary, deeply coded, camouflaged and unreadable to an outsider, was the perfect representation of his psychological state, and his offer to decipher it for her showed that he was willing to let her read him as well. The last time he referred to the idea was during the preparations for the reunion party with Ginger. After that the impulse seemed to fade.

There was every good reason why they failed to find the key. The most obvious was that it did not seem important at the time. Neither they nor the authorities believed that there was anything to be gained by bringing back painful memories.

When the prisoners returned to Britain, the few who were offered any help discovered that it amounted to little more than a medical examination and the occasional issue of extra leave. The official attitude was put in a directive from the Ministry of War which was issued in 1945 to everyone dealing with servicemen returning from a Japanese prisoner-of-war camp. They were told to advise the ex-prisoners not to say anything of their experiences since it would only upset their family and friends and could do nothing to put right what was done to them. At the time most accepted this as sound advice, and for Donald and Pamela in particular the feeling that they had arrived in their safe haven after a long voyage made them even less anxious to return to the past.

The first evidence of long-lasting damage occurred while Donald was at Hendon. In part it was simply a matter of having been away for so long. The old RAF he had known in Britain was pre-war, and still imbued with the stiff discipline of its founder, Lord Trenchard. But since then the service had been transformed by the arrival of the teenagers and youths in their twenties who had won the Battle of Britain, then by the incursion of egalitarian-minded Australians and South Africans, and finally by the more tolerant attitudes required to cope with the high tension of repeated bombing tours. To the new station officer, these modern standards of behaviour were shocking.

'When I came back the morale and discipline seemed to have gone,' he said. 'The war had ended, and everyone was drinking too much. They all looked pretty scruffy. I was horrified because my proudest and happiest moments had been in the air force before the war and now, quite frankly, I was almost ashamed of being in the air force.'

His outlook belonged to another era, and to the young flying crew on the station hauled up before him for being improperly dressed or behaving in a disorderly fashion he must have seemed impossibly remote and severe. There would have been rumours that he had been a prisoner of war of the Japanese, and presumably at first allowances were made for him. But it was more than a matter of being out of touch. The RAF was one of the two poles of his existence, and it had thrown up a barrier which shook his fragile confidence to its foundations.

He had always thought of himself as a pilot. It was not just for the prestige of the wings on his chest but because, as he said, 'the happiest time of my life was flying'. Before the war, it had released him from the drudgery of accountancy, and from the dark weight of his mother's influence. His pilot's logbook was among the few possessions that he kept with him through prison camp, and, when he returned, he imagined that flying would again be part of his freedom. But in March 1946 a medical examination showed that, although he was physically fit, he suffered from colour blindness. He suggested that this must be a result of his blindness at Sham Shui Po and would in time disappear. But the Medical Board banned him from night-time and combat flying, and rubbing salt into the wound, entered on his record their conclusion that the defect was 'unknown on entry as pilot'. In other words he must always have been colour-blind, and the implication was that perhaps he had not really been fit to be a pilot in the first place.

'That's a load of old rubbish,' he raged. 'It's the effect of malnutrition.' But he was not believed, and it seemed to him that a slur had been cast on what he prized most. Years later it still stung. 'They had no idea about the effects of malnutrition,' he expostulated on the tape he made for his son, 'they hadn't a clue at all, no clue at all.'

He was restricted to daytime flying, a decision which effectively ended his career as a RAF pilot. Despite the prestige of his job at Hendon, he felt it as a rebuff. Quite soon, the stress of the position began to mount, and as it did so he found it increasingly difficult to cope with unexpected memories of the camp which broke his concentration. The sense that he was losing control made him anxious and bad-tempered. For the moment he could still hold things together, and in September 1946, when further reductions in the force were made, his superiors recommended that he be retained for a further eighteen months. That was the high-tide mark of his RAF career, and thereafter the tide began to ebb.

By the end of the year, it was clear that he could not cope with the strain of Hendon's busy schedule, and in April 1947 he was transferred to Wymeswold, a much smaller station in Nottinghamshire. With lighter responsibilities, the job should have been easier, but in the narrow confines of a provincial station he was thrust more into the life of the base, and there was less to shield him from the high spirits of his young successors in the cockpit. He was still clinging on to his sanity, but only just. With a fog of anxiety clouding his mind, his adherence to rules and regulations had the rigid grip of a drowning man. More than ever he felt entirely alienated from the new RAF, and it was evident that they felt the same about him.

'This was an experience I wouldn't want to go through again,' he admitted to Christopher, his son. 'I was completely anti-social. I was an officer on the station, yet in the evening I did not mix with the other officers at all. I felt almost as if I were unclean. There were parties going on in the mess with a hell of a lot of drinking, and it was all foreign to me. I'm sure there wasn't the slightest interest in me, they were more concerned with boozing it up.'

What made it worse was that he could not understand what was happening to him. He had no self-confidence, he could not concentrate, and his temper would erupt uncontrollably. He and Pamela were living in a flat near the base, and she did her best to look after him. It was not the love she had expected to give to a man who had been so competent and high-spirited when he left, but she believed that she could rescue him from the pit into which he was sliding. There were times when the strained look left his face. She would take him dancing and, if the band played some of the old Benny Goodman music they had danced to before the war, they could still recapture the past. Sometimes in the evening when they sat alone in the flat, he clung to her as though she were his only hope and she could soothe the fear from his eyes.

At other times, a trivial incident might provoke an outburst of rage. In a pub one evening, she recognized a wartime friend and introduced him as someone she had danced with. When he left, Donald's calmness dissolved into fury as he accused her of having arranged the meeting behind his back. The quarrel lasted for three days. They made up as passionately as they had fallen out, but both were frightened by the violence of his reaction.

Eventually the RAF recognized that he was no longer capable of doing his job. In September 1947, he was relieved of his duties, following an adverse report from his commanding officer, and ordered before a medical board. Having heard the evidence of his reclusive habits and unpredictable, explosive behaviour, they made a preliminary diagnosis that he was suffering from 'affective disorder', and recommended that he receive treatment at a psychiatric hospital near Woking.

'It was a shattering experience,' he said. 'But I wasn't functioning at all. My morale had gone completely. My concentration seemed to have gone to hell – I could not concentrate.'

While they waited for his admission to hospital, Pamela took him back to Tunbridge Wells, where she found the flat overlooking the Common. She was in the last weeks of pregnancy, but she had her parents and friends at hand and she recalled it as a happy period. Without the strain of his RAF duties, Donald became calmer and more rational, and in October Joanna was born. They revisited old haunts, and pretended that normality went deeper than the surface. In February 1948 he was admitted to Woodside psychiatric hospital near Woking, and she rented accommodation near by so that she and the baby would be able to visit him.

For a man who had survived over three years in a Japanese prison camp, Woodside presented a particularly terrifying aspect. No one was tortured there and food was plentiful, but doors were locked and the men in white coats had as much power over their patients as guards did over prisoners. Under the pressure of war they had evolved an interventionist approach which was designed to return patients to active duty as quickly as possible. Drugs such as the early amphetamines were administered to combat depression, and hyperactivity or mania was treated by inducing deep, coma-like sleep with large doses of insulin. In the nearby mental hospital of Belmont, Dr William Sargant had popularized the use of electro-convulsive treatment in cases of depression when drugs failed to work. As administered in its experimental form, ECT employed huge voltages with so little preparation that bones sometimes broke as bodies arched under the impact of the current and blood spattered the walls from bitten tongues and lips.

The ultimate weapon of the men in white coats was brain surgery. In the 1930s the usual operation was a frontal lobotomy, in which the entire frontal lobe of the brain was removed with an instrument rather like a giant corkscrew. But in the aftermath of the war this was superseded by the more delicate leucotomy, in which major neural connections between the lobe and the rest of the brain were snipped away. In Woodside a number of strangely placid patients with bandages round their heads illustrated what the outcome might be. It was enough to jolt Donald out of his incapacitated state and into the cold clarity that he felt in the presence of danger.

'I saw the terrible things that were happening,' he recollected, 'doing awful operations and turning people into cabbages, and I wouldn't allow them to touch me in any way. I decided that it was my fight and I was bloody well going to win it. They wanted to give me shock treatment, but I wasn't having that.'

Unfortunately, the hospital took his refusal to accept treatment for fear of becoming a vegetable as evidence of paranoia. Instead of offering any other treatment or attempting to understand the cause of his fears, his case was sent back to the RAF medical board, which accepted the psychiatrists' judgment that he was suffering from 'affective disorder paranoiac state'. It was the end of his career. In April he was ordered to 'proceed home and await instructions'. There he was informed that he was to be invalided out of the service. He had four months' leave owing to him, and when this finished on 6 October 1948 he ceased to be an officer in the RAF.

It seems fairly clear that Donald was suffering from post-traumatic stress disorder, a condition first recognized in the aftermath of the Vietnam War, whose commonest symptoms are flashbacks, loss of concentration, sleeplessness, high anxiety and aggression. In the standard definition offered by *The Diagnostic and Statistical Manual III* used by American psychiatrists, these are precipitated by the sort of stress which 'would evoke symptoms of distress in most people and is generally outside the range of such common experiences as simple bereavement, chronic illness, business losses or marital conflict'. As examples, it lists earthquakes, car accidents, physical injury and such deliberate man-made disasters as bombing and death camps, and explains that 'The disorder is apparently more severe and longer lasting when the [cause of stress] is of human design.'

Treatment today is based on bringing to the surface the fear and shock that was first experienced, often in group-centred therapy sessions, and sometimes simply by listening to the patient's account. In 1983, the realization that former prisoners of the Japanese were still suffering from their treatment persuaded the British government to offer them free health assessments. During the next fifteen years, over a hundred consulted Dr Keron Fletcher, an RAF psychiatrist. Interviewed for a Channel 4 documentary in 1998, he recalled his findings: 'It was amazing – forty-five years after the war, I'd ask a question like, "What was the worst part of your wartime experience?", and they'd break down and cry. They were still getting sleepless nights. I reckon that over half had significant symptoms.'

Neither diagnosis nor treatment was available in 1948, and when Pamela took Donald and the baby back to Tunbridge Wells that summer he had sunk as low as he could. There were periods of normality, but increasingly they were broken by bizarre behaviour. As though looking after Joanna were not enough, Pamela had to deal with Donald's agitated and mad advice about how to do it. In the immediate post-war years, all baby food had to be prepared, and some of the first solid food she made for Joanna was mashed potato and milk.

'You can't feed her that poison!' Donald shouted in a rage. 'Don't you know potatoes give you cancer? You'll kill the child.'

She tried to appease him, explaining that it was on the list of recommended baby feeds, but he would not be convinced. Potatoes were killers. It was the first of his remarks which bore no relation to reality, but over the ensuing weeks they became more frequent. Terrified by the growing signs of mental instability, she would burst into tears, which infuriated him to wilder outbursts.

'I would turn to my mother for help,' she remembered, 'and she would talk to him, but he could be perfectly normal with other people. I even went to talk to the vicar – there really was no one else – and all he could say was that a lot of men came back from the war behaving oddly and that I just had to put up with it.'

Donald felt equally tormented by the knowledge that he was out of control. One evening his condition reached some sort of crisis.

'I had been all tensed up,' he recalled, 'and suddenly tears started running down my face. I don't know what it was, but all at once my whole body and mind became clear. It felt as if a complete weight had been lifted off my shoulder. I thought: "There's no point to all this worrying." And from that moment, I got back faith in myself.'

This seemingly spontaneous recovery produced such a sense of relief that neither questioned how it came about. Donald at least was convinced that his problems were solved, and the past was over. In his late sixties, when he made a tape recording of his life story for his son Christopher, the phrase he repeatedly used about the prison-camp experience was 'There's no point in going back over it. The past is over.' Indeed, when he came to that point in his life, his usually strong, fluent delivery became broken and mumbling. 'I think I've told you about my experiences as a prisoner of war,' he said at last, and after a long pause added emphatically, 'In fact I know I have.' A reference to the war stuttered to a halt, and the subject was dismissed with a curt, 'I think I'll gloss over that.'

Clearly an emotional shift did take place which enabled him to cope. The strain of trying to return to the career which once had made him supremely happy, and now made him supremely unhappy, had precipitated a nervous breakdown. Sometimes madness is the only reasonable response to an utterly intolerable situation. When the tears came, they must have signalled that at some emotional level he felt able to let the past drop away, and with it went the conditions which gave rise to the unbearable pain. Tentatively he and Pamela began to rediscover their happiness in each other.

Yet even then Pamela sensed that what had happened in the camp might represent unfinished business. Although she was reluctant to test his newfound lucidity, she tried to ask him about the war, but this time it was he who deflected her. 'I can think of more interesting things to talk about,' he would say defensively when she raised the topic. Her tentative efforts to return to the diary were pushed aside in the same way.

Perhaps by then it was too late. The tears after his breakdown were the result of a deep psychological adjustment. Donald had broken with his past, and that included the festering emotions of anger and fear and humiliation that prison-camp conditions had created. In *The Railway Man*, Eric Lomax wrote of his determination in 1945 to leave behind the memories of his torture and humiliation in a Japanese prison camp. 'I didn't understand yet that there are experiences you can't walk away from,' he observed, 'and that there is no statute of limitation on the effects of torture.'

Donald was now thirty-six, with a wife and child to support and no job. Long before – almost, it must have seemed, in another existence – he had been an accountant. It was the only saleable skill he had, and he scoured the employment columns while Joanna crawled around the floor beneath his feet. But in 1948 the war boom was over. Manufacturing industry was contracting nearly as fast as the armed forces had done, and laying off skilled and unskilled employees alike. The classified columns, which still bulged with advertisements from former middle-ranking officers seeking an opening in sales or administration, now carried almost as many from production and administration managers seeking any sort of job at all. Nobody was advertising for an accountant, let alone for a part-qualified accountant who had not practised for over a decade.

On his return from the Far East, he had had three years' accumulated pay, but by the summer that had practically all gone. Before the war they had lived extravagantly on nothing, but being married was more expensive. Pamela required a certain standard of living, and a baby's needs devoured banknotes faster than mother's milk.

'I can always get work as a cook,' Pamela volunteered once, but he could not bear the idea of living off his wife's income. Then, just as they were growing desperate, an advertisement appeared for what seemed like an ideal job with the Iraq Petroleum Company. He was called for interview. To his immense relief, a glowing reference from his former commanding officer and his experience of life in a hot climate counted for as much as his qualifications, and he was offered the post. It sounded ideal. The accommodation was free, the salary was generous and it came tax-free, but when he got back to the flat that evening he gave Pamela the news with a sombre face. When she heard what he had to say, she screamed.

His job was in the Middle East, and, because he was on probation for the first two years, he would not be allowed to take his wife out with him.

'I thought, what have we done to deserve this?' Pamela recalled. 'We've had barely two years together, and now we're to be separated again. It did not seem bearable.'

In an emergency, he had always responded with icy clarity, not letting fear or anguish deflect him from doing what had to be done. This was the only way he could find of supporting his family, and he had to take it. In the last few weeks before his departure, she clung fiercely to him and he did his best to comfort her. In September 1948 he left for northern Iraq, leaving her to a loneliness she thought had gone for good.

Aspects of it were different. There was not the fear that he might be dead. They could speak every night on the telephone. She had Joanna to look after, and she was pregnant again. Her parents lived near by, and with three generations on hand her days were filled with family matters. It was a town she had grown up in, and she had never found it difficult to make friends. But, at the heart of it all, there was a space. No one to share the shape of her life, and at night no body in the bed beside her.

'I was absolutely devastated. I missed him always, every minute, but most of all at the end of the day,' she recalled. 'It seemed so unfair. I'm afraid I cried a lot, but there was nothing to be done. You just had to put up with it.'

The centre of Iraq's fabulously rich oil-producing region was the town of Kirkuk. Almost 150 miles north of Baghdad and far from the irrigated valley of the Tigris–Euphrates, the area would have remained an empty desert were it not for the discovery of oil in the 1920s, which had spawned storage tanks, extraction pumps, several settlements for expatriate oil-workers outside Kirkuk itself and the perpetual smell of gas. All this was owned by the Iraq Petroleum Company, itself a subsidiary of Standard Oil, then the largest petroleum company in the world. IPC's massive profits were split with the government of Iraq, and its influence on political affairs was enormous. Until the overthrow of King Feisal II in 1958, a major plank of Britain's foreign policy was to sustain the king in power in order to safeguard its access to Iraqi oil and to protect IPC from nationalization.

Within this petroleum empire, Donald's job could hardly have been less demanding. Initially it consisted of supervising the ledgers and accounts kept by the company's Iraqi book-keepers. He lived in one of the company's expatriate settlements known clinically as K-3. Over time his responsibilities increased, but a job he did not love never called from him the sort of dedication he had given the RAF. Nevertheless, he was widely liked. He played tennis well, and there was something about his large, calm presence which was immediately reassuring. The crises which are endemic in oil production did not upset him. He himself felt more relaxed than ever. He did not look for responsibility, and never pushed for promotion. Almost, it seemed, he was without ambition. But, in the middle of the desert and over 150 miles from the nearest town, K-3 had the atmosphere of a frontier settlement, and it was more important to be a good man than a hotshot thruster. He lived in the bachelors' block where the parties were riotous, the cocktails were mixed in dustbins, and practical jokes endemic. Beds were apple-pied, doors were booby-trapped so often that the sound of falling metal buckets was one of the block's trademark sounds, and one hungover bachelor woke after a party to find a donkey in bed beside him.

One month in twelve he was allowed home on leave, and after the second leave he brought out Pamela and his two daughters, Joanna aged four and Carolyn aged two, to live with him in K-3.

Coming out of the BOAC airliner into the searing heat of Baghdad with two children in tow and the prospect of a six-hour car journey ahead, much of it across tracks and dried-up wadis, Pamela's first instinct was to hate it, but the profits of IPC were so enormous that it could afford to cushion its expatriate employees against the worst discomforts of desert life. They lived in a bungalow, but it offered a way of living which seemed the height of luxury after the penny-pinching restrictions of post-war Britain. They had an amah to look after the children and a houseboy to take care of the housework. The company supplied a gardener and a free taxi service to take them shopping and to the club and to the Olympic-sized swimming-pool. A free primary school provided an excellent education for their children. There was, it seemed, no material want unsatisfied, and better than all of that, the two of them were reunited once more.

In her happiness, Pamela took it all at face value. It was the first time she had lived so far away from her parents that she could not visit them, and she felt homesick, but it counted for nothing beside the security of sharing her life again with the man she loved. There was a dance at the club most weekends, and on each occasion the purely physical sensation of being in his arms restored an old pleasure.

It did not take long to discover the reality below the surface. The summers were blindingly hot, the average daytime temperature was 110 degrees, and the air-conditioning units in the bedrooms were noisy and inefficient. The days began at 5.30 when the men went to work, and the women occupied themselves with coffee mornings and dressmaking until 2.00 p.m. when work on the oilfields ceased. A siesta occupied the afternoon, and then there was tennis and the club. Sometimes there were weekend expeditions up into the hills, or an occasional week's holiday in Tripoli on the North African coast could be arranged, but otherwise its few hundred inhabitants did not leave K-3.

They made an attractive couple, good-looking and sociable, with her vivacity and flair allied to the charm of his quiet solidity. Joanna went to the company's school, and an amah helped look after Carolyn. When Pamela became pregnant with their third child, it seemed to her like the seal on their rediscovered intimacy.

She was older now, however, and more aware of the shadows beneath the surface. The parchment-covered notebook was among the possessions that she had brought out with her, and one evening after she had put the children to bed she asked him whether he would let her read it at last.

'Why?' he asked in surprise. 'Why would you want to read about that awful time?'

He made it sound like an intrusion, and a little uncertainly she answered, 'I think it's important. We've never really talked about what happened to us in the war.'

Suddenly he flared up. 'What happened in the war was that you went dancing at the Savoy with Eric Maschwitz while I was locked up in a prisoner-of-war camp.'

The attack was so unexpected, she stared at him appalled. 'But that's unfair. You mean I was never supposed to go out at all?'

Seeing her outrage, his mood abruptly changed once more. 'I don't think either of us need rake up those memories again,' he said calmly. 'The war's over and forgotten. Besides there are more amusing things to read than my old diary.'

It was easier to let the moment pass than provoke another outbreak of anger. The diary's contents, she recognized sadly, had sunk a little deeper from view. Soon they would become inaccessible. She went to pour them both a drink.

Like many couples, they tended to accept the roles that their friends made for them, that she was the outgoing one and he the reserved. In K-3 the distinction was cruder than at home where old schoolfriends knew the shyness behind her showing-off, and fellow pilots who shared his deep love of flying instinctively understood some of the passion beneath his self-control. Here the difference came closer to caricature, and imperceptibly he found himself thrust into the background. Eventually it triggered a scene she never forgot.

She so obviously loved dancing that she was never short of partners at the club dances. There were more men than women, and the bachelors queued up to dance with her. One evening she came smiling off the floor and with a mock elaboration of courtesy asked him for the pleasure of the next dance. It should have been an unnecessary request. Dancing after all was what had first drawn them together, and they always enjoyed it. This time he dourly shook his head. She was hurt by the refusal.

'Why not?' she asked.

'I don't feel like it,' he answered.

She could not understand the sudden coldness. 'But what's happened?' she demanded.

'Nothing has happened,' he insisted shortly. 'I just don't want to dance.'

At last she concluded that she was being punished. 'What have I done wrong?' she wailed, but the only answer was a stony silence.

The reason for his refusal was simple jealousy, she decided, but, as was to become clear, there were more complex causes for the abrupt changes of mood. What had happened in prison left Donald peculiarly ill-equipped to deal with frustration. It touched the deep reserve of anger built up by years of helplessness, and provoked quite unreasonable spasms of rage. While he was in the RAF, his mounting frustration had sent him spinning out of control. What enabled him to regain command of himself was the tearful moment when he removed himself emotionally from the cause of it. This need to walk away from upsetting situations dictated the pattern of his behaviour. By himself it was quite easy to avoid frustrating circumstances, but when he was with Pamela her behaviour was liable to trigger feelings too powerful and spontaneous to be held under.

In a revealing passage in his taped life-story, he remarked how well he had played tennis before she came out. 'I've never felt so relaxed in my life,' he said. 'My reflexes were lightning fast, in fact in my volleying and service I was a top-class tennis player.'

That ease began to go when Pamela came out to join him, and some of the old symptoms triggered by his beloved RAF reappeared. 'My concentration started to slip back,' he noted. 'Suddenly the anti-social thing was back. My confidence started going.' Among other things, it affected his tennis, and he imagined that people were laughing at him because he was playing so badly. 'I think this was the most humiliating thing that ever happened,' he said, 'because I think Pamela was probably watching, and here was I, who had been a good tennis player, making a complete fool of myself. That was a very very shattering experience.'

Where she was concerned he had no defences. His behaviour when she came off the dance floor was triggered by more than simple jealousy, it was an emotion that threatened the edifice of his sanity.

The birth of Christopher in 1952 introduced another facet to their relationship. Donald liked the idea of having a son, and the boy always intuitively understood that his affection was something which could be counted on whatever happened. Nevertheless, with children, the controlled expression of feeling which was becoming his habit did not provide enough stimulus. Pamela was inevitably the centre of their emotional life, while he was perceived as a distant, regulating force. Soon after his birth, they moved from the desert to the relative sophistication of Kirkuk. The expatriate life allowed the children such freedom that all of them grew up thinking of it as a kind of paradise in which the sun shone all day, where their friends would be waiting by the enormous swimming-pool, and there were parties every week.

'Our life was extraordinarily privileged,' Carolyn recalled. 'It must have been like that in the British Raj. We had servants to look after us, and a sense of wonderful liberty.'

The liberty had strict limits. From the age of six or seven the girls were sent back to Britain to be educated. For them summer holidays took on the quality of a return to the promised land. They would turn up in school uniform under grey skies at Heathrow, and emerge into the dazzling light and heat of Baghdad, and the prospect of parties and sunshine and poolside friendships.

The outcome for their parents was less boisterous. When the girls departed, the bungalow was left empty, with nothing to buffer the growing disparity of need between the two adults. On the one side there was a man who needed to maintain his remoteness to keep control of his sanity, on the other a woman who yearned for overt affection. Each made the other's love treacherous – she was the person who aroused his deepest feelings, and he was the only man she wanted.

Alcohol has always played a prominent role in expatriate communities, and in Kirkuk gin cost just six shillings or 30p a bottle. To dull the sharpness of unexpressed feeling, they began to drink, and the alcohol exaggerated their differences. The emotion which then surfaced most frequently was anger. As the years passed, the returning children became aware of the frozen atmosphere and sudden arguments which ended in tears. But while Donald could restrain his feelings – *had* to restrain them – Pamela's emotions and drinking easily flew out of control.

'I know I provoked him, but I didn't know why,' Pamela said looking back. 'It was so difficult to disentangle one feeling from another. We would be very close and somehow end up shouting at each other.'

But it was the closeness that bred the shouting, and it was still there when the shouting stopped. She was in her early forties when she became pregnant again. It was a baby she desperately wanted in order to bridge the widening rift, but news of her father's illness forced her to fly back to Britain in the summer of 1960. He rallied, and she decided to return to Iraq with Carolyn, now aged eleven, whose holidays were just beginning. Worrying about her father, and anxious about her marriage, she caught the flight back, but while they were still in the air she felt an agonizing pain in her womb. The four-month pregnancy had ended in a miscarriage. The anguish of her loss found expression in a record that she had brought back with her from London. It was the soundtrack of *South Pacific*, and Carolyn used to hear her playing one track in particular time after time.

'It was called "This Nearly Was Mine",' she remembered. 'I heard it so often I almost knew it by heart, but it's only now I realize that she must have played it for the child she lost.'

From then on everything seemed to go bad for them. To dull the grief, Pamela drank more, and the arguments became more high-pitched. Then in 1961 they lost their privileged position in the sun, when the republican regime which had overthrown the king three years earlier nationalized IPC's assets. The expatriate community quickly dispersed, and at Pamela's urging Donald decided to buy a house in Tunbridge Wells. She had missed being close to her parents, and looked forward to visiting them again, but, soon after they moved in, her father died. The loss was made worse when a quarrel over his belongings pushed her always prickly relationship with Brigit into outright estrangement.

Donald's experience with an oil firm had helped him get another job quickly, this time with a subsidiary of the conglomerate Trafalgar House, which was drilling for water in Libya. Soon after his arrival, he saved the company from a large loss by uncovering a network of fraud in its overseas operation. In recognition he was quickly promoted, and, finding himself appreciated, he gave the work a degree of attention it had never commanded in Iraq. He commuted into London, and the entire family found themselves together again for the first time in ten years. In this renewed proximity the sudden alterations of mood which had crippled his love for Pamela began to corrode his relationship with his daughters as well.

It was Joanna who was most prepared to confront him. In what was almost a stereotype of the 1960s rebellion against the older generation, her whole outlook represented a challenge to her father's tightly controlled nature. Impassioned and idealistic, she espoused causes like banning nuclear weapons, played pop music performed by people he damned as 'retarded teddy boys', and wore sweaters so tight and skirts so short they seemed a direct affront to good taste. With no less commitment, she also confronted him over his treatment of her mother, and indeed of any other member of the family who aroused his anger.

'I always used to hide behind her,' Carolyn confessed. 'She was never afraid of him.'

Christopher's memory of these years has a significantly different emphasis. Between him and his father there existed a warm though unspoken bond, which was typified by Donald's response to his son's request to read the diary. The boy was only about twelve years old, but the event had made an impression because within the family the diary was regarded as a forbidden topic. At first his father had tried to discourage him.

'There's nothing important in it,' he said, 'and translating it would be a very laborious process.'

For once in his dealings with his father, Christopher had persisted, and surprisingly Donald agreed to show him how the code worked. The parchment-coloured notebook had been taken out, but in the end his father had been forced to put it aside. The reason, as Philip Aston would eventually discover, was that by then Donald himself had forgotten how the code worked. The key to unravelling the past had been lost.

Nevertheless, the boy understood the significance of the gesture – he and his father were on the same side. In later life, when Christopher talked of the same quarrels as his sisters, his memory was not of Donald bullying the others, but of the mother and daughter allying against him. 'Father was the odd one out,' he recollected. 'There was almost a conspiracy against him. All he wanted was a quiet life.' Specifically he pointed out that, although there were explosions of temper, his father did not respond to attack, but instead retreated into himself. That too was something his daughters remembered – he would not argue or try to defend himself.

Among traumatized prisoners of war, this is such a common mode of behaviour that it is almost a symptom of their condition. With terrible lucidity, Eric Lomax described the part it played in the gradual breakdown of his first marriage: 'Of course it takes more than one person to create what Milton called "disconsolate household captivity" and my withdrawals into cold and blank anger in the face of hostility, pulling my shell around me and locking it tight, cannot have made things easier. Confrontation threatened my whole being, triggering flashes of memory that I could not articulate to anyone, and most tragically of all, not even to my wife.'

Donald betrayed one other unmistakable legacy of the camp – he ate prodigiously, even greedily, finishing up other people's leftovers. It was a habit that he was to retain to the end of his life, and one typical of those who have suffered starvation. Perhaps he could have functioned well enough, keeping the memories at bay, had he not felt so deeply about Pamela, but the very intensity of his feelings ensured that any wayward act or word of hers would trigger the explosion of all the locked-in anger. Carolyn recalled that as the destructive spiral grew worse she would be awakened by the sound of raised voices, and would sit huddled at the top of the stairs wishing with every fibre of her body that they would stop.

At the end of the 1960s they decided bitterly that they could no longer live together. Pamela rented a flat on Mount Ephraim at the top end of Tunbridge Wells, and tried to build an independent life, helped by her daughters and a wide circle of friends in the town. Donald seemed to become entirely solitary. It was almost a commonplace that she was so sociable and he so remote, but now it became extreme. He kept to his regular schedule of driving up to London every day and returning at night, but he saw no one on his return, while she could scarcely bear to spend a moment by herself. In each it was a measure of their unhappiness at being separated. As Christopher observed, 'They might not have been able to live together, but they certainly couldn't live apart.'

At the first opportunity, they came back together again. In 1971 Joanna got married, and the need to plan the wedding gave them the excuse they needed to talk, and the talk led to the renewal of their old intimacy. Nothing had changed, however, and their relationship quickly returned to its tempestuous, destructive form. Its shape was becoming blurred now. They made a habit of blaming the place they were living in for any shortcomings in their marriage, and in the attempt to find a solution they kept moving house, but always within Tunbridge Wells and its neighbourhood. 'I think we lived in fifty-five different homes,' she said extravagantly. Alcohol, which had begun as a palliative for Pamela, was rapidly becoming an addiction, and it made her loud and demanding. His behaviour at home grew more violent, not to her but to objects that she loved. Letters and photographs were burned, china ornaments she valued were given away, mementoes of her past were destroyed.

Again they flew apart. This time Pamela went to stay with Joanna, who, with her new husband Richard Wilkinson, had emigrated to Australia. It was a more terrible repetition of their first separation. She was drinking more, and despite Australia's greater tolerance it was becoming embarrassing. Yet even that handicap did not obliterate her continuing appeal. 'She had a talent for relating to people,' Joanna said. 'She lightened up a room the moment she walked in. She was a very stylish woman, but also very funny, with a dry, ironic, almost camp sense of humour. It was a winning combination.'

Still she could not live without Donald, and on her return they tried yet again to live together. They were in their late fifties now, old enough to understand what was happening, and to give each other room.

For all his tightness towards his own family, Donald's attractiveness was immediately apparent to an outsider. In 1974 he acquired another son-in-law when Carolyn married Stuart Morris, 'a long-haired, bearded leftie' by his own description, who should have been anathema to him. Instead the young man found in the older what he called 'an ideal father-figure'.

'He was a tall, striking man, with an undeniable dash to him,' Stuart explained. 'In some ways he behaved like a typical pilot, always drove too fast and had that outlook which is ultra-conservative, but doesn't much care for the rules. I think he was probably happiest on long walks by himself in the country. He was very much a loner, but a natural leader, the sort of officer you would follow anywhere.'

Yet, when they came together again, the elegant, amusing woman and the dashing, natural leader were as emotionally destructive as ever. There could be no rational explanation for how they felt about each other. Perhaps it was the key to his remoteness that she hungered for, and he wanted the secret of her ease with people, for they dug into each other as though to excavate whatever lay within. Neither could really pretend to be in control in the other's company any longer. Talking about that period in her life, Pamela lost all her animation.

'He would ring me up, and I would go to him,' she said dully. 'I loved him, what else could I do?'

What Donald remembered of those days was the strain of coping with the vastly more complex work that Trafalgar House demanded of him, then coming home to a marriage that was blowing itself to pieces. Even when they were living apart, he could not help responding to her pleas for help. 'She used to ring me up,' he told Christopher, 'and I used to go across to her flat and stay with her in that flat all night, comforting her and trying to keep her off the drink. Then I had to get up in the morning and drive forty miles to London and do a responsible job.'

When Pamela finally recognized that she needed professional help, it was Donald who drove her down to the respectable-sounding treatment centre in Sussex. To his consternation, she was put in a bare unfurnished room which to his experienced eye looked like prison. Both the doctor and Pamela's brother, who had come with them, assured him that there was nothing to worry about, but later that night he received an anguished call from Pamela pleading to be taken away. He raced down to the centre and, when the nurse asked what he was doing there, replied, 'I've come to take my wife home.' Even recounting the story on tape several years later, a note of hair-trigger aggression came into his voice, as he told how the nurse answered flatly, 'You can't.' 'Oh can't I?' he replied. 'You try to stop me.' The menace conveyed by his voice is unmistakable, and the nurse evidently appreciated the danger, for a doctor was hastily summoned, and responsibility for Pamela was signed over to Donald. At the level of hero and heroine, knight and maiden, they still functioned. It was ordinary living that defeated them. Carolyn eventually found her mother a more suitable place for treatment, and there she gradually recovered.

The strain had told on Donald to such an extent that mistakes crept into his normally meticulous figures, and in the effort to catch them he worked later and later at the office. 'I would stay up all night because I wasn't confident I had done it right,' he said. 'I would check and recheck it, and suddenly realize I had made the most stupid mistake. Then I would get in a bit of a panic because the damn thing had to be presented the next morning.'

Sensing that he was beginning to slip, and that too many people had found errors in his work, he asked for early retirement. Professionally it made sense, but it removed the last solid structure in his life. Recognizing the danger that their relationship presented to her fragile sobriety, Pamela had gone out to stay with Joanna in Australia again, and he was left living alone in the large house they had shared in Mayfield in Sussex. Donald had taken to gardening in a rather wild way, growing quantities of kale which he would leave as a present heaped up outside Carolyn and Stuart's door. There were long solitary walks with his dogs, but apparently nothing else. When Carolyn went to see him, she was shocked.

'He was living like a hermit in one room,' she said. 'He had everything there, his bed and clothes and a place to cook. It was all very neat but rather fusty as though he didn't wash much. It almost looked as if he had gone back to the prison camp.'

His loneliness must have been intolerable, otherwise he would not have taken to reading the lonely-hearts advertisements, nor have replied to one from a comfortably off widow in her fifties. Soon afterwards, in 1978, he telephoned Pamela in Australia.

'He said he wanted a divorce,' she cried, as though the pain of it was still fresh twenty years later. 'I couldn't believe my ears, and when he said it again I couldn't believe he meant it.'

What prompted the call was his meeting with Cynthia, a wealthy widow who had advertised for a partner, and with whom he had started an intense physical affair. Pamela flew back from Australia immediately, but it was too late. Three days after her return he announced that he proposed to marry Cynthia.

It must have seemed to him like an escape from the past, from memories of the camp, from the love of Pamela, from emotions he could not control. He never pretended that he loved Cynthia, but for just that reason she seemed to present no threat to his mental stability. With her he could relax, and to Stuart, accustomed to his officer-like reserve, there was something shocking about the sudden coarseness of Donald's conversation when he talked about their life together. More ominously, he who had been so restrained in his drinking now ordered in whisky by the case.

At first it seemed that Pamela would fall apart completely. Rather than oppose the divorce, she drowned her days in a blur of alcohol and misery. It is not a time from which much has stayed with her except the pain, until again she decided to get help. What she recovered to was a life of grinding poverty, mitigated by one unexpected act of generosity – Donald had paid the rent on her flat. On her birthday another came in the form of flowers from him, with a brief, tender note. On several occasions he telephoned to find out how she was, and she fancied that in their talk there was more than a trace of the old warmth. Jealously she hoped that Cynthia was aware of it too. But, just as she pulled herself back from the brink, Donald was plunging towards it.

He and Cynthia lived in a cottage near Yeovil in Somerset, not far from the Devon countryside in which he grew up. Soon the outline of catastrophe began to emerge. His new wife drank with a heavy persistence, and, released from his self-imposed control, Donald joined her. To Carolyn and Stuart, who kept in touch with them, the signs of mental deterioration were obvious: his temper grew more wayward, he cared less about his appearance, and memory lapses became more common.

When he went out to Australia in 1981, Joanna immediately noticed how unfocused his mind had grown, and how old he appeared. It occurred to her that he had come to put things right with his children.

'I think it was a pilgrimage for him,' she reflected. 'He had a sense he wasn't going to live, and he had come to sort things out.'

With Christopher that was easy. His son had come out to stay with Joanna and Richard in 1974, and, after a succession of jobs in catering and publishing, had at last found something that fulfilled him. At the age of twenty-eight, he had just gained his pilot's licence. In the clear Australian sunlight, he took his father up in a little Tomahawk trainer. It was flying as Donald had experienced it, with the ground below visible from the cockpit, and the whole expanse of sky offering freedom in every direction. Briefly he let himself enjoy an almost forgotten taste, then abruptly anxiety flooded in and he begged Christopher to take him down.

On the ground, he recovered himself and, turning to Christopher, said, 'One day you'll fly me from England to Australia.'

'I remember my astonishment,' Christopher remarked. 'Flying was just a hobby, and I had no thought that I could make a living from it.'

It took his father's financial and moral support to help him cross the vast gulf between a private and a commercial pilot's licence, but he had clearly inherited the flair and application that Donald had discovered in himself when he briefly escaped the accountant's desk. Once qualified as a commercial pilot, he quickly raced through the ranks to become a senior first officer with British Airways, flying jumbo jets on long-haul routes.

'I never forgot what Dad said,' he acknowledged, 'and, when I was flying the London–Sydney route, I always felt as though I was flying with him. I am just sorry he wasn't alive to see me do it.'

It was harder to make things right with Joanna, and Donald's first attempt to do so ended disastrously. He adopted his familiar prescriptive style, telling her how she should lead her life, and with a directness learned in childhood and developed by Australian manners Joanna let him know she did not need any lessons from a father who had so spectacularly failed her. She told him of the impact of his years of emotional coldness, the harshness of his rules and prohibitions as she was growing up, and the way he had belittled her achievements so that she had always had to fight for self-respect. Before she finished it had become a shouting match, and they parted with a fury which on Joanna's side left her so upset she could not eat all day. But when she returned home that evening she found a shaken Donald waiting for her. In gingerly fashion they talked through what had gone on between them.

'It was a cathartic experience,' she said. 'We resolved a lot of things, not everything, but in the end we arrived at an understanding.'

Reconciliation had come very late. When her father left for home the next day, she knew that she would not see him again. Later that year, he made a tape for Christopher recounting his life's story. The voice is controlled and coherent, and studiously free of emotion. It is hard to quarrel with the reasonableness of his conclusion. 'It was nobody's fault. When your mother last saw me [before the war], I was a fit, active man. Seven years passed, and when she met me again I was a shadow of my former self. It's quite understandable that she began to drink. No one was to blame. But there's no point in going back.' It was reasonable, but only half true.

The last acts in Donald's tragedy took place very rapidly. In October 1983 his outbursts of wild behaviour had become so marked that his doctor recommended him for treatment in Yeovil's psychiatric hospital, but when he went there no permanent bed was available, and he was sent home. On 2 November 1983 he was examined at his own request by a psychiatrist who concluded that he needed help urgently, but, even with that diagnosis, no place could be found. Two days later, neighbours in the village of Chiselborough heard screams coming from their cottage and called the police. When they arrived, they found Cynthia bruised and bleeding and an incoherent Donald shouting violently. It was clear that he had attacked her in the course of a drunken quarrel, though what it was that finally pushed him over the edge of self-control was never explained. He was arrested and charged with causing grievous bodily harm with intent. Carolyn received a call from the Somerset police to tell her that he was being held in custody, and immediately went to visit him.

'Seeing him in a police cell was the most distressing sight,' she said. 'He was a broken man. He didn't know where he was or why he was there. I think at times he believed he was back in Sham Shui Po.'

He was charged the next morning, and on police advice was denied bail. By a bitter irony, his size, which had led the Japanese guards to make him a particular target in prison camp, was also the reason why the police feared that he would be a danger to his wife if released. But, when Stuart and Carolyn went to say goodbye to him after the hearing, they found Cynthia in the cell kissing him. Pamela, who wrote to him giving her support, received a card back from Exeter prison, where he had been taken. In its attempt to reassure her, it had a flavour of his wartime letters, and it was written in capital letters as if he were still subject to Japanese camp regulations. But now it also had the wild incoherence of a mental breakdown.

'Was touched by your card – full [of] warmth and affection,' he had printed. 'Never felt so well. Vacate your flat now and move to the croft [the cottage where he and Cynthia lived] your new permanent home w[h]ere we all and admire [and] love you. Burn *all* hot water bottles we have super log fires roll on January. I love you but care for Cynthia.'

He appeared in court a week later. Cynthia made it clear that she did not want him punished, and he was so obviously confused that he was taken away while the magistrates decided what should be done with him. The reality was that the mental health services had failed him as spectacularly in 1983 as they had in 1948. Understanding that his father could not survive the experience of prison, the family decided that whatever the cost he had to be given psychiatric help. Christopher had found a private hospital, Ticehurst in Sussex, which would look after him, and the court agreed to remand Donald to their care for twelve months. Once he was receiving proper treatment, it was not long before the staff agreed that he presented no danger to visitors.

The hospital was only half an hour from Tunbridge Wells, and one afternoon an elegantly dressed lady in her sixties approached the girl at the reception desk. Her name, she said, was Pamela Hill and she had come to visit Squadron Leader Donald Hill.

'Of course I had to go to see him, I couldn't not have gone to see him,' she said indignantly.

What she said to him no longer exists in memory, but perhaps it could be imagined. Soon afterwards she returned to Australia to visit Joanna, and while she was away a crisis occurred. Ticehurst was expensive, and in less than a year the fees had eaten up all Donald's savings. Rather than let him be returned to the custody of the court, Christopher, Carolyn and Stuart decided that cheaper care had to be found for him. It was complicated to vary the court order and so, to save time and money, Christopher simply kidnapped him and flew him first to Scotland where he was working, then south again to a hospital which Carolyn and Stuart had found in Northampton. At last a health system which had failed Donald so badly worked for him. Retrospectively the paperwork for his transfer was completed, and, once the twelve months' supervision required by the custody order was up, the family were free to take him anywhere. It does not seem to have been a hard choice.

When Pamela came back from Australia, she found that Donald was in a nursing home in Tunbridge Wells within walking distance of her flat. It was natural to drop in to see him when she passed by. Soon it was no less natural to direct her walk towards the nursing home, which had a fine situation near Mount Ephraim looking over the town. And not much more time had elapsed before it was her daily habit to visit the man she had first loved so long ago.

'It was desperately sad to see him there, but he liked it,' she said. 'Sometimes the matron would ring up to say he was upset, and ask me to come round. It was always me he wanted to see, and when I came he was quite happy again.'

Day by day, their old intimacy returned. In the autumn of 1984 he insisted on taking her to the Spa Hotel. As they walked slowly along the road he stopped to buy her some flowers. 'Darling,' he said awkwardly, 'you know you're the only one I have ever loved.'

It was not 1939, not even 1946. 'It's a bit late for that now,' she answered sadly.

'No, no,' he said, 'it's not too late. I want to marry you.'

'Darling,' she exclaimed, 'it's impossible, you're already married.' Then she saw his anguished expression, and relented. 'We could always say we're married.'

A look of pure relief came into his face. 'We will *always* be married,' he declared exuberantly.

In the prosaic surroundings of the Spa Hotel lounge, they sat facing each other, and he whispered to her that he took Pamela Hill to be his wife to love and to cherish in sickness and health till death parted them. From his little finger, he took the gold ring she had given him forty-six years before at their engagement. 'With this ring,' he said softly, 'I thee wed,' and slipped it on her finger.

It is doubtful if anyone who saw the elderly, slightly battered-looking couple exchange kisses in the corner of the lounge would have realized that they were bride and groom, but it would be nice to imagine that someone did notice the look on their faces.

In the cold of winter, Donald's strength faded. He looked healthy, and still possessed a prisoner's appetite, absent-mindedly eating his granddaughter Lauren's sandwich and her peppermint creams when she and her parents paid him a visit, and then devouring lunch. But his heart was gradually failing. Christopher came down from Scotland to see him, and found him sitting in an armchair but desperately weak.

'At the door, I turned to say goodbye, and he was looking at me,' he said. 'There was a terrible sadness in his eyes as though he knew we would not see one another again.'

The next day, on 25 February 1985, the matron took Pamela aside, and told her that Donald's heart had begun to give up, and he was on his way out. The doctor came, but could only confirm the matron's opinion. While Carolyn took Lauren to be cared for by friends, Pamela sat with her arm round Donald in the chair. Before her eyes his life began to fade away.

'I told him that all the things I had said to him in the bad times I wished I hadn't said, and I told him that I loved him, and that we would always be married, and I told him that I had never stopped loving him since the first time we danced together all that time ago.' She blinked rapidly, refusing to cry. 'They say that the dying can hear right to the end, that hearing is the last thing that goes. I'm sure he heard what I was saying and that he took it with him.'

Carolyn returned, and they took the dying man's hands, talking to him so that he who had been so solitary in life would know at the very end the comfort of being loved. Then very peacefully, so that they were aware of it only by a slight relaxation in his body, Donald died.

CHAPTER 10

THE DIARY DECODED

My love, my love, no, there is no waking
From that long bed or that sleep.
My love, my love, the heart is here for the taking,
And we can take, but not keep.

George Barker, 'Wild Dreams of Summer, What Is your Grief?'

The parchment-coloured notebook was among the pitifully small parcel of Donald's possessions which Pamela took home after his funeral. Apart from his pilot's logbook, there was almost no other documentary evidence to bear witness to his life. Each crisis had swept away more of his belongings, so that, instead of the steady accumulation of possessions that most people make, the record of his days had been reduced to this single document. He had saved it from Japanese guards, from the restless house-moving, and from the repeated urge to destroy everything inessential to existence. Whatever was in it had meant that much to him.

The notebook's cardboard cover was beginning to poke out at the corners through the brown manila-paper cover, but holding it in her hands Pamela was determined that the diary must be read. It contained something that had cast a shadow across his life and as a result had darkened hers. Yet the contents held less significance for her than the secrecy. That was what had really haunted their marriage. She needed to drive out that ghost.

In material terms, the years following Donald's death were the hardest Pamela had to endure. His pensions from the RAF and his employers had gone to Cynthia. But for a discretionary

RAF pension and help from her children, she would have found it difficult to survive. Distracted by illness and poverty, she struggled to find someone who could unravel the mystery Donald had left behind. The problem was simply that his disguise for the diary had been too good. When she sent the notebook to the Imperial War Museum, the staff there concluded that it was no more than a mathematical aid. Like them, the RAF Museum at Hendon concluded that it was simply an interesting artefact from the prison camp, and saw no reason to devote resources to examining it further.

When Colonel Quayle of SSAFFA found Dr Aston, she did not let her hopes rise too high at first, but with his discovery that it was indeed a diary it became difficult to keep her excitement in check. Then as the summer of 1996 arrived, and nothing further emerged, she began to grow anxious. In February, she had reached her eightieth birthday, and there could not be many more attempts if this one failed. Had she known Philip Aston's state of mind, her anxiety might have come close to desperation.

He was not the sort of person to abandon a project, but the end of July now loomed as a deadline. After that date, preparations for the new semester, the extra work generated by a fresh generation of students and the sheer mass of research and publication that he had put on hold meant that he would not be able to return to the diary for six months or longer.

'If I can't solve it by the end of the month,' he said to Linda bleakly, 'I'll have to send it back.'

What he had come up against was the one part of the code that was not susceptible to purely logical analysis. Here the computer had proved itself helpless. It generated great quantities of mathematically analysed patterns, but the pattern that Donald had created came out of his own heart and mind, and no software existed to follow human hopes and inhibitions. In its entry under 'Cryptology', the *Encyclopaedia Britannica* notes 'cryptanalysis is as much an art as it is a science. The reason is that success in cryptanalyzing a cipher is as often as not a product

of flashes of inspiration, gamelike intuition and most importantly, the recognition by the cryptanalyst of pattern and
structure at almost the subliminal level in the cipher.'

For months Philip had methodically picked away the layers of
Donald Hill's encryption. Now he had reached a point where
logic could go no further, and his cryptanalyst's mind had to
sense rather than deduce the key to the cipher. At first the
frustration of dealing with fuzzy intuition rather than the clear-
cut certainties of maths prevented him making the final leap.

'When you decipher a code, you don't get it half right,' he
pointed out. 'It's either completely right or completely wrong.
There were a number of possible approaches to this problem,
but there was just one answer, and that's what I had to find.' In
fact it was literally staring him in the face, but to recognize it he
had to make an unconscious shift which finally brought his
dogged, problem-solving mind into line with Donald's vulnerable, disguise-making personality.

One morning in June, Philip suddenly woke with a picture in
his mind of the inside cover of the notebook. At the foot of the
page, Donald had written his name out in full, DONALD
SAMUEL HILL, and beside it his fiancée's, PAMELA SEELY
KIRRAGE. Idly Philip began to count the number of letters in
their names – there were thirty-four. The blocks of jumbled
letters he was trying to decipher consisted of thirty-four letters
in each line. Immediately he saw that putting the names
together might create a keyword for rearranging them.

The purpose of a keyword is to define the order in which
variable parts of a code should be read. When he was trying to
explain the code to Christopher, Donald had written a number
under some letters in the names. Beneath the first *A* in 'Donald'
was the figure 1, beneath the second *A*, in 'Samuel', 2, and so
on until the fifth in 'Kirrage', beneath which was the figure 5.
There were no *B*s or *C*s, but under the two *D*s in 'Donald'
were the figures 6 and 7. Suddenly Philip had it. He did not care
that the secret had been there for him to see all the time, he was
simply delighted that he had got the keyword and could finally

work out the order in which the confusing mixture of letters should be read. The fourth letter in the row should be taken first, then the eighth. When he put the full solution on the screen it looked like this:

1	2	3	4	5	6	7	8	9	10	11	12	13	14	15	16	17	18	19	20	21	22	23	24	25	26	27	28	29	30	31	32	33	34
D	O	N	A	L	D	S	A	M	U	E	L	H	I	L	L	P	A	M	E	L	A	S	E	E	L	Y	K	I	R	R	A	G	E
6	27	26	1	18	7	31	2	24	33	8	19	14	15	20	21	28	3	25	9	22	4	32	10	11	23	34	17	16	29	30	5	13	12

The top row was the order of the letters in the original text, the bottom row was the order into which they had been arranged. He wrote a program to reverse the process, rearranging the columns so that the sixth letter was read first, the twenty-seventh read second, and so on. When he ran it, he saw to his despair that the block of letters had simply been scrambled into a different order. Then the intuitive part of cryptography came to his aid. There was an aptness to this romantic combination which, he was utterly convinced, made sense. So far, each step of the code had been coldly rational, a conscious mental disguise. But the key to it had to be something that sprang from the inexplicable heart.

So strong was his conviction that for the first time he dared to suppose that Donald had made a mistake when attempting to show Christopher how the code worked. Each block was made up of thirty-three rows and thirty-four columns. Instead of arranging the letters from left to right along each row, it was possible that they should have run from top to bottom. Laboriously Philip retyped the letters, this time arranging them so that they ran down each column rather than along each row. Then he applied the keyword once more.

To his amazement, coherent words like 'Japan' and 'war' began to appear on the screen. He stared at it, scarcely daring to believe what he saw, then came a tremendous sense of achievement. 'I've cracked it!' he thought. 'After all this time we can at last read Donald's story.' Reluctantly he tore himself away to concentrate on the day's teaching, but that evening, unable to wait any longer, he downloaded the diary and the program for decoding it on to a laptop computer so that he could continue reading it at home.

'I've done it!' he shouted to Linda as he came into the house. 'The words are jumping off the page, I've got it, at last I've got it.'

The next morning he continued the work, typing in every digit on every page, and unpicking each step of Donald's code until the original plaintext was uncovered and available for reading. He had to put spaces in between words, and except for full stops, which were marked as X, it had to be punctuated. A final block was incomplete, and the missing letters had to be guessed, but eventually he had just over thirteen pages of text.

The diary covered the period from 7 December 1941 to 31 March 1942, beginning with the last day of peace, followed by the confusion of the battle for Hong Kong and the demoralizing impact of defeat. The style was clear and detailed, and it did not alter when it described the disease, malnutrition and brutal beatings which the defeated men experienced in Sham Shui Po camp. What struck Philip as extraordinary was the resilience of character that emerged as Donald and his fellow captives set about rebuilding a sense of purpose and order. For the first time, he understood fully the sort of circumstances under which Donald had devised the code, and still more the phenomenal strength of mind needed to apply it.

CHAPTER II

DONALD HILL'S DIARY

Sunday 7/12/41. Much talk about war with Japan but no one seems to think anything will happen. We, the RAF in Hong Kong, are a very small crowd: seven officers and sixty men with five aircraft, two Walrus and three Vildebeeste. Group Captain Horry sails for Singapore on the *Ulysses* leaving Wing Commander Sullivan as our CO. I have the doubtful honour of being i[n] c[ommand] of our one and only flight and have three other pilots F[lying] O[fficer] Gray or Dolly, who is also signals officer, FO Baugh, or Whimpey, equipment officer, P[ilot] O[fficer] Crossley, or Junior, a New Zealander just arrived from Singapore and with very little flying experience, PO Thomson, the Colonel, our adjutant, is a V[olunteer] R[eserve] who came to Kai Tak with me from Singapore last June. Finally we have an Australian, PO Hennessy, just arrived from Singapore to start a fighter operations room. The joke is that everything is being prepared for the arrival of fighters but they are not expected for a month. With only five obsolete aircraft and one aerodrome our prospects are not rosy, and it looks as if we might finish up in the army if war comes to Hong Kong. During the day the news gets worse and all precautions are taken, everyone being confined to camp. I take a Vildebeeste with full bomb load on a test climb during which I try to imagine where would be the best place to drop them and what would be my chances if attacked by fighters. But everything is peaceful, and Hong Kong looks quite beautiful beneath.

We park the Walrus on the water and disperse the Beests, but what beautiful targets they make. The 2nd Battalion Royal Scots and two battalions of Rahjputs [*sic*] are in their positions in the New Territories, and the island is being defended by two battalions of Canadian raw recruits and, only just arrived, the Middlesex battalion man the coast defences. Finally, the [Hong Kong] Volunteers, four thousand Europeans, Chinese, Portuguese, etc. Our Navy has one destroyer, ten M[otor] T[orpedo] B[oat]s and a few gunboats. Not a very formidable force especially as we shall be completely cut off from outside help and our food and ammunition supply is only sufficient for a hundred days. Still everyone seems cheerful, I am duty officer and wonder if I shall get any sleep.

Monday 8th, I am disturbed early as the Colonial Secretary rings up to say that war with Japan is imminent. Hell, there goes my sleep, and I wake the other officers. Over breakfast we are told that we are at war with Japan. We dash down to flights just in time to hear an ominous roar of planes and nine bombers escorted by over thirty fighters appear heading our way. There's no time to do anything except to man our defence posts. The bombers pass overhead but the fighters swoop down on us and pour a concentrated fire into our planes. We give them all we've got, which is precious little. Some Indian troops get panicky and rush into a shelter, in their excitement they fire their Lewis gun. There is a mad rush for safety and by a miracle no one is hit. After twenty minutes of concentrated attack by the fighters, the Beeste with bombs goes up in smoke and the two Walrus are left blazing and sink. Finally they make off, not unscarred we hope, and we inspect the damage. Both Walrus are gone, one Beeste is ablaze, another badly damaged, leaving one plane intact. We attempt to put out the fire praying that the bombs won't explode. The blaze is too fierce and she is completely burned with two red-hot heavy bombs among the ruins. One aircraft left but no casualties to personnel. Eight civil machines are burnt out including the American Clipper. In the afternoon, bombers come over again bombing the docks and Kowloon, one stick dropping on the aerodrome. Heavy fighting reported on the frontier, the Japs said to be using one division with another in reserve.

Tuesday 9th. After a quiet but sleepless night comes a hectic morn with rumour and counter-rumour. Heavy bombing of docks and shipping and a big blaze is started in Kowloon. The Japs make a breakthrough on the Castle Peak Road. Chiang Kai-shek's army reported to be coming up behind the Japs and we realize it is our only chance of holding the mainland with two brigades against two divisions. Oil dump at Lai Chi Kok set ablaze by bombs.

Wednesday tenth. News of fighting on mainland bad and we are ordered by the G[eneral] O[fficer] C[ommanding], Major-General Maltby, to evacuate the island. We smash up all valuable equipment and burn all secret papers. All arms and ammunition to be carried with us, parties taken off by lighters proceed to Aberdeen and thence to the A[berdeen] I[ndustrial] S[chool]. I left late in the afternoon on the last lighter with twenty men and all the arms and ammunition. Aerodrome strewn with all kind of obstacles to prevent use by the enemy. Chinese loot our mess as the lighter leaves. When just off the waterfront, bombers appear and our skipper takes fright, have to use force before he will proceed. Heavy shelling and bombing of Stonecutters [Island] which is bombarding the Japs advancing down Castle Peak Road. We are fired on by our coastal defences after rounding Davis [Point] but we run up a Union Jack and all is well. Arrive Aberdeen and get everything off just before dark. The AIS is full of naval personnel, all trying to find accommodation and food. After a mad scramble, manage to find a bed and retire early, tired and hungry.

Thursday eleventh. Commander Millet, O[fficer] C[ommanding] AIS, asks me to form anti-aircraft and defence posts for Aberdeen as RAF only people with machine-guns. I fix up four posts on the roof with tommy [Thompson sub-machine] gun posts on the verandahs. The AIS makes a wonderful target being half a mile from the naval dockyard. A hospital has been set up next door to the armoury. For breakfast we get one slice of bread and a little butter, and tiffin [midday meal] is the same. For supper, if we're lucky, we get hot stew. Intensive bombing of Aberdeen harbour causing heavy casualties. How we curse the bombers and wish we had a few Gladiators which would make short work of them. Jap fighters are quite slow.

Friday twelfth. Up early and drive into H[ong] K[ong].[1] Buy food, cash a cheque and have a steak at Jimmies. Send cables to Pam and Mother. HK shelled from Kowloon. All our troops evacuated from mainland. Hear that Walter Rosa, Dick Stanton, Houston Boswall and Bell,[2] who messed with us at Kai Tak, have all been killed. Small party of Indians still fighting on Devil's Peak. Royal Scots fired on in Nathan Road[3] by Chinese fifth columnists using automatic weapons but Scots wipe the whole lot out. Chinese reported assisting Japs on large scale. Amazed at sinking of *Prince of Wales* and *Repulse*,[4] also Jap successes against Americans. No one, however, doubts the final outcome and we realize that HK is only small fry in a tremendous issue.

Saturday thirteenth. I set up anti-aircraft positions on Bennetts Hill and Reservoir Hill w[ith] RAF personnel. C[ommanding] O[fficer Sullivan] goes to battle hqrs leaving me in charge. Dolly goes to Little Saiwan and the Colonel to Stanley. After much sweated labour, get guns etc. in position. Whimpey is in charge of Reservoir Hill and I of Bennetts [*sic*] Hill. I return to AIS for the night and at midnight there's a hell of a commotion and everyone is roused as the Japs are supposed to have landed on Aberdeen Island. Whole thing is a farce and return to bed.

Sunday fourteenth. Set up positions on Bennetts and start digging holes in side of hill for billets. Junior and I dig like mad but, owing to rocks, make little progress. Quiet day except for a few air-raids. Bed extremely hard and rain comes in.

Monday fifteenth. Contact Canadians who have positions at

[1] The town of Victoria, the colony's capital, on the north side of the island of Hong Kong.

[2] All 2nd Bn Royal Scots.

[3] Main street in Kowloon.

[4] British battleships sunk by Japanese air attack.

foot of Bennetts. They are very helpful, bringing us hot tea and helping us in our digging. Am now in the army without a doubt and under the orders of Major Baillee [*sic*] of E Battalion, Winnepeg [*sic*] Grenadiers with hqrs at Wanchai Gap. More heavy bombing of Aberdeen harbour, heavy casualties to Naval personnel caused by explosions of torpedoes and depth charges.

Tuesday. Japs attempt landing at Lye Mun but party wiped out by six-inch gun. Heavy shelling by Japs of Wanchai Gap and Stanley bombed. Driving the staff car into HK, I have a lucky escape as a stick of bombs meant for the *Thracian*[1] in Deep Water Bay drops on the road just behind me.

Wednesday. Hennessy goes to Canadian hqrs on Col Sutcliffe's staff. Intense bombing and shelling of island defences. One stick aimed at us misses. Another day of hard work and very little food. During the night enemy warships shell the island and shrapnel shells burst right over our heads giving us an uncomfortable time. Two cruisers and one destroyer had been seen the previous night. One six-inch shell of British make struck the AIS and knocked a large hole in the wall of MTB repair shop, also completely writing off my car.

Thursday. Enemy succeeded in landing on island last night and forced their way into Happy Valley despite heavy casualties. Scots and Canadians fail in attempt to drive them out. Japs in large numbers assisted by fifth columnists. Landing covered by intense artillery and naval bombardment. News muddled and rumours of all kinds rife.

Friday nineteenth. News still confusing but Japs push into Wong Nei Chong Gap. My positions were designed against attack from the west, not east, and we have to improvise a new line. Lt. Campbell takes a party of men to go to the assistance of Canadians trapped in Wong Nei Chong, their place being filled by Chinese Volunteers. Major Giles R[oyal] M[arines] arrives with a small party. Eventually the Chinese go, much to our relief, as they are much too jumpy. Junior is now in charge of

---

[1] First World War destroyer.

Bennetts with Giles and myself commanding a sector running from the foot of Bennetts to Mt. Nicolson. Situation very tense and we spend a sleepless night. Pours with rain all night and bitterly cold. Everyone soaked through and half dead by the morning as we had no protection against the weather. Spend half the night pouring rum into semiconscious men who are dead tired after sleepless nights with very little food. We have no reserves and everyone has had a gruelling time. A Canadian sergeant returns to our pillbox at midnight in a state of mental and physical collapse and reports that all his party have been killed. A few hours later another Canadian arrives in a similar condition and with the same story. Worst night I can ever remember, and never was dawn more welcome.

Sunday twenty-first. Naval personnel recalled by the Commodore for defence of the dockyard, leaving us seventy Canadians. We all carry a good supply of grenades as the Japs are very skilled at getting to close quarters without being spotted. The Jap soldiers wear rubber shoes and are as stealthy as cats. They carry a bag of grenades, automatic weapons and light rifle of quarter-inch calibre. They always attack at night and from all directions. Their snipers seem to be everywhere. Japs now using their mortars and artillery much more, being firmly entrenched on Shu Shun Hill. Our artillery do some excellent shooting at Shu Shun and Japs run in all directions. No one seems to know where the Japs are or how many there are. The High Command, whose daily communiques reveal nothing, seem to know less than anyone else. Chiang Kai-shek's army reported attacking Japs in the rear and we are told to hang on as they will be with us in a few days.

Monday. Japs break through Middle Gap and now very close to us. Scots take a heavy toll and retake some positions, but Japs always come back in strength. There is no doubt now that the Japs have a very large force on the island, well equipped and experts in this guerilla warfare. Spend the night on continuous watch. The men very jumpy as every sound has to be investigated. If only one could see them instead of this hide-

and-seek. In several cases Japs have crept up to pillboxes and dropped grenades down the airshaft, killing everyone.

Tuesday twenty-third. Several Canadians who had been given up as lost return with amazing stories. Many wounded Indians come through our lines kitless but not broken. Heavy shelling of Bennetts. Just before dark, enemy starts terrific bombardment of our positions. Hundreds of shells whistle just over our heads. Major Baillee rings up constantly and seems very jumpy about our positions. At two am he orders us to evacuate our positions and retire to Aberdeen. We are amazed at such an order but apparently the Japs have broken through over Mt Nicolson, turning our left flank. We collect our small force and start our retirement. Heavy firing coming from Wanchai Gap, where fierce fighting is going on. What a forlorn sight we make groping our way back through the hills in the dark. Finally reach Aberdeen, the Canadians going up Mount Gough and I take my men to the AIS. Atmosphere depressing and everyone falls to sleep through exhaustion. Up early, lucky for me, as a bomb lands on my bed as I leave the room wrecking everything including my kit. AIS heavily shelled causing many fires and casualties.

Wed twenty-fourth and Thursday Xmas Day. The retire-ment order was a mistake and back we go to Bennetts with guns and equipment. Just as we reach the top the Japs open up on us with mortars. We have no protection and lie flat. The shells land right amongst us. Man next to me hit, also several others. Piece of shrapnel glances off my helmet and am half buried in flying debris. If we stay we shall all be killed so order the men to disperse and dash for cover, and miraculously we make it. During the barrage I had noticed that one of our previous posts was still manned by Canadians who obviously had not received the order to withdraw. C[or]p[ora]l Blueman A.C., Canadian, volunteers to go with [me] to try and get them out. We climb on our bellies through the thickest undergrowth but are fired on several times. Finally we get within hailing distance and get them all into a pillbox. We collect all the arms and equipment which we can't carry, pile them in the pillbox, and throw a couple of grenades into the pillbox. As we start back, everything goes off at once and we have to duck flying bullets. Eventually we arrive intact at the AIS. No one seems to know where the Japs are, so back we go to a new position guarding the bridge over Aberdeen reservoir.

My party consists of twelve Canadians and ten RAF. Up to midnight all is quiet, although every sound indicates Japs to the men. Soon after midnight heavy firing starts just across the bridge. The Japs' weird war-cry is plainly heard, and soon a small party of Canadians retire over the bridge. They report heavy attack by Japs who crept up on them and broke through. We open up with everything we have across the bridge. The Canadians are badly rattled, even their officer seems to have lost control of his men. The Japs start shelling us and confusion sets in, and the men start leaving their posts. A scene I never wish to see again, I am in an awkward position as I have no command over the Canadians.

Just as they start moving back [up] the road, Major Baillee advances down the road waving a revolver and shouting to his men to get back to their posts. Some obey and some don't. The major is highly excited and his voice rings through the night calling his men all the names he can think of. The Japs must have a good idea of our positions. He calls his officers and men all the names under the sun and shouts for volunteers to cross the bridge. The Canadians refuse to budge so I, more [out] of a desire to back the major than of any thought of heroics, go across with him. We reach the other side safely, whereupon he is violently sick, and I realize he is drunk. Through overwork he worked himself into a state of complete collapse, and should have been releaved [*sic*] of his command earlier.

We retire still intact. We can hear the Japs' wild animal calls and they appear to have gone another way. Most of the Canadians have disappeared and with the few left we set up a mortar which fires its first shell into a nearby tree, explodes, blowing the operator's right arm off, and another man nearly loses a leg. Get the wounded into a dugout where there are some others badly wounded and try to stop their bleeding. We only have bandages and several of them are in danger of bleeding to death. Their moans are terrible and although I keep ringing up for an ambulance, none arrives. What a horrible mess, and I try to restore some kind of order. After a good talking-to, the men pull themselves together and go back to their posts. Thank God the ambulance arrives at last, also Lts Campbell and Park. Campbell threatens to put the major under arrest, and Baillee threatens to put every Canadian under arrest.

Comes the dawn and most of the Canadians have disappeared. What a Xmas Day, empty stomachs, tired out, and heaven knows what is going on. At ten am a message arrives saying their [sic] is a truce until midday. This news is immediately followed by a terrific bombardment of our positions. Not my idea of a truce. More Canadians melt away, leaving our line practically undefended. I gather the few remaining men together and proceed to climb Mt Gough hoping to join up with our main forces. When we reach the top and strike the main road, we run into several hundred Canadians in retreat from Wanchai Gap. Wanchai Gap is the most vital sector of all and this means the end. We are told that island surrendered at three-thirty, over an hour ago. The troops have no arms and are completely worn out. A scene I will never forget with ammunition dumps going up everywhere and the Japs pouring hundreds of shells just over our heads into blocks of houses across the road. Finally the barrage stops and white flags appear from all the houses. The troops have got hold of quantities of beer and are singing to releave [sic] their shattered nerves.

I am too stunned to describe my own feelings but decide to try and escape. The Japs are reputed never to take prisoners. With Junior and three of my men, we grab an Austin Seven and decide to make a dash for Aberdeen to try to get a boat. The engine won't start but it's all downhill. By now it's dark and the road is very narrow and tricky. We throw away our arms and get aboard. What a ride, crashing through barbed wire and roadblocks in the dark, but the old Austin showed her worth and we finally coasted into Aberdeen without seeing any Japs. We go straight to the AIS and get hold of Chinese boy who says he will try to get us a boat with food and water. Then, to our horror, we discovered that the building had been locked and we could not get out as the Japs were outside. What a disappointment, and we had nothing to do except find somewhere to sleep not having had a real one for ten days. My old room was a complete shambles, so slept on the floor.

Friday twenty-sixth. Woke to a beautiful morning, being unnaturally quiet and peaceful, so that the last few weeks seemed as nightmare. We were all under orders for the dockyard. Spent most of the morning smashing up thousands of bottles of beer and spirits for fear the Japs would get drunk and run amuk [sic]. Got a car and set off for the dockyard passing hundreds of Chinese laden down with loot. On arrival at the dockyard, we're told to go to the detention barracks, the men being locked up in the cells, and we went to China Command.[1] Had a real wash and shaved off my fortnight's growth of beard. The Colonel [Thomson] was in hospital having received a bullet through the neck, eight of our men were dead and several missing.

We had no kit, so I decided to try and get back to the AIS. The only transport I could find was an old dairy farm lorry. Whimpey and Frank came with me. Soon we ran into several thousand Japs marching along the road looking tired and ragged. An officer signalled us to stop, made me turn the lorry while troops climbed in the back. He indicated by signs that I was to drive them to HK. The troops seemed baffled by our blue uniforms but were quite friendly. Dropped our load and once more set off for the AIS. Passed hundreds more Japs, but after some nasty moments finally reached our destination. Found most of our kit, and got safely back. Just as I was congratulating myself on a good day's work, a Jap officer came up and ordered

---

[1] Headquarters in Victoria of the defence force.

me back into the lorry. Whimpey and Frank got off. He directed me by hand signs to drive to Courtland's Hotel which had been taken over by the Japs. The few remaining residents looked pretty scared. More troops piled in and after a very trying drive through Kennedy Town, we finally reached the St Louis Industrial School, where they all got out. We had passed hundreds of troops and the streets were littered with dead Chinese.

I was beginning to think my work was done when several officers started arguing and kept pointing at me and looking aggressive. Suddenly one of the officers whipped out his sword and I thought they had decided to bump me off, but to my amazement he produced a bottle of beer, nipped the top off with his sword, and handed me the bottle. I was then given a loaf of bread. Apart from one or two soldiers, they had treated me very well. My wings seemed to fascinate them. By now I wanted to call it a day, but another officer got in the lorry and off we went back to the hotel. He had some beer with him and handed me the bottles to open. I stopped the van and wedged the tops off on the mudguard. This seemed to amuse him and he tried to do the same on the dashboard with drastic results.

Once more the van is loaded up with troops. Another officer takes over who is not so pleasant and I get half an inch of bayonet in my bottom for being too slow. Back to the School where another terrific argument starts. I want to go back with the van, but two officers decide to drive me back in a Ford Ten. They don't use any lights and we have several narrow escapes from hitting lamp posts. Suddenly I see we are heading for one of the islands in middle of the road, and shout a warning. Too late, and there's a terrific crash and we finish up on our backs. By now I am fed up, so bowing politely I leave them and walk the two miles to China Command.

Saturday. Five of us sleep in a small office. All our water has to be drawn from a stream near by. No one knows what is going to become of us and everyone tries to guess at our future destination. Some Jap officers inspect us.

Sunday twenty-eighth. More troops arrive from Stanley and report that Japs raped and bayonetted nurses in St Stephen's Hospital, also killed the wounded. Colonel Smith, whose wife was one of those killed, goes nearly mad and tries to get at the nearest Jap. Several atrocity stories come to light and atmosphere becomes very tense. Two destroyers and one cruiser anchor off the dockyard, followed by a victory parade including a flypast of sixty bombers and fighters. All very galling.

Monday twenty-ninth. News is that we are to be moved to the mainland at dawn tomorrow, and that we will be given no transport and can only take kit that we can carry. The GOC and Commodore are treated the same as everybody else. Obviously we are going to be humiliated. For dinner we open all the tins in store and eat royally, washed down with beer and champagne. Pack what little kit I have, also any tinned food left over.

Tuesday. At dawn we prepare to move off. Frank and I sling our kitbags on a pole coollie [sic] style. We sling blankets round our neck. We are determined to bear our humiliation without a murmur – our day will surely come. We form into units and after two hours' waiting move off, over six thousand strong. Arrive at the ferry and, after another long wait, are ferried across to Kowloon, where we form into units again. Off again but where no one knows. After a mile or so, we come back into Nathan Road. By this time we begin to feel the strain and have to rest frequently. Each unit has its own guard. Thousands of Chinese line the streets, a few jeering but mostly quiet and some are in tears.

It would appear that we are going to Sham Shui Po, several miles away. Our guard is a decent fellow and seeing we are having a rough time allows coollies to carry our kit. Eventually we reach SSP barracks eight hours after leaving China Command. A battle for billets commences. The whole camp has been stripped of every useful article by looters, and had also been bombed. All doors, windows, furniture and fittings had been taken, leaving just hulks of buildings. Even in peacetime it was an awful dump, but now it looked as if a typhoon had hit it.

We found a small hut, and then a tremendous hunt started for anything resembling a bed. Found some horsehair and wrapped into one of my blankets. Several men had been here for days, being captured earlier on. Two W[arrant] O[fficers]s had been tied up with wire, stripped of everything, and left for three days without food or water after having seen several of their comrades bayonetted. We get rice twice a day which tastes foul and does not alleviate our hunger.

Wednesday thirty-first. Moved to a slightly bigger hut, the Wing [Commander Sullivan] moving in with us, the men are in another hut close by. There are over six thousand men in the camp with no sanitation and rotten food. We have no lights and go to bed soon after dark. We have one meal at nine and another at five consisting of soggy rice, and are permanently hungry. And so ended nineteen forty-one.

Jan first. A new year which we hoped would see the end of the war. We hear no news, only wild rumours, and we all wonder what our people at home are thinking as we are unable to tell them of our safety. Soon adapted ourselves to our surroundings and began fixing our rude quarters into some sort of shape. Bits of wood and attap made windows, and no kind of scrap was wasted. Had no eating utensils, any old tin had to suffice. Cigarettes very scarce, but luckily we had brought some with us.

Second. Our camp adjoins the main road, and the Chinese sell us foodstuff at exorbitent [sic] prices. We have three hundred dollars and add considerably to our stock of food. My boy, Ah Cheung, brings a basket of food and I slip him some money to get some more.

Third. Take it in turns to go [to] the wire. Often the Chinese, usually boys, grab the money and run away without giving anything in return. Junior put in charge of messing, and we open a tin a day.

Fourth. Our chief danger is flies, which swarm everywhere spreading dysentery, and the added menace of cholera. We have practically no medical supplies as the Japs have taken them all for their own wounded, which run into thousands. Just as we get to bed, a lorry arrives and we are disturbed by the squealing pigs. Thirty for six thousand men. We all assist in chasing them, and put them in a hut.

Fifth. Each receive a small lump of fat with our rice, very unappetising.

Sixth. My batman, Cpl Moulton, who was my fitter, is a great little scrounger and handyman. Manage to buy a camp-bed for ten dollars at the fence. Sheer luxury but the canvas is rotten, and during the night it collapses and lands me on the floor.

Seventh. Moulton fixes my bed but breaks my rice bowl. Buy a tin of coffee and some vegetables. We make a stew in a bucket and do we enjoy it. Many of the troops have Chinese wives and girlfriends who bring them food. Japs get very strict about buying food at the wire, and many Chinese get beaten up, women being stripped naked in full view of everyone. Indians are getting unruly. Several deaths from dysentry [sic].

Eighth. Florrie and her amah arrive with more food. She tries to cross the road but I signal her back. No parcels get through as a general is expected to visit us. My boy also arrives. What a disappointment.

Ninth. Jap general arrives with an escort of twelve cars, and troops manning machine-guns in lorries. He drives to the guards' hut, steps out, has his photograph taken, and drives off without a word. What a farce. Many wild rumours but as usual no truth in them.

Tenth. Bed collapses again during night. Our roof leaks from the effects of a bomb, but so far the weather has been perfect. The flies swarm everywhere due to the filthy condition of the camp. All buying at the fence stopped, the Japs torturing any Chinese who come near the fence.

Eleventh. Florrie arrives again and I receive a parcel of bread, butter, milk and tomatoes. What a treat, and the six of us make short work of it. Rumours even wilder: Tokyo reported bombed, Japs suffer severe naval defeat, Hitler committed suicide, and Japs evacuate Malaya. Have grand supper of coffee, bread, butter and jam.

Twelfth. All buying definitely stopped, many Chinese beaten up.

Thirteenth. Many sick with tummy trouble. One feels fairly fit but completely lacking in energy. Twenty Scots arrive from Fan Ling, amongst them being Potato Jones who commanded the company at the Shing Mun Redoubt, and Lieut Thompson who was hit by a grenade and is practically blind. Japs refuse to take him to hospital, which will probably cost him his sight. Florrie brings another parcel. I throw a message to her across the road screwed up in a cigarette holder.

Fourteenth. Everyone's stock of food running low. Rumours still wild, but always good news and we think things are going well.

Fifteenth. Florrie comes again, but Japs won't allow parcels through. Get some soya beans which help the rice down. Junior falls down and nearly breaks his leg.

Sixteenth. Start Japanese lessons. Florrie arrives again, and this time I'm lucky. Whimpey gets a blue mood and refuses to talk to anyone.

Seventeenth. Florrie's amah arrives with more food.

Eighteenth. Sentries wire up streets facing camp and shoot a man and a woman for trying to sell food. Florrie turns up again but can't get her parcel through. What a girl. Two Chinese bodies washed up near fence. Everyone feeling weaker due to lack of proper food. Rumours and counter-rumours so contradictory that I don't believe anything. Some real news would make such a difference.

Nineteenth. Now get three meals of rice a day but quantity the same. Rice by itself is awful muck, but we save our small stock of milk and sugar for our evening tea. Over hundred men arrive from Queen Mary's hospital.

Twentieth. More men arrive in lorries, some unable to walk, and dressed only in pyjamas and socks. Troops give a concert including a dance band. Cigarettes very scarce.

Twenty-first. Fight between Middlesex and Indians. Rice ration very short.

Twenty-second. All Indians moved out of camp. Canadians being moved tomorrow, destination unknown.

Twenty-third. Disturbed early by troops detailed for work at Kai Tak, a three-mile walk. Wonder how they'll make out on the diet.

Twenty-fourth. Navy are moved from the camp, and we are going into Jubilee Buildings.[1] Usual mad scramble for accommodation. Wing gets peeved with Brigadier McCleod and tells him a few things. News is that we have withdrawn in Malaya and that there's a rumpus at home about HK and Malaya, and quite rightly too as both places were very weak in defences, especially aircraft, and men have had to fight against overwhelming odds. We all hope these blunders will soon be rectified.

Twenty-fifth. Move into Jubilee, which is much more comfortable and on the waterfront. The six of us have three rooms and even a bathroom. What a relief after our squalid hut. Junior has planned to escape with several others. They hope to get to Mirs Bay in a junk, and then fifty miles over land to Wai Chow, which is still in Chinese hands.

Twenty-sixth. Junior gets up at five to contact the Chinese who is escaping and is going to arrange for the junk to pick the rest of the party up tomorrow.

Twenty-seventh. Junior up at five and contacts the junk but doesn't get away. Frank and I up at six and go down to the jetty which is now the only place one can buy food. We get seven lbs of sugar. It is pitch dark and we have to wade some distance to the junk. The Chinese are very cunning at avoiding sentries, but several have been shot.

Twenty-eighth. GOC talks to all officers and NCOs about morale, which is very low, and warns us against disease. We are all staying up late tonight and are having a late meal to feed the

[1]Married quarters when Sham Shui Po was a barracks.

escapists: Junior, Capt Scriven and Capt Hewitt. Whimpey is also due to go, but one of their party backs out and upsets their plans, which is to swim to the mainland then walk to Wai Chow. A perfect night with a bright moon and as still and quiet as a graveyard. We sit up until two o'clock playing cards by the light of the moon. Finally they go and we get some sleep.

Up to thirty-first. Junior and Whimpey's escape[s] don't come off due to the junk not turning up and Whimpey's raft collapsing. Many Chinese escape, and some Europeans, many being captured and brought back. Japs machine[-gun] all junks moving by day. Many cases of dysentry and typhoid.

Feb first. Japs stop all food coming into the camp. Whimpey and Junior due to try again tonight. Four of us get up at two to wait for the trading junks. Several hundred in queue. Sampan arrives at four and we buy sugar, milk and sardines. Whimpey goes just before midnight, it being very light. Shortly after, we hear rifle fire and we pray that he made it.[1] Bullets fly past our verandah. Junior gets off at two am in one of the trading junks.

Second. We feed well today as we get rations for six. We are all a bit on edge, wondering how they got on.

Third. Frank and I up at four and go down to the jetty. The Japs have locked the gates, but we make a hole and get through. Japs hold a parade to count us as they caught three gunners last night. On parade the Japs spot that we are two short and ask the Wing why. He says he has no idea but they were with us last night. They seem perturbed about escapes.

Fourth. Up at three and down to the jetty, but the sentries are awake and shots start whistling near by. This happens every half-hour and we take shelter. After two hours and no sampan turns up and bullets getting too close, we retire to bed.

Fifth. Japs now wise to escapes and we have to parade again at eight for two hours. Another parade at one, which takes over four hours. All very annoying and they don't seem very clever at

---

[1] Both officers succeeded in escaping and returned to active service as pilots. Flying Officer Baugh was killed before the end of the war.

counting us. They don't take precautions to prevent escapes, but seem very surprised when it happens. In the Jap army to escape is to desert.

Sixth. Wake up to find the others busy dressing and packing. They have been ordered to be ready to move at short notice, but I am not included. No one knows what it's all about. Just time for brief farewells and they are gone, driven off in a car and what luggage they have follows in a lorry. I am now the only RAF officer left. A sad day for me to lose such grand companions in distress, especially the Wing. Someone brings me a parcel which Florrie had brought me. The Japs have started to allow a limited number through. A large tin of cocoa, milk, butter, soap and biscuits. How the others would have enjoyed it. I go down to the fence and see Florrie and have quite a long chat with her. She has been interned at Stanley for a fortnight. She seems very cheerful and is coming again tomorrow. What a girl. Sentry offers me ten cigarettes for my gold wristwatch, a twenty-first birthday present from Billie.[1] When I refuse, he indicates my gold signet ring given to me by Pam. I would not part with either for the world, so no business is done. Roy Haywood and Ken Glasgow come and have evening cocoa with me. Spend hours these days thinking of home and family, especially Pam. Thank God for you, Pammy darling, your memory is ever with me. I still have your photograph, signet ring and cigarette case. I will never lose them.

Seventh. Eight officers move into the flat including a Chinese called Evans. In my room, I have Captain Chippywood and Lieut Tressider. Ian Blair and Mathers of the Punjabis bring along some chapatties, which go down well with butter and marmalade. Roy Haywood and Glasgow join us and spend a pleasant evening. Ken had been to Kai Tak on a working party, and been roughly handled by a sentry, but an officer apologised and gave him a tin of plums which he brings along.

Eighth. Shave my beard off and feel a new man. Florrie turns

---

[1] DH's sister.

up and I get another good parcel. I had told her if she wanted to get a note to me to bore a hole in a bar of soap and put the note inside. She has made a good job of it. Poor kid, the Japs have turned her out of her home. I keep trying to stop her bringing me parcels, but she tells me to mind my own business.

Ninth and tenth. A Jap general is due to arrive, and after a two-hour wait on parade he arrives and goes in a few minutes. Florrie turns up again and I get within ten yards of her. She appears to be in tears. I get a note to her and tell her not to bring any more food, but she just smiles and says she will be here again Sunday. News bad, Japs having landed on Singapore Island. Things look grim.

Eleventh and twelfth. Another parade and we are kept standing for two hours and nearly freeze to death, several men pass out. One has to go to bed fully dressed to keep warm. Chippy keeps us constantly amused with his antics.

Thirteenth. Electricity is turned on and we find a bulb. What luxury. Still very cold, and news still bad. Had slight attack of stomach poisoning. Give men a lecture on discipline as some troops in camp, not RAF, are getting unruly. GOC says he will hand control over to Japs unless men snap out of it. My men behaving very well. On the evening parade, camp commandant asks if I miss the others and says that perhaps in two months I shall be with them. Bitterly cold, difficult to keep warm.

Fourteenth and fifteenth. Florrie brings a huge parcel including a Chinese mingtoia blanket, sheet and pillowcase, and food. What an angel, and one day I hope to repay her. Another death from dysentry and many more sick.

Week ending twenty-second. Slightly warmer but was thankful for that blanket. Singapore has fallen, which is a severe blow. Cholera outbreak in colony, and we fear it will reach the camp as sanitary conditions are awful and men in very low state, especially Scots. Two men killed at Kai Tak in landslide. At GOC's conference, he gives us the daily news from BBC as there is still a set working. Japs shoot two Chinese who were marched through the camp on to the jetty where [they] were shot in the back. Food bad and little of it, but worst of all practically no medical requisites.

Week ending twenty-ninth. Florrie turns up every few days, and tells me the Japs have turned her out of her flat and pinched all her jewellery. I wish I could help her, and I tell her to leave the colony. Governor's chief of staff and retinue visit the camp. Another two hours on parade. Much warmer, and Chippy, Tressider and I cut each other's hair off. We look extremely funny but it feels cool. Two Scots escape and Japs have rigid check on evening parade. Wet and cold again and running short of footwear. Owing to fifth columnists in the camp, Japs suspect we have a wireless, so GOC orders it to be destroyed. A three-hour parade in the rain, and Japs search our rooms. They find a couple of wireless sets. No more BBC news now, just wild rumours. Two Scots who escaped have been shot. A proclamation is read to us forbidding escapes, all who are caught will be shot, and severe reprisals taken against our comrades. Malnutrition very noticeable. Personally I feel very fit thanks to Florrie's parcels.

Week ending seventh March. Japs interview my wireless people, but I had prepared them for it and the Japs get nothing out of them. Florrie still sending parcels. Chippy also gets one from his wife. The women of HK are doing grand work, little do they know the difference their presence and gifts of food make to us. Usual two parades a day and life is becoming a little monotonous. Japs send for me, and I am escorted out by George, the Jap WO, and a Portuguese interpreter. I am taken to the camp commandant's office where the officers are very pleasant and give me some cigarettes. I ask the English-speaking guard commander about the RAF officers, and he says they will soon be back, being in Canton or HK.[1] The WO takes me to his flat, where he proceeds to question me through the interpreter about the RAF, where we kept our stores, and how their air force compares to the RAF. He wants me write my

[1] They were in fact held in Shanghai.

answers down on paper. I refuse to answer most questions, but I give my opinion of their air force which is far from complimentary. Am also asked if they could have reduced HK earlier by bombing indiscriminately. I write some lines of nonsense about raids on London e★★.[1] Manage to pinch a handful of cigarettes before I go back to camp. Cigarettes run out and we smoke dried tea leaves, which are pretty foul. Another parcel including cigarettes and curry.

Week ending fourteenth. Getting warmer and diet beginning to have effect. Many men with beriberi or swelling of ankles and have difficulty in walking. Feel fairly fit but lack energy. Common sight to see several dead bodies in sea. George orders all ranks to salute him ★a★sh★★ep★★sent★★hem★k★★o★we.

Twenty-first. Florrie turns up in her best effort looking charming. Suspect Rangoon has fallen and Japs have a big celebration. Outlook looks decidedly grim. Troops put on an excellent concert and George attends. Have started brewing wine from raisins. Japs say officers are to be paid, so shall be able to send some to Florrie. Wthr hot and acquire quite a tan. ★★e★ow★★★t★n★f★ur★★sm★★tada★★ith★u★★i★ex★★★a★f★n★as-★★cr★★ours start to malign our people in the camp. Make most of a pair of wooden clogs as I only have v old pair of shoes.

Thirty-first. Japs have another search and confiscate all electrical kit, including Chippy's immersion heater. No meat for over a week and everyone gets one rice pot. Celebrate the twenty-fourth birthday of Ray and T

---

[1] The remainder of the diary is incomplete, and some numbers cannot be deciphered.

EPILOGUE

The translated diary was presented by Philip Aston to Pamela on a sunny autumn day in 1996 at the university, but it was not until she was back in the privacy of her own home that she dared read it through. At first its matter-of-fact tone surprised her. There was nothing here to be concealed. The existence of Florrie did not shock her. She had learned about her from Donald after the war. It would have been strange if he had not found a girlfriend, and she was glad the girl had proved so generous with food and clothing. It was only as she read about the punishing conditions in Sham Shui Po camp, and discovered the hunger and the brutality he endured that she saw how the experience had come to be locked away.

Whatever happened his spirit must not be broken. 'We are determined to bear our humiliation without a murmur,' he had declared, and the phrase told her what she had never before understood. All through those terrible years it was not the enemy he had feared, but himself. No one must guess at the shame and degradation he felt. His self-control was the one thing he could still take pride in. If that went, he would break utterly.

Then she came to the entry barely a week before St Valentine's Day: 'Spend hours these days thinking of home and family, especially Pam. Thank God for you, Pammy darling, your memory is ever with me.' Reading the words which he had hidden so carefully, she began to cry.

'If only he could have talked about those feelings,' she said later. 'We might have found a way through all the secrecy. We might have found a way of sharing the burden.'

Yet, as she wept, she finally realized why he had found it impossible to tell her. Even after he returned home he could not escape the prisoner's instinctive secrecy. To reveal feelings so profound was still to risk being broken.

Long after she had finished reading, an unexpected but profound sense of peace took hold of her. The diary had revealed to her something quite different from what she had imagined. The code had hidden not dark secrets, but his vulnerability. Reading his actual words seemed to remove a mask that had distorted his character. It felt as though the man she had first loved had been restored to her.

Above all, she could not forget the significance of Philip Aston's discovery. The key to the code came from the two names, Donald and Pamela, locked together. That alone made sense of the jumbled letters, and that alone made sense of the tangle of their lives.

ENVOI

Soon after the manuscript of *The Code of Love* was delivered it became apparent that Pamela Hill was dying. When I had first met her, almost three years earlier, I was expecting a frail old lady – she was eighty and suffering from cancer – but encountered instead a genuine romantic heroine, someone who was beautiful, funny, stylish, hugely entertaining and, at the same time, difficult, temperamental and utterly beguiling. Those were the qualities that I valued in her as our friendship grew, and especially in the course of preparing and writing the book. What I did not appreciate until after it had been finished was her strength of will.

The cancer made it increasingly difficult for her to swallow, and by the end of 1999 she had grown painfully thin. Nevertheless, whenever I saw her, she declared fiercely that she was going to live to see the book published. It seemed a hopeless ambition. She was taken to a hospice for the terminally ill, but staged a remarkable recovery and came out again. By a prodigious effort, the publishers accelerated production so that, on her eighty-third birthday in February 2000, I was able to put an advance copy in her hands. She could just whisper her pleaure, but it was the look of relief that I really remember. A few days later she returned to the hospice and it seemed impossible that she would ever leave it alive.

On the actual day of publication there was a launch party at a bookstore in Tunbridge Wells, where she lived. As I stood up to talk about her, the door was thrown open and, to my astonishment, Pamela appeared, swathed in blankets and propped up in a wheelchair pushed by her carer. During the next twenty minutes I told an audience of over one hundred people about her life, aware only of her sitting five feet away, her blue eyes fixed on me with blazing intensity, her face skeletal and as pale as death, yet with her last energies ferociously holding death at bay.

When I finished speaking, there were questions, and someone asked whether she had read the book. Her carer replied that she had read it aloud to her. Another person asked what Pamela thought of it. Her carer answered that during the reading Pamela had been repeatedly overwhelmed by tears, and kept saying it had told the truth about her and Donald. Not realising how ill she was, the questioner persisted. 'I would like to hear Pamela herself tell us what she feels,' he said. There was complete silence. Then, with the tiniest breath she whispered, 'I feel that now I can let myself die.'

Six days later her life, which had been shaped to the very end by one single love, was completed.

A NOTE ON SOURCES

My research for this book depended heavily on the personal memories and written sources of Donald Hill's family, and especially of his widow Pamela. Her sisters, Mrs Brigit Ferguson and Mrs Sheila Froom and family friends also helped with personal, and often extremely vivid, reminiscences. To fill in the gaps in Donald's prisoner of war experiences, I was aided by a piece of undeserved good fortune in having as a neighbour, Mrs Anne Sorby. As a former, longtime Hong Kong resident, her knowledge of the place is formidable, and having spent her impressionable youth in both MI5 and the Special Operations Executive, she possesses sleuthing skills beyond the ordinary. Thanks to her, I was introduced to a wealth of Hong Kong books and contacts, especially to a network of ex-prisoners of war whose help was invaluable. The Imperial War Museum's reference staff produced other diaries of Hong Kong prisoners, and those of Brigadier Cecil Templer and Captain A. White gave an especially clear picture of life in the camp.

At a late stage in writing, I had the luck to hear the tape-recording which Donald Hill made in 1982 for his son Christopher. It was not only full of detail about aspects of his life which I knew of only from others, but conveyed in the tone and timbre of his voice an immediate sense of the man he was and the struggle it cost him to keep his mind and life intact. Despite this unexpected assistance, I have not found it possible to establish the heroic Florrie's identity precisely. Donald himself tried to find her after the war, but without success, a failure that troubled him deeply since he felt that he owed his survival to her efforts. It is, however, probable that she did not survive the war. Like many Hong Kong Chinese, she suffered from malnutrition and ill-treatment by the occupying forces. The only clues that Donald left were that she was Christian, westernized, in her mid-thirties and the wife of a serving British police officer. Unfortunately the wholesale destruction of records by Japanese occupation forces during the Second World War has so far made it impossible to find a list of officers in the pre-war police service.

After the hardback edition was published, a call from Dr Goorney, a psychiatrist who had known some of those treating Donald in his last years, enabled me to establish the real name of the heroic Florrie. During a rambling talk about the war, Donald had revealed that her name was Foo Ling. It seemed he had tried to find her after his release to acknowledge his debt to her, but could find no trace of her. it is probable that she did not survive the war. Like many Hong Kong Chinese, she suffered from malnutrition and ill-treatment by the occupying forces.

But of course the most puzzling and rewarding source of information has been the notebook in which he kept his coded diary. More often than not it has seemed utterly baffling in its opacity, but at times it becomes quite clear, as though the disguise itself were the man.